GENDER, LANGUAGE AND DISCOURSE

Is language sexist?

Do women and men speak different languages?

Gender, Language and Discourse uniquely examines the contribution that psychological research – in particular, discursive psychology – has made to answering these questions. Until now, books on gender and language have tended to be from the sociolinguistic perspective and have focused on one of two issues – sexism in language or gender differences in speech. This book considers both issues and develops the idea that they shouldn't be viewed as mutually exclusive endeavours but rather as part of the same process – the social construction of gender. Ann Weatherall highlights the fresh insights a social constructionist approach has made to these debates, and presents recent theoretical developments and empirical work in discursive psychology relevant to gender and language.

    Gender, Language and Discourse provides the most comprehensive and up-to-date discussion of the gender and language field from a psychological perspective. It will be invaluable to students and researchers in social psychology, cultural studies, education, linguistic anthropology and women's studies.

Ann Weatherall is a Senior Lecturer in the School of Psychology at Victoria University, Wellington, New Zealand. Her research interests are in the areas of feminist and discursive social psychology, gender and language and social psychology. Her previous work has been published in various scholarly journals.

WOMEN AND PSYCHOLOGY
Series Editor: Jane Ussher
Centre for Critical Psychology,
University of Western Sydney

This series brings together current theory and research on women and psychology. Drawing on scholarship from a number of different areas of psychology, it bridges the gap between abstract research and the reality of women's lives by integrating theory and practice, research and policy.

Each book addresses a 'cutting edge' issue of research, covering such topics as post-natal depression, eating disorders, theories and methodologies.

The series provides accessible and concise accounts of key issues in the study of women and psychology, and clearly demonstrates the centrality of psychology to debates within women's studies or feminism.

The Series Editor would be pleased to discuss proposals for new books in the series.

GENDER, LANGUAGE AND DISCOURSE

Ann Weatherall

First published 2002 by Routledge
27 Church Road, Hove, East Sussex BN3 2FA

Simultaneously published in the USA and Canada
by Routledge Inc.
29 West 35th Street, New York, NY 10001

Routledge is an imprint of the Taylor & Francis Group

© 2002 Ann Weatherall

Typeset in Sabon by Mayhew Typesetting, Rhayader, Powys
Printed and bound in Great Britain by MPG Books Ltd, Cornwall

British Library Cataloguing in Publication Data
A catalogue record for this book is available from the British Library

ISBNs   0-415-16906-2 (pbk)
0-415-16905-4 (hbk)

To my daughter Paris, my feminist mother Kathleen Weatherall, my grandmother Helen Weatherall, my nana Doris Grady and my great-grandmother, suffragette, Elizabeth Anne Hall.

CONTENTS

ACKNOWLEDGEMENTS

I wish to thank Victoria University of Wellington, New Zealand for granting me fourteen months' sabbatical in order to complete this book. Thanks also to the Centre for Critical Psychology, University of Western Sydney, Australia and the Department of Psychology, University of Manchester, England for hosting me during my leave.

Thanks to all my colleagues in the School of Psychology at Victoria University of Wellington, New Zealand who have contributed to the environment that allowed me to write. For their specific comments and feedback I would like to thank Jiansheng Guo, David Harper, Sue Jackson, James Liu, John McClure and Sik Hung Ng.

I am also grateful to people outside my university for their encouragement and comments on various chapters. I would particularly like to acknowledge the friendship and support of Nicola Gavey and Marsha Walton.

The person whose input I have valued the most is John Haywood. Without his contagious enthusiasm for academic life, his belief in my work and the hours he dedicated to proofreading every chapter draft, this book might never have materialised.

INTRODUCTION

Chick, hangipants, sheila, Mrs, Miss and Ms. Words for women, do they matter? Are names as harmful as sticks and stones? Are girls better at language than boys? If women are so good at talking, why do men dominate many conversations? Is there a woman's language? Are women and men really communicating across a cultural divide or is 'I don't understand' just an excuse for not listening? If a woman speaks like a man, has she lost touch with her femininity? The answers to these questions are not straightforward. As Robin Lakoff, a key figure in gender and language research, put it: 'The questions surrounding women and language bring together some of the most agonising, complex, diverse and ultimately insoluble issues facing our society' (Lakoff, 1990, p. 199). This book is an exploration of the issues underpinning the sort of questions that get asked about gender and language.

My interest in the topics of gender and language began in 1987 during my third year of studying psychology at Otago University, Dunedin, New Zealand (NZ). I became involved with a group project on sexist language as part of a social psychology course. In our reading we discovered a debate about whether masculine generic terms such as 'mankind' and 'chairman' were sexist or not. One side of the debate was that masculine generic forms were not biased, they were just grammatical convention. On the other, was the suggestion that masculine generics functioned to disadvantage women by making them seem invisible and unimportant. Social psychological research confirmed for me that sexist language was not a trivial issue. One of the main themes of this book is to show how language is key to understanding gender and challenging sexism.

Later in 1987, Sik Hung Ng, my social psychology lecturer (and later a valued colleague), found financial support for me to travel to Christchurch to attend a lecture by Dale Spender. I will never forget my awe at her head-to-toe purple clothes and the passion she stirred in me as she spoke of the silencing of women and the work needed to make women's voices heard. Fired up by Spender's lecture I became committed to challenging sexist language practices. I wrote letters to editors complaining about sexist

1

language in their publications and corrected anybody who used masculine generic terms in my presence. I had been converted to, and continue to hold, the belief that language is important in the ways women are thought about and how women's social disadvantage is perpetuated.

Language issues are political issues. Language not only reflects women's social position but can be used to challenge it. Feminist resistance to sexism and patriarchy has often involved harnessing language (consider terms such as 'wimmin' and 'herstory'). Feminist campaigns use slogans to mobilise action; instances include 'deeds not words' (women's suffrage), 'girls can do anything' (equal employment opportunities) and 'no means no' (rape awareness). Knowledge about the relationships between gender and language is important because it can inform strategies for engendering social change for the better.

Of course, I am not alone in my interest in and concern about gender and language issues. An indication of public interest is that newspapers regularly publish articles on sexist language issues. Even during the time I was writing this introduction there was a newspaper report about an Australian politician (Queensland Premier Peter Beattie) who was rejecting the suggestion that 'sheila' was politically incorrect, claiming instead that it was an authentic and unique part of an Australian language (*The Evening Post*, Wellington, NZ, 16/07/01). Scholarly concern with the topic is evidenced by recently edited volumes, which include works within anthropology, art history, cultural studies, education, linguistics, literary studies, women's studies, philosophy, psychology and psychoanalysis (e.g. Coates, 1998; Holmes, 2000; Holmes and Meyerhoff, in press; Livia and Hall, 1997; Mills, 1995; Wodak, 1997). The attention and controversy around issues of gender and language signal that there are some important matters at stake. This book teases out what those matters are.

A brief history of gender and language

The earliest concerns about gender and language can be traced to linguistics and to feminist theory and political practice. Gender has been invoked as an explanation for all manner of linguistic variation, including vocabulary innovation (e.g. Jespersen, 1922), pronunciation (see Coates, 1986), grammar (see Key, 1975) and communication style (e.g. Maltz and Borker, 1982). An awareness of a relationship between language and women's social status can be found in nineteenth-century publications of the women's movement (see Rakow and Kramarae, 1990), in feminist campaigns about personal names (see Stannard, 1977) and in feminist philosophy (de Beauvoir, 1952). The linguistic message has been that there are important relationships between gender and language; the feminist one is that those relationships are significant for understanding and challenging sexism and patriarchy.

Although issues about gender and language have a long history, its status as a field of research developed alongside the second wave of feminism during the 1960s and 1970s. Around that time a number of articles and books were written which voiced two questions that have, until recently, divided research in the field. The questions asked about the nature and significance of gender bias in language and of gender differences in language use. In what is now a classic paper, Lakoff argued that 'the marginality and powerlessness of women is reflected in both the ways men and women are expected to speak and the ways in which women are spoken of' (1973, p. 45). In one of the first overview essays, psychologists Cheris Kramer, Barrie Thorne and Nancy Henley asked, 'Do women and men use language in different ways? In what ways does language – in structure, content and daily usage – reflect and help constitute sexual inequality? How can sexist language be changed?' (1978, p. 638). These questions set the agenda for research on gender and language for some time.

Kramer *et al.*'s question about gender differences in language continued a long tradition within psychology of asking about differences between men and women. However, where Kramer *et al.*'s concern was to challenge a social system that supported gender inequality, earlier work on gender differences was based on assumptions of women's inferiority (see Chapter 2). For Kramer and her colleagues, power was key to understanding patterns of language and communication. The important feminist insights were that language reflects men's power and social advantage and it also reflects women's relative lack of power and their social disadvantage.

Feminist language researchers established that men's power was manifested in language in a number of complex ways. Spender (1980) identified one of these when she argued that in the past men have had control over language (as philosophers, orators, politicians, grammarians, linguists, lexicographers and so on), so they encoded sexism into language to consolidate their claims of male supremacy. Spender's work highlighted an important avenue for feminist action: to ensure that women are involved in all facets of language and communication. Recording women's views and disseminating accounts of their experiences are important strategies for ensuring equitable and accurate representation of women in texts. The importance of being involved with developments in language and communication was discussed in Spender's (1995) more recent work on gender issues and the internet. Spender argued that women must be involved as users and innovators of the world wide web; otherwise it will develop to serve and promote men's interests over women's.

Spender's (1980) work attended to the powerfulness of those who can exercise some degree of control over language. People with public speaking rights, those who record and communicate ideas, and the information-rich are all in a position to exercise some power over language – to use the power of language and communication to promote particular social and cultural beliefs and suppress others. However, language is not just a tool for manipulating meaning, nor merely a vessel for the containment of ideas. Another source of power is how language is used by speakers when communicating with each other.

The idea that there is power in language use was an important part of early research on gender differences in speech styles. For example, one suggestion was that men used interruption as a way of wielding their power over women in conversation (Zimmerman and West, 1975). Another way in which power may be expressed in language use is in the way people address each other. Conventionally in English it is more formal and respectful to refer to another using a real name rather than a nickname. However, those in positions of power are more able to ignore convention. Men, on the whole, are more likely to challenge norms of language and communication because they are generally in more powerful positions than women. For example, bosses (probably male) may refer to workers, using their nicknames or terms of endearment, but not the reverse. Men are more likely to break a social norm of inattention between strangers by making street remarks or wolf whistling, because they have more power.

Lakoff (1973, 1975) strongly endorsed the idea that language reflected women's secondary status in society. According to this mirror model, the few words that refer to strong, intelligent, sexually active, independent women and the plethora of negative and sexual terms just reflected negative attitudes towards women in society (Stanley, 1977). More frequent comments about how women look and what men do are a form of power because they set up the desired attributes expected of each gender (Miller and Swift, 1976).

Early feminist language research firmly established that patterns of language and communication reflected gender differences in social power and the different cultural values associated with women and men. However, many feminists wanted to argue that language not only reflects men's power but actively establishes and maintains negative attitudes towards women and their secondary social status. Thus an early debate was about the significance of sexist language and gender differences in speech. The issue was whether language just reflected men's power or whether it also perpetuated it.

The debate about the significance of language bias was particularly important for feminist campaigns, dating from around 1970, against the use of sexist language forms. Lakoff (1973) argued against campaigns to change the language because she thought that language change followed social change and not the reverse. However, if it could be shown that sexist language not only reflected sexism but helped to perpetuate it, then a stronger case could be made against its use.

Social psychologists made an important contribution to campaigns for sexist language reform by providing empirical evidence that certain features of language do encourage a cognitive bias against women (e.g. Crawford and English, 1984; Wilson and Ng, 1988). The theoretical perspective used to explain the impact of sexist language on thought and behaviour was Edward Sapir and Benjamin Whorf's theory of linguistic relativity, where language provides people with their guide to social reality (Whorf, 1956).

According to linguistic relativism, the way the world is seen and experienced is largely due to the symbolic guide language provides. Unfortunately, endorsing linguistic relativity marginalised research on sexist language in psychology. In the 1970s and 1980s the dominant cognitive focus of the discipline meant that perception and information processing, not language, were taken to be the primary mechanisms involved in people's understanding of the world. Berlin and Kay's (1969) work on the universal perception of colours supported the dominant cognitive view. They found that people from different cultures perceived colour in the same way despite vast differences in colour terminology.

In some ways, social psychological work on sexist language that endorsed the influence of language on thought was theoretically ahead of its time. The idea of linguistic relativity – that there is not just one way of seeing, thinking and talking about the world – is one that is consistent with recent developments in social psychology (see Chapter 4). So, early empirical work on sexist language endorsed a theoretical perspective of the impact of language and thought that would not gain wider support within the discipline for another ten to twenty years. However, other aspects of the early work were more typical of the time when it was conducted. For example, an assumption underlying psychological research on sexist language was that words have a fixed and stable meaning, which can be measured. Experiments were conducted to show that the term 'girl' was sexist because it had less positive connotations than 'woman' did (e.g. Kitto, 1989). Psychological research increasingly recognises that context is central for understanding words, and cultural meaning systems are implicated in the production of concepts that we have words for.

Gender, language and power

The perspective that I develop in this book is most consistent with the ideas associated with linguistic relativity and poststructuralism. That is, language not only reflects and perpetuates gender but language constitutes gender and produces sexism as a social reality. In addition, the idea of power that is used in this book moves beyond that used in early gender and language research.

In the past, feminist language researchers viewed power as something outside language; men had power over language to define meaning and they showed their power in the language they used during interactions.

However, power can be thought of as part and parcel of language, not as separate from it. The notion of discourses of gender (see Chapter 4) begins to capture the idea that language is imbued with power.

Much psychological research proceeds on the assumption that absolute and universal truths about human behaviour can be discovered through the accumulation of appropriate research. However, in her early work on gender, language and communication, Henley (1977) recognised that the language of science had often been used to justify the dominant social and moral order. Henley noted that interpretations of psychological research on gender were often status-quo-preserving and self-serving for academics. Henley's recognition of politics in science has some parallels with developments in feminist poststructuralist theory (see Weedon, 1987). According to feminist poststructuralism, the truth of what 'being a man' or 'being a woman' means can never be objectively established because knowledge about gender is produced and reproduced within a patriarchal social order.

An aspect of the ideological power of language is conventions of speech. Cameron (1995) argued that 'verbal hygiene' or standards of appropriate ways of talking are fundamentally ideological. Norms about speech are powerful forces that influence people's perceptions and evaluations of others. Ideas about women's speech, for example, can be seen as constructing a double bind for women. Women's speech is believed to be grating and trivial, therefore easy to ignore. However, for a woman to talk in a low pitch about serious matters is to be dismissed as a real woman. Questioning standards of speech and norms of language is one way of exposing the dominant social order.

Gender and language researchers have not always been successful at reflecting upon the ways in which politics enters into their empirical work. For example, many studies take for granted that there are gender differences in language use and that careful research will establish what the true and enduring differences are. However, theory and research on gender differences in language have often turned to women's disadvantage. A poststructuralist insight about the interdependence of power and knowledge underlies the perspective that is taken in this book on gender differences and speech styles.

One of the original questions asked about gender and language was 'how can sexist language be changed?' (Kramer et al., 1978). An assumption that underlies this question is that particular linguistic forms can be identified and defined as sexist. A lot of mileage has been made from the notion of sex bias in language (see Chapter 1). However, another idea about language stemming from poststructuralism (see, for example, Gavey, 1989) is that meaning is tied to broader sense-making systems or discourses. If the significance of words depends, at least in part, on their position within broader systems of meaning, then sexism in language is more than a matter of just words.

Feminists following the discursive turn in psychology are building a body of work that looks at sexism in language from a different perspective (see Wilkinson and Kitzinger, 1995). Feminist discursive psychology is post-structuralist in the sense that it investigates language as a complex and dynamic system that produces meaning about social categories such as gender. This work can seem quite removed from the original concerns that defined the gender and language field. However, it seems clearly relevant for understanding how language constitutes sexual inequality. One of my aims in writing this book is to encourage the gender and language field to engage with feminist discursive psychology.

In this book I have attempted to build upon the social constructionist approach to gender and language developed by psychologist Mary Crawford (1995) in *Talking difference*. Like Crawford, I argue that a focus on gender differences in language, with its assumptions of essential and stable qualities, disregards the variability, complexity and dynamism of linguistic behaviour in ongoing social relations. Notions of enduring, measurable gender differences in speech fail to advance an understanding of sexual inequality and patriarchy.

Crawford's (1995) claim that research on gender differences in speech is neither feminist nor scholarly is developed further in this book. Ideas of difference, despite intentions to the contrary, tend to support rather than challenge the status quo. Furthermore, a focus on difference is neither necessary nor sufficient for a complete understanding of how women and men speak. Important questions for gender and language research are asking how gender is produced and sustained through patterns of talk, through the organisation of social interaction, through social practices and in institutional structures. These questions take the field beyond the notion of difference that was so central to its founding questions.

Crawford (1995) defined the focus of her book as examining questions about women's and men's speech. She bracketed off the issue of sexist language as an important but somewhat separate issue in the gender and language field. A unique aspect of this book is that it begins to blur the boundaries between the study of women's and men's representation in language and the study of the way they use language. Language about women (and men) and women (and men) speaking are both aspects of one process – the social construction of gender.

A social constructionist perspective is tied up with poststructuralist ideas. It holds that meanings associated with male and female are not fixed or static. Rather, understandings of gender are contextually (culturally, historically and locally) specific. Around 400 years ago, to be female was to be an inferior form of male (see Laqueur, 1990). Now to be female means to be different or opposite to male. There may be a time in the future when male and female are just two of several sex/gender categories (see Chapter 4). The meanings of words also vary depending on their local

7

linguistic context. The term 'bird' may be considered demeaning when referring to an independent woman, but it certainly causes no offence in discussions of what is for Christmas dinner. 'Girl' may be used to trivialise the status of a woman but it may also be used as a way of expressing a kind of power (e.g. 'girlpower') or sisterhood.

Feminist research following the founding questions about gender and language has shown how language reflects and helps to perpetuate a social system that, on the whole, benefits men more than women. More recently, social constructionist approaches have highlighted that language is also imbued with ideological power – where ways of talking and knowing about the world can be linked to dominant cultural beliefs and values. This book follows feminist language research from its original concerns about sexism and gender difference in speech through to its current engagement with social constructionist and poststructuralist ideas.

Book overview

The ideas touched on in the discussion so far are discussed more fully in the rest of the book. In Chapter 1 the topic of sexist language is considered in detail. The trouble stirred by sexist language issues is evidence that rules about words are neither trivial nor neutral but deeply ideological. Aside from sexist language, the second issue that has historically occupied gender and language research is that of gender differences in language use. Outside the gender and language field there has been considerable debate about whether questions of gender difference are worth pursuing. Chapter 2 examines the issues raised in that general debate and considers why there is a lack of consensus about exactly what aspects of cognition and behaviour differentiate women and men. Chapter 2 also discusses research on sex differences in verbal ability and voice, to illustrate the more general pattern of non-closure in sex difference research.

The theme of sex difference in speech continues in Chapter 3, on women's language. Chapter 3 considers the issue of gender differences in speech styles and shows how theoretical explanations for difference have also functioned to disadvantage women. Chapter 4 considers a social constructionist approach by outlining the impact of the discursive turn on the field of gender and language. The aim of the chapter is to examine the kinds of insights that a theoretical shift from essentialism to social constructionism brings to the concerns that have typically occupied gender and language research.

The contribution made by ethnomethodology (EM) and conversation analysis (CA) to issues concerning the gender and language field is considered in Chapter 5. An ethnomethodological perspective is particularly pertinent to the field of gender and language because it was from that approach that Kessler and McKenna (1978) developed one of the earliest social constructionist analyses of gender within psychology.

Chapter 6 addresses directly the topic of gender identity and its relationship to language and discourse. It examines the different assumptions made by social psychological and sociolinguistic perspectives on the relationships between language, discourse and identity. In two important approaches, communication accommodation theory and the study of linguistic variation, language has been treated as the site where identity is expressed and reflected. A discourse conversation analytic approach from psychology shifts attention to how and why identity categories are used and made relevant in social interaction.

The final chapter (Chapter 7) looks back over the ground that has been covered in the book and highlights the strengths and limitations of theory and research conducted before and after the discursive turn. The book ends by considering what may follow after the discursive turn in the gender and language field.

1

SEXIST LANGUAGE

Introduction

A feminist concern with words for woman in the English language has a long history that continues today. Issues concerning sexism in language and feminist endorsement of non-sexist language policies attract public comment as well as academic attention. In fact, the ongoing ridicule in the media of concerns about sexism in language is one form of evidence that rules about words are not neutral but deeply ideological. For example, the headline 'Try a little togethern' used by *The Economist* (Johnson, 1994) was written to undermine a feminist lobby to ban job titles marked with feminine suffixes (e.g. waitress, actress). The reason for dropping '-ess' endings is that they seem to imply that the role is less important than when the ending is not used, which is typically the case when the terms are used to refer to men in the same roles (e.g. waiter, actor). Another example was the *Sunday Times* (UK, 23/03/97) article headlined 'Women may give Ms a Miss', which argued that 'Ms' was being shunned by a new generation of women because of its association with aggressive feminism.

Butler (1990a) suggested that a sense of trouble tends to arise when there is some kind of threat to a prevailing law. The trouble provoked whenever feminist issues are raised about words and women is, I would argue, an indication that issues of sexist language are inextricably tied to the prevailing social and moral order. To say that rules about words are closely intertwined with dominant social belief systems is not to say that a non-sexist language would naturally and inevitably lead to a non-sexist society. The important point is that language about women is not a neutral or a trivial issue but deeply political. Cameron (1995) made a similar point in her work on verbal hygiene: rules about language and standards of 'correct' speech reveal information about patterns of power and privilege in society.

Challenging sexism in language and making trouble with words can be an important feminist strategy to engender social change. However, it seems to me that the solutions offered to the problem of sexist language are somehow less important than the issue itself. One reason for this is that there is no simple relationship between linguistic forms and non-sexist language. For example, words that are marked for gender can be construed as sexist (e.g. chairman) or supporting a feminist political agenda (e.g. wife basher). Similarly, unmarked forms may include women (e.g. chairpersons) but exclude women's issues (e.g. partner abuse). Furthermore, a natural and inevitable link between bias in language and social discrimination seems unlikely. Nevertheless, language issues have a strong political component.

The aim of this chapter is to explore the issue of sexist language and to examine the contribution psychology has made to debates about the significance of sexist language. Sexist language is not just about the words used to describe women but also how they are used and to what ends. A shift from a concern about sexist words to sexist discourse reflects a profound theoretical shift in some areas of psychology and in the gender and language field, which is detailed in later chapters. Much of the discussion on sexist language in this chapter is predicated on the rather simplistic assumption that language is a stable system of meaning that has an existence outside its users. Despite the limitations of this assumption, the awareness about gender issues that feminist attention to sexist language has created makes the issue important in its own right.

Discussion of sexist language in this chapter will be confined to my mother tongue, the English language, although it exists and has been analysed in other languages too (see Pauwels, 1998 for a comprehensive overview). Also, the topic seems to be as troublesome in other languages as it is in English. For example, women's insistence, in the French cabinet, on the title Madame la Ministre, despite 'le ministre' being a masculine word in French, created such an uproar in France that it attracted international media attention (e.g. *Dominion*, NZ, 11/03/98; *Independent*, UK, 10/01/98). The newspaper articles reported an open letter from the French Academy to the French prime minister which argued that the women cabinet ministers were committing grammatical nonsense and undermining the feminist cause.

This chapter will begin by describing the features of English that have been identified as sexist, and reviewing the psychological research that has investigated the impact that sexist language has on the way individuals think and behave. An important theme of this chapter is that language not only transmits social information about discrimination against women, but it also reveals how successful feminists have been in promoting a greater awareness of language change as important in social and political change. Throughout the 1970s and early 1980s many works appeared that critically detailed sexist language and provided evidence of its significance (e.g. Miller and Swift, 1976; Nilsen, 1977a, 1977b; Thorne and Henley, 1975; Thorne, Kramarae and Henley, 1983; Vetterling-Braggin, 1981). In

11

the 1990s investigations into language change were indicating that the continued work of feminists was impacting on language (Holmes, 1993; Pauwels, 1998). English is evolving so that fewer 'sexist' forms are used; there are new ways to label experiences of oppression (e.g. sexual harassment); there are new words to celebrate the resilience of women (e.g. abuse survivors), and more words to describe barriers to women's achievement (e.g. glass ceiling, mommy track). An exciting development is the appearance of new words and phrases that seem to challenge normative assumptions about gender (e.g. gender bending, Bob's your Auntie). Furthermore, discursive work (discussed in detail in later chapters) suggests that non-sexist language has become normative, with the use of sexist forms typically being accompanied by a self-correction or an explanation for their use (see Edley and Wetherell, 1999; Hopper and LeBaron, 1998).

Sexism in the English language

The idea that language treats women and men differently is not new. Feminists have long voiced their concerns about the ways in which women are represented in language. Penelope (1990) documented an early challenge to sexist language from St Hildegarde of Bingen, who in the eleventh century attempted to construct a non-sexist language alternative. Lana Rakow and Cheris Kramarae (1990) edited a collection of articles from *The Revolution*, a radical American women's rights periodical published from 1868 to 1871. They found that a substantial amount of writing in *The Revolution* drew attention to (what I would consider as) sexist language. Issues discussed in *The Revolution* included the more frequent use of terms of endearment when addressing women than when addressing men, and men's renaming of women after marriage.

Consideration of the relationships between language and sexism in society has been evident for a long time in some feminist philosophical writings. For example, Simone de Beauvoir (1952) noted that in male-dominated cultures the term man:

> represents both the positive and the neutral, as is indicated by the common use of man to designate human beings in general; whereas woman represents only the negative, defined by limiting criteria, without reciprocity.
>
> (de Beauvoir, 1952/1988, p. xv)

In this brief quotation, de Beauvoir insightfully anticipated ideas that were to become central to later empirical work on sex bias in language. During the 1970s and 1980s considerable social science research investigated the psychological significance of using the term 'man' generically – that is, using man to refer to a person whose gender is unspecified or unknown. De

Beauvoir's observation that man is generally regarded as 'both the positive and the neutral' also pre-empted a later concern that the addition of adjuncts (e.g. lady doctor) and suffixes (e.g. poetess) detracts from connotations of potency that the unmarked forms (e.g. doctor, poet) normally invoke.

While feminists have long demonstrated an awareness of gender and language issues, a focused academic interest in sexist language has been relatively recent. Inspired by the American feminist movement of the late 1960s, a large literature on the topic has emerged (e.g. Bergvall, Bing and Freed, 1996; Coates, 1986; Graddol and Swann, 1989; Henley, 1989; Hill, 1986; Key, 1975; Kramarae, 1990; McConnell-Ginet, Borker and Furman, 1980; Mills, 1995; Penfield, 1987; Smith, 1985; Spender, 1980). Many forms of sexist language have been identified, but feminist social psychologist Nancy Henley (1987) suggested that they might be classified into three types: language that ignores women; language that defines women narrowly; and language that depreciates women. I will use Henley's typology to organise the following discussion. However, it is important to note that the three types are very broad, and some issues, such as bias in traditions of personal naming, straddle all types. Also the three types are not mutually exclusive – language that defines women narrowly may also depreciate and demean.

Before discussing sexism in language at greater length, I would like to make a point that seems to me to be very important. Although words can define, depreciate and demean women, the same words may also inspire resistance and rebellion against that negative meaning. Thus, sexist language should not just be thought of as constructing women as invisible or passive and silent. Sexism in language may also inspire resistance and demonstrate women's agency. A similar point was made by Judith Butler:

> One is not simply fixed by the name that one is called. In being called an injurious name, one is derogated and demeaned. But the name holds out another possibility as well: by being called a name, one is also, paradoxically, given a certain possibility for social existence . . . thus the injurious address may appear to fix and paralyse the one it hails, but it may also produce an unexpected and enabling response.
>
> (1997, p. 2)

Invisible women

One way in which language can be considered sexist is that, at a symbolic level, it makes women seem invisible. One aspect of the invisibility of women in language is their absence as the subjects of stories or topics of articles. Some empirical evidence of women's absence was provided by

Caldas-Coulthard (1995), who analysed the content of a sample of American newspapers. Caldas-Coulthard found that news items were more likely to be written by men than women and were also more likely to be about men. Furthermore, Caldas-Coulthard found that men were more often quoted as saying things than women and were more often attributed as being the agents of action than women. Hence, in news reports women are not only ignored by not being the writers and subjects of stories, but are also marginalised by being denied the role of active agents.

Religion has long been criticised for effectively undermining women's existence through language style choices. For example, Miller and Swift (1976) criticised major Western religions for their patriarchal world view which, they argued, gets maintained by the use of metaphors and symbols that are male-oriented. Referring to God with words such as father and king evokes the image of a god that is male – a myth that is attacked in feminist humour (e.g. when God created man she was only joking) and by those directly involved in religious organisations (see Gross, 1996).

Feminist activists such as Dale Spender have responded to women's exclusion. The response has included writing books that recover and publicise stories about and by women – stories that have, for a number of different reasons, been hidden and forgotten. In her book *Man-made language* Spender (1980) argued that just because women, historically, have not been the influential thinkers and have not had the opportunities to influence language does not mean that women have not had great thoughts or held important theories of language. Rather the knowledge that women have produced and the meanings they have generated have not always entered the public arena like those produced by men. The reason for women's relative invisibility in the public arena is that women have not always had straightforward access to the technologies and institutions that transmit information from one generation to another.

A well-documented aspect of women being ignored in language is the use of masculine forms, such as 'chairman', 'mankind', 'guys', 'helmsman' and 'fireman', when referring to people in general or a person whose gender is unknown or unspecified. Conventionally these forms, called masculine generics, are the grammatically correct way to generally refer to an unspecified person or to a group of people. But of course such words are also masculine-specific terms and can be interpreted as excluding women. Arguably, terms such as 'chairperson', 'humans' and 'helm' are more neutral than their masculine generic equivalents because they have no gender marking.

Although conventional, Ann Bodine (1975) documented that masculine generics are not natural, trans-historic aspects of English grammar, but are the result of specific efforts by particular grammarians in the past. She found that the first grammatical rule supporting the use of a masculine pronoun to refer to people in general or a person whose gender was unknown, arose in the eighteenth century. Kirby, an English language grammarian writing in 1746, wrote: 'The masculine Person answers to the general name which comprehends both Male and Female; as Any Person, who knows what he says.' Kirby's rule was introduced as legal usage by a British Act of Parliament in 1850. It was not until that time that masculine generic forms became conventional in written language.

Despite the prescriptive grammarian movement to eradicate 'he and she' or 'they' as gender-indefinite referents, these forms have persisted, especially in spoken English (Baron, 1986). However, during the 1970s the formal grammatical rule prescribing masculine generic forms attracted explicit and vehement criticism. Feminists viewed masculine generics as both ambiguous and discriminatory because they could be interpreted as being masculine-specific or neutral and thus, in some cases, be interpreted as not referring to women at all (e.g. Martyna, 1980a, 1980b). As one anthropologist noted:

> If you begin to write a book about man or to conceive a theory about man you cannot avoid using this word (man). You cannot avoid using a pronoun as a substitute for this word, and you will use the pronoun 'he' as a simple matter of linguistic convenience. But before you are halfway through the first chapter a mental image of this evolving creature begins to form in your mind. It will be a male image and he will be the hero of the story: everything and everybody in the story will relate to him.
>
> (Morgan, 1972, pp. 8–9)

Masculine generic forms seem to exacerbate an existing tendency for a prototypic person to be considered male (e.g. Broverman, Vogel, Broverman, Clarkson and Rosenkrantz, 1972; Hamilton, 1991). I found an example of this tendency in an analysis that I conducted of children's conversation. When the children used personal reference terms, the majority (88 per cent) were male terms (Weatherall, 1998). Many of the male terms were used when the children anthropomorphised objects. For example, the train was Mister Train, while the different-shaped train tracks were Mister Turny and Mister Downhill. A toy dog was assigned a masculine gender and called Joey, and masculine-specific terms were used for job titles (e.g. fireman). In addition both the girls and boys referred to each other as guys. I didn't ask the children why they referred to things as he, but Wood (1997) cited the experience of a mother who asked her 6-year-old daughter why she called stuffed animals 'he'. Her daughter replied that there were 'more hes than shes'. So, at least for one girl, the impression gained from the world was that it contained more male entities than female ones.

A masculine impression of the world may also be, in part, due to the prevalence of male characters in children's stories and the masculinisation of children's toys (e.g. Thomas the tank engine). Nilsen (1977b), in early work in the field of education, documented the pervasive sexism in children's books and classroom materials. Nilsen found that books were overwhelmingly oriented towards boys, and gender was depicted sex-stereotypically. The bias concerned Nilsen because it gave children the impression that males are more important and that females' contribution to society is trivial (see also Cooper, 1989).

In *Girls, boys and language*, Swann (1992) provided a comprehensive analysis of the role language plays in providing children with equal opportunities in education. Referring to books she said:

> Educationists have been concerned about sexism in print resources because of the local, or immediate effects this may have; for instance, the predominance of male examples in science textbooks may suggest to girls that science isn't really for them; in assessment tasks, girls or boys may be disadvantaged depending on whether male or female experiences are drawn upon. But there is also a concern about continuing, more general effects: that the female and male images conveyed to pupils contribute to their sense of what is normal for girls and boys and women and men in our society; that children's reading material helps reinforce gender as a social division, and perpetuates inequalities between girls and boys and women and men.
>
> (Swann, 1992, p. 96)

Of course, it is not only books and reading materials that may perpetuate inequity in education. Teachers' language, such as the way they talk to pupils, may also impact on the learning experience. An area of education that Levi (1995) criticised for patronising and excluding females was physical education. Levi pointed out that comments like 'last one across is a big girl's blouse' were frequently used by men, and these had the effect of discouraging women from participating in outdoor activities. The way in which talk-in-interaction functions to reproduce and support a gendered social and moral order is central to discursive social psychological approaches to gender and language.

A study of language bias and its consequences, using a traditional social psychological approach, was Hamilton's (1988) research on the influence of different words for homosexuality, on people's judgements of groups at risk of contracting Acquired Immune Deficiency Syndrome (AIDS). Hamilton analysed the content of newspaper articles reporting on AIDS, and discovered that almost all references to homosexuality were gender-neutral – for example, 'gay'. She found that people interpreted the terms generically (i.e. referring to both women and men), which resulted in the assumption that gay women and gay men were at equally high risk for contracting AIDS. So in this research the use of gender-neutral terms encouraged an over-estimation of the degree to which lesbian women were at risk of acquiring AIDS.

In Hamilton's (1988) research and in many other studies on generic language, the use of unmarked or gender-neutral terms seemed to function to increase the perceived salience of women as subjects. In many contexts – for example, in children's stories or job advertisements – the increased relevance of women leads to more accurate comprehension. However, in Hamilton's research the use of neutral terms resulted in a misperception.

The term 'partner-abuse' is another example of an inclusive word that may lead to a false impression of the gender of the referent. Women are far more likely to be victims in violent relationships than men (French, 1992), but the gender-neutral term may disguise that fact. A friend of mine whose job involved drafting plans for architects provided a further example of generic language use – with an interesting twist. She told me that she encouraged the use of the term 'draftsman' in the business that she worked for because it meant that clients tended to mistake her for an architect, and treat her with more respect!

Although there are exceptions, psychological research on masculine generic terms tends to assume that such words function to disadvantage women and that gender-neutral forms are favoured by feminists advocating English language reform. Interestingly, the corrective strategies for features of sexist language vary across languages. In general, English-speaking feminists advocate making terms neutral or unmarked for gender. However, in other languages the recommended strategy has been to make terms gender-specific, as was the case with the French women cabinet ministers who wanted to be called 'la ministre' even though 'le ministre' was the correct grammatical form (see also Michard and Viollet, 1991).

The lack of direct correspondence between language forms (e.g. gender-marked or gender-unmarked generic forms) and effects (gender issue being highlighted or hidden) shows that the relationship between language form and symbolic meaning is not straightforward. Sometimes discussions of bias in language imply that particular words (e.g. 'girl' to refer to an adult woman) or word forms (words ending in '-ess') naturally and inevitably define women negatively. Other times it is claimed that particular words are offensive because they seem to reflect and perpetuate bias and stereotypes (e.g. referring to a sexually active woman as a 'slut'). Language policies can be a useful strategy for ensuring that the language used in institutions and in formal publications is not blatantly offensive. However, it is important to remember that words are not simply and transparently sexist. A word that at one time may have negative connotations may at another time be reclaimed and acquire positive associations (e.g. dyke, queer). Also terms may be considered more or less offensive depending on who is speaking and who is being referred to. Consider, for example, the difference between a male boss referring to his female secretary as 'girl' and close women friends addressing each other as girl. So, the relationships between words and their meanings are complex. Feminist language campaigns may be criticised for promoting over-simplified perspectives on how words and the world are related. Nevertheless, heightened awareness of the politics of words is an important outcome of feminist language campaigns.

In the past, linguists and grammarians interested in language change have suggested that women more than men tend to be 'guilty' of intro-ducing new words or changing the pronunciation of old words (see Coates, 1986). I would like to suggest that, in the twenty-first century, women are continuing to show a 'talent' for creative language use by inventing forms that draw attention to gender issues; examples include 'herstory', 'cyber-gURLs' and 'wimmin'. Playing with words has long been a technique used by feminist writers to draw attention to male dominance in language and society. For example, Mary Daly used slashes and hypens to shift word meanings to highlight women's issues. 'Re-fusing', for instance, was defined as 'an essential to the process of the Self's re-membering, re-fusing' (Daly, 1978, p. 67). Daly's subversive use of words did not follow any rules to ensure a non-sexist language – rather it mobilised language in ways that highlighted and challenged taken-for-granted beliefs about the social and moral order. *Webster's first new intergalactic wickedry of the English language*, conjured by Mary Daly in cahoots with Jane Caputi (1987), highlights that the imaginative and playful use of language is at least as effective as 'non-sexist language rules' for subverting masculine meanings in language.

Another aspect of language that has been interpreted as emphasising male prominence is the order of precedence given to feminine and mascu-line terms in parallel constructions. Smith (1985) noted that in language the etiquette of 'ladies before gentlemen' is, in Shakespeare's terms, 'more often followed in the breach than the observance'. The more usual word order is to place the male term first, as in husband and wife, brother and sister and host and hostess. Like the grammatical rule for masculine generics, the historical roots of the tendency to place male terms first have been traced back to the work of prescriptive grammarians. Wilson (1560, cited by Bodine, 1975) outlined the order-of-mention rule, 'the worthier is preferred and set before. As a man is sette before a woman.'

More recent work on language use has shown that male primacy in parallel constructions is not absolute but depends on context. After study-ing how people produced a range of parallel constructions, McGuire and McGuire (1992) suggested that people's word-order preferences reflected more general cultural beliefs regarding gender-appropriate spheres of activity. So that in traditionally female domains, such as within family contexts, there was a more pronounced female primacy (e.g. Mum and

Dad). Outside the family, male primacy was more pronounced (e.g. Mr and Mrs, male and female).

Another feature of the English language which can be understood as obscuring women is the relative lack of lexical resources to refer to women and women's experiences. For example, words to describe sex and sexuality overwhelmingly deal with men and men's experiences. Germaine Greer (1970) in *The female eunuch* was among the first to note the lack of terms that adequately encode women's experience of sex. She pointed out that all the linguistic emphasis of words and labels describing the sexual act (e.g. fuck, shag, screw) had been placed on the penetrative act performed by an active male on a passive female. Men's sexuality is validated by widely used terms such as 'virility' and 'potency', but everyday ways of symbolising a positive, healthy, sexually active woman are not widespread. However, in particular subcultures of women – for example, in lesbian communities – sexual terms for women that are generally thought of as negative may be used in more positive ways (for more recent studies of sexual slang, see James, 1996; Sutton, 1995).

Women defined narrowly

The narrow definition of women in language refers to the observation that women are more often discussed in terms of their appearance and their family relationships, whereas men are more often discussed in terms of what they do (Key, 1975). The power to define women in terms of their marital status is seen starkly in cultural traditions of naming. Naming and naming practices have been an important aspect of the study of languages because of the insights they provide into the world view and social hierarchies of a culture. The types of names given, the systems through which they are bestowed, and the ways they are used in social interaction vary widely from society to society (Alford, 1987). In the case of Anglo-American-influenced cultures, naming practices reflect the patriarchal nature of society, where a male is the head of the family, and descent, kinship and title are traced through the male line. Another feature of the patronymic Anglo-American tradition is that boys are commonly named after their fathers (Otta, 1997).

A significant aspect of naming practices is that they constitute cultural conceptions of the self and the self's relation to others in society (Strathern, 1992). Typically in English-speaking societies, individuals are distinguished at birth by an individual name; this practice supports dominant notions of the importance of individual identity for a sense of self. So the name represents an important aspect of self, an anchor to selfhood (Allport, 1963). Generally the bestowed name also identifies an individual as male or female. Butler (1993) argued that personal naming at birth is a performative act, one that 'initiates the process by which a certain girling is compelled' (p. 224). The labelling and naming of gender at birth can be understood to be performative because it requires the referent and people responding to that referent to act in accordance with relevant gender norms and expectations. Consistent with Butler's argument are studies that show that adults respond to the same infant differently, and interpret the behaviour of that infant differently, depending on whether they are told that the child is a girl or a boy (e.g. Burnham and Harris, 1992; Condry and Condry, 1976). Differential treatment of boys and girls even occurs when the adult feels that their behaviour towards the child is independent of their gender.

The practice of a wife taking a husband's surname defines women narrowly – that is, in terms of their family. Furthermore, when a woman is referred to by her husband's first name as well, as in Mrs John Smith, she is rendered both subordinate and invisible (Baron, 1986). The assumption of a man's name on marriage suggests that the woman is merely an extension of her husband or part of her husband's estate. A further problem with the practice is, as Spender (1980) noted, the difficulties it creates with tracing maternal rather than paternal lineages of descent. Some women have tried to resist the symbolic meaning of name-changing by not changing their name when they marry, or hyphenating their birth name with their husband's name. However, neither maintaining one's birth name nor using double-barrelled names fully resolves these problems. Keeping your father's name as a protest against assuming some other man's name still perpetuates an androcentric naming practice. Also, having the same name as your partner can be understood as a symbol of commitment to a relationship, rather than a reflection of patriarchy. Yet regardless of the effectiveness of the strategies used to resist traditional name-changing practices, women's attempts to defy social customs are a deliberate confrontation of inequitable systems of naming.

Apart from documenting the demographic characteristics of women who decide to keep their name after marriage, existing research on women's surnames has largely focused on two different aspects of marital name-changing (see Duggan, Cota and Dion, 1993 for a review). One line of work measures people's impressions of women who comply with or defy convention. For example, Scheuble and Johnson (1993) examined White American college students' attitudes towards women's surname decision. Most respondents thought that it was okay for women to keep their own name. However, in general, men were less accepting of women keeping their name than women were. Women planning to marry later and planning more liberal work roles after children were less likely to indicate that they would change their name on marriage.

A second line of enquiry investigates factors that correlate with the decision to change or not change name at marriage. For example, Kline, Stafford and Reiss (1996) compared women who were name-changers with

women who were name-keepers on a range of demographic and relationship measures. They found that name-keepers were significantly older,
were more educated and had higher incomes than name-changers. Name-
keepers and name-changers did not differ in terms of marital satisfaction,
love towards their husbands, perceptions of mutual control or commitment
levels, but they did consider different issues when making their decision
about marital naming. Women who changed their name were more likely
to describe the name-change as symbolic of a commitment to the partner-
ship and family, whereas name-keepers were more likely to mention
identity issues.

Another feature of naming conventions in English that defines women in
terms of their relationship with others is that titles preceding women's
names have traditionally varied according to whether they are married or
not (Mrs or Miss). In contrast, the equivalent title (Mr) comes before men's
names regardless of their marital status. Jespersen (1911) documented that
both female titles stem from the word Mistress: Miss being used to refer to
a girl and Missis (Mrs) to an older woman. Master is still used in some
situations as a title for boys, and Mister (Mr) for men, but these forms
have not developed as marital status markers.

Miller and Swift (1976) suggested that patriarchal societies' need to
identify whether a woman was married or not coincided with the industrial
revolution. At this time women started to work outside a community
where all personal information about its members was shared:

> Under these circumstances a simple means of distinguishing
> married from unmarried women was needed (by men) and it
> served a double purpose: it supplied at least a modicum of infor-
> mation about a woman's sexual availability, and it applied not so
> subtle social pressure toward marriage by lumping single women
> with the young and inexperienced.
>
> (Miller and Swift, 1976, p. 99)

A relatively recent strategy to remove the inequity in titles has been the
introduction of the unmarked title 'Ms'. Allegedly, Ms was first introduced
by American mail-order firms to save on the cost of enquiries about the
marital status of customers. Indeed, Baron (1986) documented discussions
about Ms in the context of business writing in the 1950s. Whatever its
origin, since the 1960s Ms has been adopted by women who object to
having a title that is marked for marital status.

There has been some research on people's perceptions of women who
use 'Ms' as a title. In a questionnaire study, Heilman (1975) found that
American undergraduate students rated course descriptions as less
enjoyable and less intellectually stimulating when taught by a 'Miss' or a
'Mrs' than when taught by a 'Ms'. Connor, Byrne, Mindell, Cohen and

Nixon (1986) asked people in a North American shopping mall to read and rate fictional paragraphs about achieving women. They found that female characters (one a college student, one a professional) described using the title Ms were rated as less honest than those described using Mrs or Miss. In a Canadian study, Dion and Schuller (1990) found that a hypothetical working woman preferring the title Ms was judged, by business people, to be like a man and attributed personality traits consistent with those attributed to a successful manager.

So, has Ms become a parallel term to 'Mr'? Pauwels (1998) noted that for Ms and Mr to become equivalent the use of 'Miss' and 'Mrs' would need to be abandoned, which hasn't happened. So despite intentions to the contrary the addition of 'Ms' may have aggravated the linguistic bias in titles for men and women, by providing even more information about women. For example, Ms is associated with feminism and widowhood (Wood, 1997). Pauwels suggested that a better option to address the gender imbalance might be to introduce new titles for men, which could provide more personal information about, for example, marital status.

Regardless of its success at remedying the imbalance of the personal title system, the use of Ms has consistently attracted controversy. The *New York Times*, for example, refused to print Ms, even if a woman preferred that title, until 1987 (Wood, 1997). More recently, the Business and Professional Women UK (BPW) attracted considerable media attention when their national president suggested that Ms was too closely associated with radical feminism and it was seen by clients as aggressive. The President of the BPW suggested using the uniform title of Miss (e.g. *Scotsman*, UK, 27/03/97; *The Times*, UK, 26/03/97; *Mirror*, UK, 26/03/97; *The Dominion*, NZ, 27/03/97). Similar to many issues concerning sexism in language, the importance of the issue is highlighted, paradoxically, by the way it is trivialised. Some examples of headlines around the time of the BPW conference were: 'Feminist title a Ms-take', 'UK style – A name with a ring to it' and 'Death by Ms adventure'. The 'trouble' around the use of Mrs, Miss or Ms can be understood as another demonstration of the links between language and the dominant moral order.

Research on gender and personal names, other than that on surnames and titles, also exists. Studies have suggested that there are stereotypes associated with names (see Otta, 1997). Those stereotypes may affect an individual's self-concept as well as impacting on the perceptions and behaviour of others towards the bearers of those names. For example, in a British study, Petrie and Johnson (1991) found a relationship between the perceived sex-typing of a name and the degree to which an individual with that name was sex-typed. In an American study, Zweigenhaft, Hayes and Hagan (1980) compared the self-ratings of men and women with ambiguous names (e.g. Kim, Leslie) with those of men and women with clearly gendered names (e.g. Mark, Pam). They found that ambiguously named men were not significantly different in their self-ratings from gender-clear named males, but ambiguously named women rated themselves higher in status and lower in femininity than women with gender-specific names.

Hypocoristic names (truncated forms of first names) and nicknames are an interesting subset of personal names because they are susceptible to relatively quick innovation and loss. In a comprehensive cross-cultural study, Harré (1980) found that a lot of importance was attached to giving and having shortened names or nicknames. Harré argued that people who have no nicknames are seen as less important, 'it may be better to be called Sewerage than merely John' (Harré, 1980, p. 81). There has been some research on sex bias in patterns of nicknaming. Poynton (1989) noted that in Australia male names tend to get truncated (e.g. Christopher to Chris), while the addition of suffixes was common for female first names (e.g. Christine to Chrissy). The suffixes -y and -ey, like the -ette and -ess suffixes mentioned earlier, tend to have diminutive connotations. Nicknames also seem to reflect beliefs about the sexes. For example, Phillips (1990) found that female nicknames tend to be based on appearance (e.g. Blondie), whereas male nicknames tend to be based on activity (e.g. Chaser) (see also Otta, 1997).

Women depreciated

Henley (1987) suggested that language not only ignored or defined women narrowly but might also demean them. An aspect of the English language that has been identified as derogating women is that masculine forms of words tend to have more positive connotations than feminine ones. To illustrate with examples used originally by Lakoff (1973), compare the connotations of 'bachelor' and 'spinster', 'master' and 'mistress' and 'lord' and 'lady'. Even words that have the same form (e.g. professional, secretary) may have more positive connotations when applied to a man than to a woman. When being referred to in terms of the opposite gender, 'tomboy' has positive connotations while 'sissy' is used as an insult. The fact that it is generally viewed as a compliment when a woman is likened to a man (e.g. she thinks like a man) and an insult when the reverse happens (e.g. he's a real old woman) is a further example of how language can be considered sexist. Perhaps more importantly though, the differential meanings associated with terms for women compared with terms for men further illustrate how language provides evidence of a social and moral order where men and masculinity are valued more than women and femininity.

In comparison to languages such as French and German, English has fewer linguistic forms that are used to indicate gender. One of the ways in which gender is marked in English is by the use of suffixes and adjuncts.

Two suffixes which are commonly used to indicate that a female is being referred to are '-ess' (e.g. actress, waitress) and '-ette' (e.g. suffragette, nymphette) (see Baron, 1986 for a thorough review of the use of feminine suffixes in English). The use of an adjunct (e.g. woman doctor, male nurse) is a less obvious technique for indicating the conventional gender of the term. The marking of feminine terms has been criticised by some for implying that the world is male unless proven otherwise (Schulz, 1975; Spender, 1980). Others have argued that the addition of feminine suffixes and adjuncts has a weakening, diminishing and trivialising effect (e.g. Eakins and Eakins, 1978; Henley, 1987; Miller and Swift, 1976; Poynton, 1989). Stanley (1977) argued that feminine markers contribute to the construction of negative semantic space for women because, no matter what women do, language marks them as being different (e.g. a female surgeon, a woman lawyer), or less important, than men who do the same thing (e.g. waiter vs. waitress, steward vs. stewardess). However, in the case of adjuncts it could be argued that gender marking is not just sexist but provides information about normative gender roles in general. For example, masculine markers may also be used to indicate that a man is entering a stereotypically woman's domain (e.g. male nurse, male prostitute).

Another grammatical technique in English that may indicate the gender of the person being referred to is the use of adjectives. For example, 'pretty', 'charming' and 'emotional' tend to be used to describe women or children and not men. In contrast, words like 'stern', 'strong' and 'tough' will mainly be used in descriptions of men; when these terms are used to describe women they detract from notions of their femininity (Poynton, 1989). Using these terms in unconventional ways (e.g. referring to women as stern and men as charming) may help to undermine adjectives that function to mark (or index) gender. The slogans 'women can do anything' and 'girl power' and the subculture of 'riot grrls' (pronounced with a growl) seem to use this strategy and can be understood as feminist in so far as they are promoting a link between being female and being strong and powerful. Paradoxically the same slogans may also be thought of as reproducing the status quo because they reinforce a cultural system where strength and power are valued.

The changing nature of gendered meanings over time has also been documented as a way in which women have been depreciated in language (Schulz, 1975). Miller and Swift (1976) suggested that many words used to describe females have travelled a road that linguists call 'degeneration of meaning'. They gave the case history of 'virago' to illustrate a phenomenon which they labelled 'semantic polarisation'. Virago, like virtue, came from the Latin 'vir', meaning male person, and had admirable connotations. It usually designated a woman, but could also refer to a man of exceptional strength and courage. It gradually stopped being applied to men and was used to refer to large women or women with a bad temper. More recently a feminist publishing company chose 'Virago' as its name, which is one example of resistance to the tide of semantic derogation in the meaning of terms for women.

Lakoff (1973, 1975) argued that the semantic derogation of female words could be seen occurring in America in the early 1970s because the once neutral term 'woman' had been developing negative connotations. Lakoff argued that the terms 'lady' and 'girl' were more commonly used than 'woman' because they seemed more polite. I was provided with a firsthand example of the perception that referring to an adult female was rude when an older shop assistant admonished a younger one for referring to me as the 'woman' wanting some particular information. However, my preference in service encounters is to be referred to as a woman rather than as a lady or a girl. Lakoff argued that 'girl', because of its associations with immaturity, removed the sexual connotations associated with the label 'woman'. In some speech communities 'girl' is used positively to show a kind of sisterhood, but using 'girl' can seem patronising and demeaning, especially if the speaker is a man. A relatively recent case that suggests that 'ladies' is still not always an appropriate female reference term was when a sports commentator's use of 'ladies', to refer to female athletes, during the Sydney 2000 Olympics was criticised in a newspaper commentary for being anachronistic and out of place (Chadhuri, 2000).

Inspired by studies of semantic change, one of my first forays into empirical research aimed to explore the role of individual psychological functioning in the semantic derogation of words associated with women (see Ng, Chan, Weatherall and Moody, 1993). In this study, I asked a sample of New Zealand university students to learn nonsense words that were associated with pictures of men and women. I assumed that the words would acquire meanings through the learning task and that the meanings that had been acquired could be measured. The results suggested that the nonsense words that had been consistently paired with men's or women's faces acquired connotations consistent with masculine and feminine stereotypes respectively. In addition, students who had unfavourable attitudes towards women (as measured by an Attitude Towards Women scale) downgraded the evaluative connotations of words associated with female pictures and upgraded the evaluative connotations of words associated with male pictures. Although the assumptions about meaning in this study can be criticised, the study was interesting because it gave some indication of how individual cognitive processes may mediate between culture and language change.

Another area of English that has been criticised for trivialising and deprecating women is metaphorical language. In a more recent study, a colleague and I considered the relationships between metaphorical language and dominant social beliefs about women (Weatherall and Walton,

1999). The data for this research were metaphors that students used to refer to women and to sexual experiences. We found that many source domains are used in metaphors about women, including immaturity (e.g. babe), animals (e.g. bird, bitch), clothing (e.g. blue stocking, bit of skirt), food (e.g. tart, sweetie pie), vehicles (e.g. town bike) and furniture (e.g. mattress). Animals are used as a source of metaphors for men as well as women, but the animals used to refer to women tend to be either domesticated (e.g. cats, kittens, chickadees) or hunted for sport (e.g. foxes) (see also Baker, 1981). Many of the metaphors we collected seemed offensive not only because they tended to sexualise women but they also constructed women in passive object positions in sentences that use metaphorical constructions (e.g. 'Looks like he's going to take the wood to the beaver').

Cognition and sexist language

A substantial body of psychological research has investigated the impact of sexist language forms such as masculine generics on cognitive processes such as perception, comprehension and memory. This work is interesting not least of all because, despite feminist critiques of 'male-stream' methodologies, it shows how experimental and empirical methods can be harnessed in support of feminist agendas. The research has repeatedly demonstrated, for example, the (negative) consequences for women that masculine generics have on the interpretation, comprehension and recall of material. Empirical studies have shown that masculine generics are under-stood as referring to men only (MacKay and Fulkerson, 1979; Moulton, Robinson and Elias, 1978), and that people gain a predominantly masculine impression when they are used (Cole, Hill and Dayley, 1983; Schneider and Hacker, 1973). In addition they are perceived as being sexist (Briere and Lanktree, 1983; Murdock and Forsyth, 1985). Falk and Mills (1996) in a review pointed out that virtually every published study has indicated that masculine-marked terms (e.g. chairman, fireman) even when used generically are interpreted as referring to men only.

It has been assumed that masculine generics are sexist because the words 'he' and 'man' have inherent masculine meaning. Some psychological research has argued that the fixed (male-specific) meaning of masculine generic forms can be established using research techniques drawn from cognitive psychology. For example, a proactive inhibition procedure is a method used in cognitive psychology to demonstrate that words belonging to the same category are more strongly associated in memory than words from different categories. So, if you are asked to remember lots of words belonging to the same category (e.g. types of flowers), the accuracy of your recall will decline as the number of words you are presented with from within a category increases. However, if you are presented with a word

26

from a different category (e.g. a type of car), your recall will improve again. Ng (1990) used a proactive inhibition procedure to suggest that 'man' and 'his' were cognitively coded as having a masculine-specific meaning only. Using the proactive inhibition technique, Ng showed that the terms 'man' and 'his' were more frequently recalled after memorising a list of feminine words than after a list of masculine words. Thus 'man' and 'his' were stored in the masculine but not the feminine cognitive category.

An assumption made in Ng's (1990) research was that there is a simple mapping between words, meanings and their representation in memory. More recently it has been argued that social interaction rather than cognition mediates between words and their meaning. However, despite debates about the relative importance of cognitive processes and language in use for successful communication, Ng's study showed that a cognitive approach to language use could be used to demonstrate the significance of sexist language.

Experimental psychological research has also investigated how individual characteristics such as age (e.g. Hughes and Casey, 1986; Ng, 1991), gender (e.g. Crawford and English, 1984; Henley, 1987), attitudes towards women (e.g. Jacobson and Insko, 1985), sex typing (e.g. Briere and Lanktree, 1983), and religious beliefs (e.g. McMinn, Lindsay, Hannum and Troyer, 1990) are implicated in people's use, interpretation and evaluation of sexist language. Of all the factors that have been studied, gender has been identified as influencing the use and interpretation of masculine generics the most.

Research has shown that girls and women more than boys and men tend to be disadvantaged by the ambiguity of masculine generic forms. For example, MacKay (1979) investigated the impact of using the generic 'he' on attitudes towards and comprehension of written material taken from a university textbook. The study showed that female participants had lower comprehension and personal relevance scores for a paragraph using the generic 'he', than for paragraphs using 'they'. Similarly, Crawford and English (1984) were interested in how masculine generic references could affect cognitive performance. A sample of participants was asked to read and later recall information about an essay on the work of psychologists. Crawford and English found that essays written using masculine generics led to better recall of factual content for males, whereas essays written using other generic forms produced better recall in females.

An explanation that has been put forward to account for sex differences in the interpretation and recall of information written using masculine generic forms is that the meaning associated with masculine generics is different for men and women (Spender, 1980). For men, words marked as masculine are always inclusive of them, regardless of whether they are being used in a gender-specific or generic way. So, masculine words tend to make men think of themselves, and men will tend to use masculine forms in a gender-specific way. Women are more likely to use masculine terms in a more truly generic way because that is the only way that they may include themselves in the reference group. Consistent with this explanation, sex differences have been found in the interpretation and use of masculine generics. Moulton, Robinson and Elias (1978) found that women used fewer masculine generic forms and more true generics than men. Martyna (1980b) found that women were more likely to draw a generic interpretation from 'he' and 'man' than were men. Nevertheless in Martyna's study masculine generic forms were interpreted more often as sex-specific than gender-inclusive.

Some social psychological research suggests that girls may be personally as well as cognitively disadvantaged by the use of masculine generic forms. Henley, Gruber and Lerner (1988) measured self-esteem among school children who had read stories using masculine or neutral pronouns. They found that boys had more positive change in self-esteem in the masculine pronoun condition, while girls had more positive self-esteem change in the neutral pronoun condition. Consistent with Henley *et al.*'s findings were those of McArthur and Eisen (1976) who found that pre-school boys' achievement and perseverance were increased by hearing a story about male accomplishment, and girls' achievement was increased by hearing a story about female accomplishment. These kinds of research highlight the importance of language in the development of children's understanding of themselves as gendered in a patriarchal society.

Another line of research on masculine generics has investigated how speakers are evaluated. For example, Johnson and DowlingGuyer (1996) found that participants in their study expressed less willingness to see counsellors who used masculine generic forms and rated them as more sexist than counsellors who used more neutral terms. In addition, Johnson and DowlingGuyer found that the impact was most evident with women and feminist participants, who expressed even less confidence in counsellors using masculine generic forms than in those using more inclusive language. Interestingly, no such negative evaluation was found for speakers using masculine generics in the context of religious sermons (Greene and Rubin, 1991)!

The effectiveness of communication in some contexts seems to be influenced by the use of masculine generic forms. In a study of persuasion, Falk and Mills (1996) found that the use of masculine generic forms inhibited the persuasion of women and not men. Women respondents did not consider appeals using masculine pronouns as being directed towards them. McConnell and Fazio (1996) found that participants' beliefs about sex roles, rather than their own sex, influenced how persuasive participants found a message. Those with more traditional gender-role beliefs were more influenced by language using masculine generic forms than participants with more liberal beliefs.

The main message from work on masculine generics is that, when used, they tend to exclude women and they promote an androcentric view of the world. Virtually every published study on the topic has shown that masculine generics tend to be interpreted as masculine-specific (Falk and Mills, 1996). The consequences are far-reaching – the use of masculine generic forms may impact on women's ability to recall material (e.g. Crawford and English, 1984) and even have a negative effect on girls' self-esteem (e.g. Henley, Gruber and Lerner, 1988). Thus, the social psychological research forms a useful body of evidence to support feminist calls for language change.

Psychological research has not only investigated the impact of sexist language on cognitive processes such as comprehension and recall, but also its applied consequences. Questions of interest have included whether the process of attracting applicants to jobs is affected by the occupational job title used, and whether the way candidates are described impacts on how they are evaluated as applicants. An early empirical study by Bem and Bem (1973), which investigated the impact of gender-marked language on job discrimination, was used as part of a legal testimony in a sex discrimination case in America. They found that job advertisements which used language that reflected the traditional sex role of occupations discouraged opposite-sex applicants. For example, an ad describing a position for a telephone lineman using the masculine generics 'he' and 'man' discouraged women applicants. Bem and Bem found that significantly more applicants would apply for opposite-sex jobs when the ads were worded using sex-inclusive terms.

The use of masculine generics in legal contexts has also been found to discriminate against women. It has been argued that, historically, where a law was about punishment and a masculine generic form was used, it was asserted that women were included. However, where a law was about privileges or benefits, courts held that women were not intended to be included within the terms of the legislation (see Spender, 1980). Related to this argument, Hamilton, Hunter and Stuart-Smith (1992) tested whether a jury's decision would be influenced depending on whether jury instructions used masculine or truly generic forms. In an experimental study, mirroring a real trial, Hamilton *et al.* found that jurors who were given instructions using masculine generics were less likely to give a female defendant a charge of self-defence and more likely to decide on a charge of murder than when instructions were worded using more neutral terms.

The above studies illustrate how language can influence people's perceptions and behaviour. A different, but related, area of research investigates the link between language and attribution processes. Of interest is how different verbs are regularly associated with different kinds of causal inference, a phenomenon that has been called the implicit causality of verbs (e.g. Brown and Fish, 1983; Semin and Fiedler, 1988). A robust finding is that in sentences with action verbs (e.g. X compliments Y) the sentence subject is most likely to be seen as the cause of the action, whereas for sentences with state verbs (e.g. X likes Y) the tendency is to see the sentence object as causal (but see Edwards and Potter, 1993 for a critique of this approach).

Related to work on verbs and causal influence is work that investigates whether gender of the sentence subject or object influences verb causality. LaFrance and Hahn (1994) documented a disappearing agent effect, which occurs when, regardless of verb type, more cause is attributed to the sentence subject when the sentence object is female compared with when the sentence object is male. In contrast, when the sentence object is male less cause is attributed to the sentence subject. Hence, the implicit causality of verbs is influenced by sex stereotypes about levels of activity (men are more active, women are more passive). It seems that the disappearing agent effect is yet another way in which the English language can be considered sexist.

Chapter summary

Documentation of the ways in which English language is sexist and experimental research on the negative effect sexist language has on the perception and evaluation of women were two dominant aspects of psychological research in the gender and language field conducted during the 1970s and early 1980s. Although useful, this research has more recently been criticised for its assumptions about language and its over-reliance on 'made-up' examples of sexist forms, albeit that they are used to ensure maximum experimental control. From the late 1980s studies began to appear that were less concerned about the impact of particular language forms and more concerned with how everyday talk was used in various and contradictory ways to produce and reproduce the dominant social order. Researchers, such as myself, who have shifted their attention away from the impact of isolated words on psychological processes to studying the various and contradictory ideological functions of talk-in-interaction are part of the discursive turn described later in this book.

Even psychological researchers who continue using mainstream methods have tended to use more valid examples of language in their research. A notable study that combined 'real-life' examples of sexist language with an experimental study was that of Henley, Miller and Beazley (1995), who considered the verb voice (i.e. active or passive) of news media reports of violence against women. In an analysis of articles from over fifty American newspapers, they found that reports of sexual violence against women were most often written in a passive voice that tended to hide the male agency in the crime. In a follow-up laboratory study it was confirmed that readers do attribute less agency to the perpetrator of violence if the action is described in a passive voice (e.g. a woman is raped by a man) than if it is described using an active voice (e.g. a man rapes a woman).

Overall, social psychological research has demonstrated the non-triviality of feminist concerns about the impact of sexism in language. Although the assumptions underlying that work can be questioned (see later chapters), the work is important because it provides a legitimate source of evidence that features of language, such as masculine generics, do have negative psychological consequences, especially for women. Of course sexist language is not just a matter of the ways in which women are represented in language. Sexism in language can be considered more broadly as forms of language use that function to control women, and discourses that perpetuate social beliefs about women. Work that focuses on language as representation hides these aspects of sexism. However, they are highlighted in discursive approaches that emphasise language as social action.

There has been a tendency in the media to trivialise feminist efforts to challenge and change words that ignore or demean women. I have suggested that the trouble stirred up by feminist concerns is an indication that rules about language, even at the level of words, are not trivial but important. Language rules are not neutral but deeply ideological, and responses to feminist calls for linguistic change are evidence of this. A related point is that there is no linguistic change strategy that is naturally and inherently feminist. It seems that, in the case of sexist language, an increased awareness of the problem is as important for feminists seeking social change as are the solutions employed to promote non-sexist language use.

2

QUESTIONS OF DIFFERENCE: VERBAL ABILITY AND VOICE

Introduction

Sexism in language, discussed in the last chapter, was one of two original concerns of the gender and language field. The other issue was the question of whether women and men use language in different ways. An interest in sex differences in language use, like that in sexist language, has a history that predates the attention drawn to it by feminists in the 1960s and 1970s. For example, Bodine (1975) cited anthropological studies conducted by European scholars in the seventeenth and eighteenth centuries that reported differences between women's and men's speech in 'exotic' cultures (e.g. Asian, African and Pacific). It was not until the twentieth century that sex differences in the speech of Europeans were considered. One of the earliest discussions of sex differences in language as an everyday, rather than a remarkable, feature was a study by Jespersen (1922) who, in *Language: its nature, development and origin*, discussed both sex differences in verbal ability and female/male variation in language use. Psychological studies dating from the 1930s and 1940s began to chart the emergence of sex differences in children's language (see Maccoby and Jacklin, 1974).

Topics of sex differences in language have attracted such a quantity of research that Crawford (1995), in a review of the literature, suggested that virtually every possible source of language variation has been considered as potentially gender-linked. Paradoxically, despite all the research, few facets of language have been found that exclusively distinguish between the sexes (Ochs, 1992). Over the next couple of chapters, reasons why definitive answers to questions of differences have proved so elusive will be explored. An interesting issue that arises from the lack of closure on the topic of sex differences and language is when or whether questions of difference are worthy of the lay, media and scholarly attention they attract.

The area of sex differences in language covers a huge spectrum of subject matter that crosses the interests of various academic disciplines. For example, the topics of gender and voice, verbal ability and brain specialisation for language have primarily interested psychologists, with differences in language development being examined in both educational and psychological research. Cross-cultural variability in gender differences has primarily been the domain of anthropologists; and sex variation at the phonological, syntactic and semantic levels of language has been of more interest to linguists. These issues are just a sample of the kinds of sex differences in language that have been investigated.

In addition to the diverse topics, there is a tremendous variety of theoretical frameworks and methodological approaches brought to research on gender difference and language. Seemingly simple but important theoretical issues at stake include: what it means to be a man or a woman, what is language, and what are the relationships between gender identity and language. A researcher's questions and choice of empirical techniques often reveal something of their underlying theoretical assumptions. Up until recently, assumptions common to much of the research were that there are fundamental and essential differences between women and men; those differences will be reflected in the language used by men and that used by women; and systematic research will identify what the stable and enduring differences are. Work based on these common assumptions will be critically examined over this and the next chapter.

Research comparing women's and men's language use is part of a wider literature on the study of sex differences in other aspects of behaviour. The lack of compelling evidence for, or consistent explanations of, sex differences in language is indicative of a wider confusion about the nature, size and origins of other sex differences. Current confusion surrounding the biological, behavioural and/or social characteristics of men and women was illustrated in the title of an article by Rhoda Unger (1992), 'Will the real sex differences please stand up?' Questions about the reliability and validity of psychological research on sex differences are part of a set of broader arguments about the usefulness of focusing on sex differences in any type of behaviour. Those arguments appear in debates about the social scientific study of sex differences. Journals that have dedicated substantial space to discussions of whether and how to study sex differences have included *Feminism and Psychology* (1994), *American Psychologist* (1995, 1996) and the *Journal of Social Issues* (1997). Edited books have also been a forum where the issue of studying sex differences has been considered (e.g. Walsh, 1997).

This chapter will begin by outlining the major aspects of the debate about sex differences research in psychology. The dominant issues that have emerged from that debate have been important in the development of my perspective, presented in the following chapters, on questions about difference in gender and language research. Two central themes of the sex differences debate are biological essentialism/determinism (the idea that there are biological causes for sex differences) and differences as social disadvantage for women (the tendency for knowledge about sex differences to be used in a way that disadvantages women). This chapter will focus on the biological essentialism/determinism theme of the debate. The topics covered – sex differences in verbal ability and sex differences in voice – have concerned psychologists for some time. The issue of sex differences will continue into the next chapter where a broader concern of the gender and language field will be explored – gender differences in speech styles.

Debates about questions of difference

Psychology has a long tradition of focusing on differences between people. One of the major sources of differences it has been concerned with is the differences between men and women. Despite over a century of consideration, there has been little consensus about the nature, size and origins of sex differences. The inextricability of essential (whether biological or social in origin) and socially constructed differences has been suggested as one reason why satisfactory resolutions to questions of sex difference have failed to emerge (e.g. Bem, 1993; Hare-Mustin and Marecek, 1990; Tavris, 1992, 1993). In the case of gender and language, it has proved difficult to disentangle whether sex differences in voice, for instance, emerge from biological and/or socially learned differences between men and women, or whether particular voice characteristics such as pitch are 'performed' in order to enact the appropriate gender and/or sexual identity. An important issue is what comes first – are speech styles expressions of an existing identity or is the identity produced as an effect of a speech style being used (Cameron, 1997)? Essentialist approaches take an individual's language as a marker of their personal and social identity. In contrast, a social constructionist would point to instances such as Dustin Hoffman's performance in *Tootsie* or transsexuals' ability to pass (i.e. to be recognised and treated as a member of the target gender) to highlight that gender cannot be fully explained by biological causes or through social learning. From a social constructionist perspective, identity is constructed from, and is a product of, social practices.

Questions about sex differences largely presuppose sex or gender essentialism. The question of how productive gender essentialism is, and whether psychologists should study sex differences, has attracted considerable debate amongst feminist psychologists (Eagly, 1995; Hare-Mustin and Marecek, 1990; Kitzinger, 1994). The positions taken on this debate and the issues raised have parallels in the gender and language field – particularly research that asks about the characteristics that differentiate women's speech from men's.

Contributors to the debate about whether to study sex differences vary widely in their responses, from a definite yes (e.g. Buss, 1995, 1996; Eagly, 1994, 1997; Halpern, 1994; Hyde, 1994), to a resounding no (e.g. Epstein,

1997; Hare-Mustin and Marecek, 1994; Hollway, 1994; Lott, 1997; Marecek, 1995; Riger, 1997). Even when the answer is yes there is considerable disagreement about the size, significance and cause of differences. Kitzinger (1994) summarised some of the richness of the arguments on the issue, saying:

> The arguments . . . are informed by . . . theories about other key concerns . . . the nature of women's oppression; the relevance of psychoanalytic, biological and social explanations of, and challenges to, that oppression; the nature of science and the social constructionist/essentialist debate; and the effects and implications of feminist intervention in social scientific research. Disagreement and agreement about many of these issues cuts across the 'pro' and 'anti' sex differences divide.
>
> (Kitzinger, 1994, p. 503)

In the above quotation, Kitzinger noted that one of the cornerstones of debates about sex differences is gender essentialism. At the risk of oversimplification, gender essentialism may take one of two forms. Biological essentialism is where 'natural' processes (e.g. genetic, anatomical or physical) are viewed as the primary causes of gender. A second form of essentialism points to more 'social' processes (e.g. learning, modelling) as leading to the development of gender. Within the topics relevant to the gender and language field, it is sex differences in verbal ability and voice that have been assumed to have biological origins, whereas gender differences in speech are assumed to be the result of different socialisation practices for boys and girls. Variation in verbal ability, voice or speech beyond gender – with, for example, sexual orientation (but see Livia and Hall, 1997), socio-economic status or ethnicity – has largely been ignored. A corollary to many essentialist theses about sex differences is a commitment to the notion that scientific approaches will establish what the true and enduring differences are. However, even in the seemingly straightforward cases of verbal ability and voice, science has failed to explain gender differences adequately.

Researchers committed to the methodological norms of scientific enquiry generally take an essentialist approach to gender and maintain that answers to questions of sex difference can be established (e.g. Halpern, 1994). The aim of their work is to establish what the true and enduring cognitive and/or behavioural sex differences are. For example, Halpern (1994) maintains that there are brain differences between women and men and that these can be used to explain differences in verbal ability. In contrast, gender researchers like myself are unconvinced by the inconsistent evidence about brain differences, and are sceptical about the relationships posited between brain structure and psychological function.

Furthermore, influenced by ideas associated with the discursive turn in psychology, a more critical approach questions the taken-for-grantedness of gender – can all human beings be straightforwardly classified as one of two and only two sexes? Furthermore, while not denying the importance of evidence-based knowledge claims, critical approaches question the assumption that good scientific research naturally and inevitably produces value-neutral facts. Bias is most likely to enter research when the object of study is something like gender, which is loaded with social meaning.

Much psychological research has been very conventional in its approach to sex differences. By conventional I mean that the importance and naturalness of gender are assumed and a scientific approach is understood to be the most appropriate way of producing knowledge about it. As might be expected, in psychology the brain has often been proposed as the origin of cognitive or behavioural variations found between women and men (e.g. Kimura, 1983, 1992). Scientific ideas about natural selection and socio-biological arguments have been put forward to explain how sex differences in the functional organisation of the brain have evolved (Buss, 1995; Kimura, 1992). However, such explanations have been quite controversial because they almost inevitably support traditional and stereotyped ideas about the appropriate social roles for women and men (see Derry, 1996; Silverstein, 1996). Furthermore, the lack of consensus on issues concerning the existence and reasons for sex differences has led feminist researchers, in particular, to think more carefully about why comparisons between men and women seem so important and whether they deserve the attention they get (e.g. Baumeister, 1988; Hare-Mustin and Marecek, 1994).

Essentialist approaches have been, and continue to be, significant perspectives in social psychological research. An unfortunate tendency of essentialist explanations of behaviour in psychology, alluded to in the quotation above taken from Kitzinger (1994), is that sex differences have been largely interpreted as deficits in women. Carol Tavris, in her 1992 book *The mismeasure of woman*, detailed how psychology has treated male behaviour as the norm and female behaviour as opposite to it – lesser and deficient. Bem (1993) argued that the concept of a lens of andro-centrism was useful to elucidate how men and male experiences get viewed as a neutral standard or norm. In contrast, women and female experiences become, by definition, deviant and hence deficient. A similar pattern found in the gender and language field has been dubbed the androcentric rule where:

> Men will be seen to behave linguistically in a way that fits the writer's view of what is desirable or admirable; women on the other hand will be blamed for any linguistic state or development which is regarded by the writer as negative or reprehensible.
>
> (Coates, 1986, p. 15)

There have been numerous feminist critiques exposing how the scientific study of sex differences in general has been androcentric (see Bohan, 1992). Some of the most damning reviews were based on scientists' work on intelligence at the beginning of the twentieth century. Shields (1975) and others (e.g. Bem, 1993; Siaan, 1994) have argued that biological accounts of sex differences and male dominance emerged around the mid-nineteenth century as the language of science took over from the language of religion for justifying women's secondary status in society. Arguing that the underlying assumption of scientists from the late nineteenth century was that women were physically and intellectually inferior to men was a critical aspect of early feminist reviews of psychology (Sherif, 1979; Weisstein, 1968/1993). Examining how research findings are interpreted on the basis of stereotyped assumptions about women and men remains an important critical tool for feminist psychologists, including those with a specific interest in language.

An important point made by feminist critiques of sex differences research was that sexual inequality had been naturalised through scientific accounts of 'women's nature'. Some early twentieth-century scholars pointed to the nature of women's speech to support claims of female inferiority (see below). However, one of the most striking examples of the use of science to legitimate the subordination of women was Clarke's (1873, see Bem, 1993) use of the conservation of energy principle to argue that higher education was bad for women. His basic thesis was that learning led to an unhealthy drain of energy from women's reproductive organs to their brains; thus women must be excluded from education for their own good.

A report on the Royal Institution Lectures published in the *Illustrated London News* (8 July 1865) further highlights the widely accepted view, among the middle and upper classes at least, about women's 'natural' role in society at that time:

> M. Jules Simon member of the Corps Législatif of France, the eminent philosopher and philanthropist gave three lectures, in French, last week to a very distinguished audience. . . . We can only give the prominent points of M. Simon's eloquent lectures, in which he considered the position of women and the state of the family, and the questions relating to wages and strikes, etc. He commenced by expressing his opinion that man was intended for labour and woman for the charge of her family. Man's weapon is said to be the sword; but certainly that of woman is the needle.

A 'scientific' theory, which was widely held for part of the twentieth century, for explaining men's alleged superior position in society was the variability hypothesis. According to this theory, superiority was equated with variability. Paradoxically women's general verbal competence was used as evidence of their natural inferiority. Men's variable linguistic ability, from orators to stutterers, showed the naturalness of male advantage.

Shields (1975) traced the origins of the variability hypothesis to Darwin's ideas of natural selection and evolutionary progress:

> Because variation from the norm was already accepted as the mechanism for evolutionary progress (survival and transmission of adaptive variations) and because it seemed that the male was the more variable sex, it soon was universally concluded that the male is the progressive element in the species. . . . Once deviation from the norm became legitimised by evolutionary theory, the hypothesis of greater male variability became a convenient explanation for a number of observed sex differences, among them the greater frequency with which men achieved 'eminence'.
>
> (Shields, 1975, p. 86)

Shields (1975) goes on to describe the influence of Havelock Ellis, a champion of the variability hypothesis, on psychologists involved in developing tests to measure intellectual, sensory and motor abilities. Ellis's observation that there were more male geniuses led to the suggestion that genius was a peculiarly male trait – the tendency for genius being reflected in the prominence of men and not women in positions of power and prestige. Ellis's work was taken up by other scholars of the time who used it to argue for education for women that was consistent with their 'natural' place in society as wives and mothers.

Ellis's work also had an impact on language scholars. Jespersen (1922, p. 253) cited Ellis as establishing the 'zoological fact' of greater male variability. Using the variability hypothesis Jespersen manages to explain evidence for women's verbal superiority while maintaining the idea of men's supremacy:

> In language we see this very clearly: the highest linguistic genius and lowest degree of imbecility are very rarely found in women. The greatest orators, the most famous literary artists, have been men . . . there are a much greater number of men than of women who cannot put two words together intelligibly, who stutter and stammer and hesitate, and are unable to find suitable expressions for the simplest thought. Between these two extremes the woman moves with a sure and supple tongue that is ever ready to find words and to pronounce them in a clear and intelligible manner.
>
> (Jespersen, 1922, p. 253)

Over time, the variability hypothesis lost favour to the idea that the physiology of the brain can be used to explain sex differences in intelligence, language and temperament (see Shields, 1975). In common with claims about sex differences using the variability hypothesis, early research on brain structure also proceeded on the assumption of sex differences and women's inferior intelligence. For example, Franz Joseph Gall's 'cranioscopy' was used to argue that women having smaller heads than men was an anatomical indicator of women's inferior intellect.

When cranioscopy was discredited as a system for describing cortical function, the search for sex differences moved to parts of the brain. Shields (1975) documented that in the 1850s the consensus was that the frontal lobes were the seat of intelligence; once that had been established many researchers started reporting better-developed frontal lobes in males than in females. However, a bit later opinion shifted and parietal lobes were thought to be more important for intelligence. The opinion shift led to a revision of neuroanatomical findings to be consistent with beliefs about sex differences. Tavris (1993) argued that a similar type of revision of scientific findings to be consistent with sex-stereotypical beliefs is still occurring:

> Originally the left hemisphere was considered the repository of intellect and reason. The right side was the sick, bad, crazy side, the side of passion. Guess which sex was thought to have left-brain superiority? (Answer: males.) In the 1960s and 1970s however, the right brain was rediscovered. Scientists began to suspect that it was the source of genius and inspiration, creativity and imagination, mysticism and mathematical brilliance. Guess which sex was now thought to have 'right-brain specialization'? (Answer: males.)
>
> (Tavris, 1993, p. 156)

The idea that parts of the brain are more or less specialised for different cognitive functions still has currency today. Indeed, some theories about sex differences in the brain rest upon alleged truths about sex differences in verbal and spatial ability. However, as I shall explain, differences in, what is glossed as, verbal ability are not as clear-cut as is widely assumed.

Since the 1970s a considerable body of empirical research has been conducted that has tended to demonstrate that women and men are more similar than they are different. Bias in the research methods of psychological studies, rather than 'real' differences, has been held as the cause of exaggerated and distorted understandings about differences between women and men (e.g. Grady, 1981; Peplau and Conrad, 1989; Wallston and Grady, 1985). In the 1990s there was somewhat of a 'backlash' against the trend that began in the 1970s to minimise and trivialise sex differences. For example, Eagly (1995) suggested that the tendency for psychologists to minimise sex differences was a *zeitgeist*. She argued that it was important for psychologists to understand sex-differentiated behaviours, such as spatial skills, so that informed training programmes can accommodate gendered preferences. Given that some differences do emerge when we group people by gender, it does seem important to identify these so that they are not responsible for medical problems (e.g. sex-specific reactions to medicines) or social disadvantage. However, such work should proceed cautiously, mindful of feminist critiques of the rather shameful history of sex difference research.

It seems unlikely, given the level of disagreement even amongst feminist psychologists and the validity of the arguments in the 'pro' and 'anti' camps, that the sex differences debate will ever be resolved one way or the other. Nevertheless, it seems useful to understand the complexities and implications of each position.

Tavris (1992) described disagreement about whether women and men are different or the same as maximalism versus minimalism. Minimisers, usually liberal feminists, dispute the contention that universal, important or stable sex differences exist. Typically, sex differences in language, thought or social behaviour are seen by minimisers as socially, historically and culturally specific and not stable or biological in origin.

Hare-Mustin and Marecek (1990) named the inclination to ignore or minimise difference a beta bias. They suggested that a positive consequence of beta bias was that it supported calls for equal access to educational and occupational opportunities. However, they also suggested that arguing for no differences between men and women could be detrimental because it drew attention away from women's special needs and from sex differences in power and other resources. For example, pregnant women may need more frequent rest breaks during working hours. Not providing such breaks is an indication of a structural inequality that benefits men.

On the other side of the fence is maximalism, a position that has parallels with the theories of a feminist standpoint (Harding, 1986, 1992), cultural feminism (Hare-Mustin and Marecek, 1990) and eco-feminism (Tavris, 1992), which all endorse the existence of sex differences. There is an emphasis and celebration of a female nature that is unique – kinder, gentler and more interconnected with people and the environment than a male nature (Tavris, 1992). Carol Gilligan's (1982) study of women's moral development typifies a maximalist position. Gilligan used the metaphor of 'voice' to refer to an ethic of care that signified a fundamentally valuable and unique feminine morality. Consistent with a maximalist position would be where claims about women's superior conversation competence and verbal skills were used to support the necessity of women's high-level involvement in multi-national companies such as banks.

Emphasising women's unique nature leads to what Hare-Mustin and Marecek (1990) called an alpha bias – the exaggeration of differences. Hare-Mustin and Marecek pointed out that a positive outcome of a

40

maximalist position is that it can counter the cultural devaluation of women. However, alpha bias can also support the status quo when women are seen not only as different but also as deficient. Another problem with maximalism is that it tends to emphasise the differences between groups and ignore the differences within them. For example, socially privileged women and men may have more in common than two women – one of whom is privileged, the other living in poverty.

As already mentioned, in the 1990s, a new wave of feminist scientists emerged who advocated a revival of the study of sex differences (e.g. Eagly, 1994; Halpern, 1994). The revivalists have proposed that one challenge for sex differences research is to account for variation between, and within, gender categories (Eagly, 1994; Halpern, 1994). As one would hope, the new enthusiasm for sex differences research often acknowledges the sexism in early scientific work on sex differences. Hyde and Plant (1995), for example, suggested a set of guidelines to be followed so that differences research meets the highest standards of science while not being detrimental to women.

Regardless of the quality and/or interpretation of sex differences research, a perennial problem with the idea of difference is that it clears the path for explanations of differences that have some biological component. For example, Kimura (1992) has argued for a biological component in spatial skills, suggesting that women might benefit from a different training from men in the acquisition of such skills (see also Halpern, 1994). Even more controversial are sociobiological explanations of sexual behaviours which inevitably support the sexual status quo (Buss, 1995, 1996). Such explanations can be very compelling, but are overly simplistic and involve incorrect applications of concepts from evolutionary theory (see Fausto-Sterling, 1986 for a detailed critique of the sociobiological explanations of human sexual behaviour). Biological or sociobiological explanations consistently get used to support rather than challenge women's subordinated social status (Bem, 1993; Hollway, 1994; Riger, 1997). Furthermore, on their own, such explanations never fully or satisfactorily account for differences.

The consistency with which sex differences are seen to be natural and enduring is given as one reason why the study of sex differences should be treated with caution. Another reason is the pernicious way in which sex differences are used to disadvantage women. However, in addition to the practical reasons for being careful and critical of claims about the nature and origin of sex differences, there is a theoretical position that undermines essentialist assumptions altogether: that is, social constructionism. On the topic of gender, the approach supposes that sex categories are social constructs (rather than attributes of individuals) that institutionalise social and cultural power relations. Social constructs such as gender function to make male dominance over women appear natural and inevitable (Epstein, 1997; Hare-Mustin and Marecek, 1990; Hollway, 1994; Lott,

1997; Marecek, 1995). Cameron summarised the social constructionist position on sex differences when she wrote:

> If it were not for our gendered social arrangements, 'sex' as we know it – a strict bipartite classification of people on the basis, usually of their genitals – would not have its present significance. That is not to deny human sexual dimorphism; the point is rather (as it also is with race) that human biological variations assume importance for us when for social, economic and political reasons they become a basis for classifying people and ordering them into hierarchies.
>
> (Cameron, 1997, p. 24)

Referring more specifically to the psychological literature on sex differences, Hare-Mustin and Marecek (1994) proposed that it was not a body of knowledge about the true and real differences between men and women. Instead, they suggested, it was a collection of explanations of gender that were organised using an assumption of difference that would reinforce present social arrangements between the sexes. Or to put it in a different way, sex differences are 'deceptive distinctions' (James, 1997). Examples relevant to language are that women's 'shrill' voices have been used to bar them from broadcasting roles, and their preferred topics of conversation have been trivialised as unimportant or gossip.

To Hare-Mustin and Marecek (1994), and other feminist social constructionists, the sex differences question is simply the wrong question. Instead of asking about difference, research taking a social constructionist approach might examine how notions of gender difference get used to promote inequality and power differentials (Lott, 1997), or investigate how gender is created through social relations in particular contexts (Epstein, 1988). These alternatives all involve an examination of language because it is through language that meaning and knowledge about gender get constituted (see Gavey, 1989 and Weedon, 1987 for more on this point). Thus, there is a 'discursive turn' in new approaches to studying gender that continues and strengthens a long tradition of a feminist concern with language (Wilkinson and Kitzinger, 1995). The influence of social constructionist ideas and the discursive turn on gender and language research is considered more fully in later chapters. Here, the issue of sex differences in verbal ability will be discussed to highlight the issues already raised in the more general debate about the study of sex differences.

Verbal ability

There is a large body of literature on sex differences in verbal ability. The work includes a broad spectrum of approaches, from neurological studies of brain activation during verbal processing tasks (e.g. Shaywitz *et al.*, 1995) to developmental studies of language acquisition (see Brannon, 1996) to research on personality traits in argumentativeness (e.g. Rancer and Dierks-Stewart, 1987). As in general sex differences research, the work rests on an essentialist assumption of stable, inherent, measurable differences between people assigned as male and those identified as female. In the case of verbal ability the assumption is that, on average, females are better than males. In fact the existence of sex difference in verbal ability has been touted as one of the most well established 'facts' of psychology (Kimura, 1992). However, when major reviews of sex differences in verbal ability are carefully examined it seems that the assumption of innate female superiority in language is not as robust as commonly believed (Hyde and Linn, 1988; Maccoby and Jacklin, 1974). Almost certainly sex differences in verbal ability could not unambiguously rise to Unger's (1992) challenge for the real sex differences to stand up.

In part of a now classic review of the psychology of sex differences, Maccoby and Jacklin (1974) analysed the body of research that had amassed to that date on sex differences in verbal ability. Even at that time the supposed truism of female superiority on verbal tasks was heavily hedged:

> Female superiority on verbal tasks has been one of the more solidly established generalisations in the field of sex differences. Recent research continues to support the generalisation to a degree. It is true that whenever a sex difference is found, it is usually girls and women who obtain higher scores, but the two sexes perform very similarly on a number of verbal tasks in a number of sample populations.
>
> (Maccoby and Jacklin, 1974, p. 75)

A particular focus of their review was on the developmental course of any sex differences. They noted that the 'classic' studies most commonly cited as demonstrating sex difference in language development in the first few years of life were based on very small samples where differences would not even reach statistical significance in large samples. They concluded, on the basis of a large number of studies on pre-school children that had been conducted up to the time of their review, that no consistently significant sex differences in linguistic abilities were found in children of that age. In their analysis they considered the measures of verbal ability that had been used as well as the nature and size of the sample studied. What counted as measures of verbal ability varied, and included spontaneous vocalisations, length of any verbalisation and vocabulary size. So, after careful consideration of all the literature that was available to them at the time, Maccoby and Jacklin stated that the presumed language advantage of girls in the first few years of life was, at best, tenuous.

Research on children in their early school years through to early adolescence was, according to Maccoby and Jacklin (1974), more easily
reviewed because studies used larger samples and more standardised
measures of language ability (e.g. Peabody Picture Vocabulary Test,
Scholastic Aptitude Test, and the Wechsler verbal IQ scale). The conclusion they reached with regard to that literature was that there was no
evidence of sex difference in verbal ability until about age 10 or 11. It was
from this age that Maccoby and Jacklin felt that there was sufficient
evidence to support the contention that from high school through to
college years girls demonstrate superior verbal skills. Hence they
concluded:

> for large unselected populations the situation seems to be one of
> very little sex differences in verbal skill from about 3 to 11, with a
> new phase of differentiation occurring at adolescence.
>
> (Maccoby and Jacklin, 1974, p. 85)

Over a decade later, Halpern (1986; 2nd edn, 1992) also published a book
that attempted to synthesise research on sex differences. Halpern's review of
the literature on verbal abilities was far less systematic, critical and
comprehensive than Maccoby and Jacklin's (1974) work. In fact, Halpern's
synthesis of the verbal ability literature seems quite contradictory. For
example, in her initial summary of sex differences in verbal ability she
stated:

> Of all the cognitive sex differences, it is probably the first to
> appear. Females aged 1- to 5-years are more proficient in language
> skill than their male counterparts.
>
> (Halpern, 1986, p. 47)

Then she wrote this seemingly conflicting statement:

> Although verbal sex differences favouring girls in early childhood
> may be somewhat tenuous, they emerge clearly at adolescence and
> continue into old age.
>
> (Halpern, 1986, p. 47)

Unlike Maccoby and Jacklin's (1974) review, Halpern does not appear to
have considered a large body of research. Instead her claims are supported
with only a few references. For example, the evidence she gave to support
her conclusion of early sex differences was a 1976 study that had demonstrated female superiority in language skill at age 1 to 5, and a 1967 study
which reported that girls talked at an earlier age and produced longer
utterances. Support for her contention of the clearly emergent female

superiority of language from adolescence was results from a 1955 study, which had, she claimed, 'been replicated many times since they were first reported in 1955' (Halpern, 1986, p. 48). In addition she cited a study which found that more boys than girls stuttered and were poor readers, and research showing sex differences in the ability to regain language after strokes, as providing other indicators of sex difference in verbal ability.

An important problem highlighted when only a few (weak) studies are used as evidence of sex differences is that research with 'significant' findings (i.e. there is a statistical difference) is far more likely to be published than research finding no difference. A publication bias exists which means that a single study that finds a difference will be published, while many other studies finding no differences will never make it to print (see Grady, 1981; Maccoby and Jacklin, 1974). Publication bias contributes to a 'hall of mirrors' effect where multiple citations of a study and its findings achieve a (mythical) 'truth' status (Cameron, 1997). The 'truth' can then become a self-fulfilling prophecy (little girls are perceived as talking sooner or better than little boys). It seems to me that Halpern's (1986, 1992) work is part of a hall of mirrors effect, giving (alleged) early sex differences in verbal ability the (undeserved) status of fact. For example, a *Scientific American* article cited Halpern to support a claim of the well-established fact of sex differences in verbal ability.

The work of Maccoby and Jacklin (1974) and that of Halpern (1986) both attempted to synthesise the whole area of sex differences research, of which verbal ability was just a small part. As a whole, Maccoby and Jacklin's review seemed to present the most exhaustive and balanced summary of research on sex differences in verbal ability. However, Maccoby and Jacklin's review approach has also been criticised. Block (1976), for example, suggested that they applied inconsistent criteria for deciding what percentage of studies had to find a sex difference for them to conclude that there was a true difference. Nevertheless, the conclusion that Maccoby and Jacklin reached about sex differences in verbal ability was consistent with the trend of the 1970s to minimise sex differences.

After Maccoby and Jacklin's (1974) review, meta-analysis developed, which was seen as a more reliable way of aggregating research findings from a number of different studies. Meta-analysis describes differences and similarities on a continuum by considering the effect sizes of individual studies. It has been extensively applied as a way of aggregating psychological research on sex differences (see Hyde, 1990). Hyde and Linn (1988) employed meta-analysis to reassess the literature of sex differences in verbal ability. The meta-analysis was performed using both the Maccoby and Jacklin (1974) sample of studies and a large sample of studies that had been published since Maccoby and Jacklin's review. Some of the questions Hyde and Linn were interested in answering were: what were the sizes of any sex differences in verbal ability and were these declining? Were sex differences uniform across various measures of verbal ability? And what was the developmental progression of any sex differences?

Over all the studies that Hyde and Linn (1988) included in their analysis, a small effect size was found, indicating that females outperformed males. When the size of the differences was examined separately for different types of verbal ability tests, the size of the sex difference was effectively zero for five of the eight tests. For tests of general verbal ability, solving anagrams and for measures of the quality of speech production there were small effect sizes, all favouring females. When the studies were grouped according to the average age of the participants, the (small) effect size was largest for the under-5-year-olds and the over-26-year-olds. Hyde and Linn also compared the effect sizes of studies that had been published pre- and post-1973. The effect size for the later studies was small and no more than half the size of the earlier studies.

The effect sizes that Hyde and Linn (1988) found fell well short of what has been considered small, even in meta-analytic terms. Hence they concluded:

> We are prepared to assert that there are no gender differences in verbal ability, at least at this time in American culture, in the standard ways that verbal ability has been measured. . . . A gender difference of one tenth of a standard deviation is scarcely one that deserves continued attention in theory, research, or textbooks. Surely we have larger effects to pursue.
>
> (Hyde and Linn, 1988, p. 62)

If Hyde and Linn (1988) are correct and there are effectively no overall sex differences in verbal ability, then research seeking biological explanations for that difference is made redundant. An assumption of such research is that sex differences in verbal ability exist and those differences will be indexed by sex differences in the functional organisation of the brain. For example, Kimura (1992), in her *Scientific American* article, maintained that sex differences in cognitive abilities, including verbal abilities, existed, and put forward evidence that the differing patterns of ability reflected different hormonal influences on the developing brains of males and females – a position surprisingly reminiscent of nineteenth-century scientists who, as already discussed, worked on the assumption of sex differences and aimed to uncover the specific physiological causes of women's (inferior) mental abilities (see Shields, 1975; Bem, 1993).

In fact the sort of re-visioning that Tavris (1993) described with regard to hemispheric specialisation of function is also evident in the literature on the brain's organisation for language. In neuropsychology, two major brain theories have been put forward to explain sex differences in cognitive abilities (see Halpern, 1986). Both rely on the notion of verbal superiority in females, spatial skill advantage in males, and hemispheric specialisation of verbal and/or spatial ability (for a critical review of the literature on sex differences in spatial ability see Caplan, MacPherson and Tobin, 1985; Lott, 1997; Ussher, 1992). So, when brain lateralisation or hemispheric specialisation was thought to disadvantage spatial skills, guess which sex had less lateralised brains? (Answer: males.) However, when evidence emerged that lateralised brains resulted in superior spatial skills, guess which sex had less lateralised brains? (Answer: females.)

Kimura's (1992) claim of sex differences in the functional organisation of the brain has some support but is by no means uncontroversial. Comments in the literature range from complete support for the idea – 'Our data provide clear evidence for a sex difference in the functional organisation of the brain for language' (Shaywitz *et al.*, 1995, p. 607) – to absolute dissent: 'we found no evidence for such differences with either speech production or reception tasks' (Seth-Smith, Ashton and McFarland, 1989, p. 430). As Healey, Waldstein and Goodglass put it, 'one can find in the laterality literature reviews stating that no real sex differences in lateralisation exist to one citing an abundance of evidence that they do exist' (1985, p. 777).

Even when the issue of lateralisation is avoided, the concept of sex differences in the functional organisation of the brain is not forgotten. For example, Hier, Yoon, Mohr, Price and Wolf (1994) argued that the language zone within the left hemisphere was differently placed in women and men, even though, earlier, Kertesz and Benke (1989) had found no evidence of sex differences in either the inter- or intra-cerebral organisation of brains.

As already mentioned, much of the brain research has been motivated by a belief in sex differences in verbal ability – a generalisation that is not strongly backed by empirical evidence. However, even if there was more substantial proof of sex differences in verbal ability, the idea that it could be attributed to differences in the brain is spurious. First, there is no reason to suspect that the tests used to measure the brain's organisation for language (sodium amytal test, dichotic listening tests, visual field and brain-imaging techniques) have any direct relationship with verbal skill, which is an extremely complex set of behaviours. Second, as any reputable neuropsychology text will attest, anatomical, chemical or electoral differences in the brain do not imply a functional difference. As a colleague of mine put it, 'brains vary hugely – big people tend to have big brains but no one thinks that big people are more intelligent. So why would a fairly minor difference in the size of one small collection of neurones imply a major difference in language or math ability?' (David Harper, e-mail communication). Thus it seems reasonable to conclude that simple and straightforward biological explanations are inadequate for addressing the subtlety and instability of gender differences.

Even within the field of biology there is disagreement about what kinds of explanations best account for gender differences. Fausto-Sterling (1997) suggested that even choice of biological explanations depends, at least partly, upon what motivates the knowledge project. Using the example of educational reform, she argued that if the starting assumption is that there are irreducible differences between boys and girls, then biological knowledge which suggests differences between the sexes would be useful for arguing for difference-based reform. If, on the other hand, the starting assumption is that individuals should be given equal opportunities, then genetic arguments may be more useful for the knowledge project:

> Belief in hormonally induced, hard-wired brain differences of very ancient evolutionary origins is easiest to reconcile with difference-based reform – encouraging boys and girls to develop their special but rather different skills. If on the other hand, one assumes that on average anyone can learn just about anything (and ought to do so if they want to), the views of geneticists who focus on norms of reaction, adaptive plasticity and context-dependent gene action will appeal. These latter understandings of biology are more compatible with equity-based reform – the belief that given the right circumstances almost all students can excel.
>
> (Fausto-Sterling, 1997, p. 255)

If one accepts that it is possible to choose an argument to support any knowledge project, then the issue of finding the 'truth' about sex differences seems irrelevant. Fausto-Sterling's (1997) suggestion in the above quotation supports a feminist social constructionist position. That is, that the psychological literature on sex difference in verbal ability, for example, is not a record of cumulative knowledge about what the sex-differentiated language skills are. Rather, it is a repository of accounts of gender, organised to reflect and perpetuate male-dominated culture (Hare-Mustin and Marecek, 1994). A belief in female superiority in verbal skills effectively reinforces cultural stereotypes of women as chatterers, gossips and nags. It is also consistent with the idea that effective interpersonal communication is women's responsibility, and it is their fault when a message has not been understood (see Crawford, 1995).

It seems that asking whether sex differences in verbal abilities exist, or whether there are sex differences in the organisation of the brain for language, may not be very good questions, because they are too general and too simplistic. In the area of sex differences in verbal abilities, as in the general area of sex differences, answers have tended to reflect ideological positions rather than any objective truth. Bergvall (1996) confirmed, using critical discourse analysis, that scientific findings on language, gender and the brain have been reported in a way that polarises gender categories and assumes a straightforward biological essentialism. Then, following a pattern already mentioned, sex differences effectively function to support sex stereotypes and disadvantage women. It is important to remember that 'difference' is not the problem. If everybody were the same the world would be a very dull place. People do, of course, differ. What is problematic is when differences between social groups are foregrounded to the extent that differences within groups are ignored (e.g. due to ethnicity or social class). It is also problematic when differences are used as a *post hoc* excuse for prejudice and inequality – something that has occurred overtly using alleged differences in the nature of women's and men's voices.

Gender and voice

The ability to recognise the sex of a speaker on the basis of verbal cues alone would seem to be good evidence that men's and women's voices do differ in essential ways. Indeed, there are numerous studies that have reported the ability of listeners to correctly identify the sex of speakers by using only verbal cues (see Eakins and Eakins, 1978). Although it is questionable whether reliable recognition of a person's sex on the basis of their voice is important, it is this kind of evidence that supports a maximalism, where male/female differences seem both self-evident and natural. A widespread consensus that women's voices are higher pitched than men's means that voice could be a candidate for Unger's (1992) call for a real sex difference. Unfortunately, agreement that the sex of a speaker can be identified purely on the basis of voice is as far as the certainty goes. As you might expect from the discussion so far, the question of why the sex of a voice is so easily identified does not have any straightforward answer (see Graddol and Swann, 1989 and Smith, 1985 for comprehensive discussions of this issue).

One factor that has been suggested as the cause of sex differences in voices is that, on average, males have larger larynxes or voice boxes than females (Eakins and Eakins, 1978; Graddol and Swann, 1989; Smith, 1985). A typical explanation refers to laryngeal fundamental frequency, which is the average frequency with which vocal cords vibrate. It is widely supposed that, on average, adult human males have longer and thicker vocal cords than adult females do, because, on average, human males are larger than human females. The greater mass and length of vocal cords lead to a slower frequency of vibration of the vocal cords and a lower pitch. Women tend to have higher-pitched voices than men because their vocal cords are shorter and thinner (Eakins and Eakins, 1978). This explanation, however, is unsatisfactory. While it may be true that men on average are larger and therefore have bigger voice boxes, this does not account for the almost 100 per cent accuracy with which the sex of a voice

49

can be identified. The voices of large women do not get identified as male and the voices of small men are not mistaken as female.

A fuller explanation of sex difference in voice refers to formants. Laryngeal fundamental frequency (rate of vocal cord vibrations) is not the only factor that influences the pitch of voice (Eakins and Eakins, 1978; Graddol and Swann, 1989; Smith, 1985). The passage of the vibrating air from the larynx, through a series of resonators (i.e. the mouth, nose and throat cavities and past the tongue and lips), also influences pitch and other voice qualities such as breathiness. So, fundamental frequency or voice characteristics result from the interaction between the laryngeal fundamental frequency and the resonators. Hence voice pitch does not merely reflect physical size but also characteristics of the resonators, some of which are under voluntary control (e.g. tenseness of throat). Everybody can, to some extent, control the pitch of their voice. Hence, sex difference in the acoustic qualities of voice cannot be accounted for by anatomical sex differences in the vocal apparatus alone.

The claim that a simple anatomical explanation cannot account for sex differences in voice raises two questions. What are the vocal cues that people use to identify the sex of the speaker, and what evidence is there that social learning influences voice characteristics? A series of studies reported by Sachs (1975) investigated the cues that led to the identification of the sex of prepubescent children. Stimuli used in Sachs's research were generated from nine pairs of children (each a boy and a girl), who had been matched on height and weight. Each child had been recorded making isolated vowel sounds and speaking in sentences. When the isolated vowel sounds were used as stimuli, judges only performed slightly above chance level for correctly guessing the sex of the child. Despite the fairly low level of accuracy there was high consistency amongst the judges in their guesses. The judges tended to agree on which voices were from girls or boys, even when their judgement was wrong. Sachs found that it was the voices of the larger girls and smaller boys that were incorrectly identified. When the stimuli were sentences, correct judgements were well above chance level. Hence Sachs concluded that vocal sex stereotypes (lower pitch in males and higher pitch in females) are used in people's judgements of the sex of speaker, and that cues other than formant frequencies are important for correct identification of sex of voice. Other research summarised by Smith (1985) confirmed Sachs's findings with adult speakers. So even though male voices drop in pitch with physical changes at puberty, it was stereotypes about voices that tended to influence judgements of speaker sex, and judgements of sex of speaker were more accurate on the basis of speaking than from isolated vocal sounds.

The importance of speech phenomena other than absolute pitch for identifying sex of speaker suggests that there is a strong social learning element in speaking style. The potential to demonstrate that social learning impacts on voice lies in the idea of pitch range. A good demonstration of the potential that voice has to be modified by social learning was given by Graddol and Swann (1989). In one graph they showed the fundamental frequency of voices from a small sample of adults. While the average speaking pitch varied from person to person, there was a clear gap in the graph between the pitch of men's and that of women's voices. However, when the pitch range of the individuals in the sample was graphed, it was clear that the voices of women and men overlapped considerably. Hence, if men and women wished to speak using a similar pitch, they could. To do this, women would have to use the lower end of their range and men the upper end of theirs. Indeed both male-to-female and female-to-male transsexuals are able to adjust their pitch to that which is appropriate for their target gender (Knight, 1992).

Further evidence of a social learning element of voice pitch has been provided by cross-cultural studies. Graddol and Swann (1989) cited research that had found differences in the average speaking pitch across cultures – even when differences in physical sizes were controlled for. For example, the average speaking pitch for American men was lower than the average speaking pitch for a group of Polish men. In a study of gender and pitch levels, Ohara (1992) found that Japanese women used a significantly higher pitch when speaking in Japanese than when speaking in English, thus confirming the idea that speakers control their pitch levels to be consistent with social norms. Additional evidence for the impact of social norms on voice was a study cited by Smith (1985) which found that babies shift their pitch to match that of the parent they are interacting with.

The idea that shifts in pitch range (i.e. intonation patterns) rather than absolute pitch identify the sex of speaker has been the focus of a number of empirical studies. Women supposedly use a wider pitch range, and thus have a more dynamic intonation pattern than men (McConnell-Ginet, 1983). However, evidence of gender differences in intonation patterns is mixed. Interestingly, when measures of sex differences are questioned and differences in pitch range are not found, the idea of difference is not abandoned. Instead it is assumed that the measure or the method is at fault. For example, Henton (1989) criticised early studies that found sex differences in speaker pitch range because they used the Hertz scale. The Hertz scale fails to adjust for the non-linearity of pitch perception. A larger change in frequency at a higher absolute range of a female voice is needed to produce the same perceptual effect as a smaller change in the frequency of a lower-pitch voice. Henton reanalysed the data from studies showing significant sex differences in pitch range, using a logarithmic semitone scale that is close to a human perceptual scale. After the reanalysis the sex differences either disappeared or suggested that it was men who used more intonation. Later studies (see below) criticised the use of the Hertz scale.

Haan and van Heuven (1999) argued that ERB (Equivalent Rectangular

Bandwidth) was more appropriate than either the Hertz or semitone scales for measuring pitch movement in speech because their study using the ERB scale found a wider pitch range in women's speech than in men's. Daly and Warren (2001) reanalysed the data from studies that Henton (1989) had used, and once again found a greater pitch range in female speakers in the majority of cases. Daly and Warren suggested that where a greater pitch range for women was not found it was because reading tasks were used, where there tends to be less intonation anyway. In their study using a storytelling task they found that women used a greater pitch range than men. However, unlike earlier studies on pitch, Daly and Warren suggested a social rather than a biological reason for the difference, because the pitch range used was greater than could be attributed to anatomical sex differences. They argued that women were using pitch patterns to attract and maintain the interest of the listeners, which indicated their involvement in conversation and showed their interpersonal orientation. This explanation is consistent with the 'difference' theory of gender and speech which gets discussed in the next chapter.

The research on voice discussed so far shows that people can accurately identify speaker sex on the basis of voice alone. However, it is unclear exactly what aspect of voice makes speaker sex so readily identifiable. Certainly any differences in voice that are found cannot be adequately accounted for by physical sex differences. Such a conclusion is similar to that made by psychological sex difference research as a whole. In this case, it seems that individuals use their voice to accommodate towards perceived social norms of gender identity. Thus in Ohara's (1992) study, female bilingual speakers used a higher pitch when speaking Japanese than when talking in English, because of different expectations about femininity and pitch in those two cultures. The idea that pitch (or any other behaviour) gets used as a cultural marker of gender, instead of considering pitch (or any other behaviour) as being caused by sex differences, is consistent with a social constructionist approach. Evidence of pitch being used to signal gender identity has been found by studying gay men's (Barrett, 1997) and gay women's speech (Moonwomon, 1985; Moonwomon-Baird, 1997).

A problem that some feminist critics have identified with the assumption of basic differences between men and women is that male behaviour is treated as the valued norm whereas women's behaviour is viewed as lesser and deficient (Bem, 1993; Hare-Mustin and Marecek, 1994; Riger, 1997; Tavris, 1992). The lower pitch levels that characterise some women in politics (Margaret Thatcher being the classic example; Helen Clark and Jenny Shipley are the New Zealand equivalent examples) were interpreted by Coates (1986) as reflecting and reinforcing the social desirability associated with a man's voice. Coates described the behaviour of such women as assimilating to a male norm – a strategy, she suggested, they were using to increase their prestige. Indeed the fact that Margaret

Thatcher was trained to speak in a lower voice supports the idea that low pitch is viewed as desirable, at least for a prime minister.

Spender (1980) suggested that the undesirability of high pitch, like many other supposed deficiencies in women's language, is based on the sex of the speaker and not the speech itself. Thus pitch can be seen as irrelevant; it simply serves as a supposed objective excuse for devaluation and discrimination. Gill (1993) confirmed that women's voices, regardless of their pitch, do indeed get used to justify sexist employment practices in radio stations. Her research involved interviewing a sample of British broadcasters about the lack of female disc jockeys (DJs). Gill found that the broadcasters used women's 'shrill' voices as an excuse not to employ women as newsreaders. However, women's 'dusky' voices were used to justify limiting their role in radio to late-night shows (the 'graveyard' shift).

The issue of sex differences in voice highlights many of the problematic aspects of sex difference research in general. Voice was observed as indexing gender. Sex difference in voice was assumed to have a biological origin based on anatomical sex differences and that difference has been used as a (*post hoc*) justification for discriminating against women in broadcasting.

Chapter summary

One of the two issues that have historically occupied gender and language research is that of gender differences in language use. Outside the gender and language field there has been considerable debate about whether questions of gender difference are worth pursuing. The general issues raised in that debate were discussed at the beginning of this chapter. A particular problem with sex difference research is the lack of consensus about exactly what aspects of cognition and behaviour differentiate between women and men. One suggestion is that the inextricability of essential (whether biological or social in origin) and socially constructed difference is a reason why satisfactory resolutions to questions of sex difference have not been reached. This chapter discussed research on sex differences in verbal ability and voice as examples of areas that illustrate the more general pattern of non-closure in sex difference research. Despite popular belief to the contrary, Hyde and Linn's (1988) meta-analysis of studies on verbal ability is evidence that general sex differences in verbal ability do not exist. Studies on voice have found that people can readily identify people's gender on the basis of their speech, but research has been unable to isolate exactly what features of voice account for that ready identification. The theme of sex difference in speech continues in the next chapter on women's language. Issues that get discussed in more detail in that chapter are why sex differences are so hard to pin down and why knowledge and beliefs about gender differences effectively function to disadvantage women.

3

WOMEN'S LANGUAGE?

Introduction

A central characteristic of gender and language research is that it has been dominated by a single major theme – that of difference. The last chapter focused on the topics of sex differences in verbal ability and sex differences in voice, which have primarily been subjects of psychological research. In that chapter I noted that an underlying assumption common to much psychological work is that essential biological characteristics are the cause, or at least the foundation, of the verbal ability or voice differences observed between men and women. However, at best, research has provided equivocal support for the idea that biological, anatomical or structural brain differences between men and women are the cause of any sex differences in voice or verbal ability.

This chapter continues to focus on the sex differences theme that began in Chapter 2, but here the topic is gender and speech styles. Like work on sex differences in verbal ability and voice, research on gender and speech style has largely been based on essentialist assumptions. Unlike investigations into sex differences in verbal ability and voice, however, sex-specific speech styles are generally not considered a consequence of biological sex. Instead, consistent with ideas about social learning, they are seen as the result of socialisation, where people internalise socially and culturally prescribed gender roles.

The huge cross-cultural variability in the speech styles associated with men and women is used to support a social learning explanation of sex differences in language use. As Gal, an anthropological linguist, pointed out, 'male–female differences in speech have been found in every society studied; but the nature of the contrasts is staggeringly diverse, occurring in varying parts of the linguistic system: phonology, pragmatics, syntax, morphology, and lexicon' (1991, pp. 181–182). A commonly cited example used to highlight the cultural diversity is Keenan's (1974) research which found that, in contrast to Anglo-American cultural norms of speech for men and women, Malagasy men characteristically use indirect, ornate, more polite speech, while women use a more direct and straightforward style.

Cross-cultural variability in the speech styles associated with men and women validates explanations emphasising the importance of socialisation processes for the development of gender-appropriate language use. However, even for speech styles, Frith and Kitzinger (1997) noted that some psychologists still insist that biological essentialism, utilising evolutionary concepts, can adequately account for phenomena such as miscommunication in sexual relationships (e.g. Ellis, 1991, 1993). A well-developed feminist critique of how biological concepts and scientific notions get mobilised in texts to regulate and normalise gender and sexuality is Potts's (1998) analysis of Gray's (1995) *Mars and Venus in the Bedroom*.

Already evident from the discussion so far is that the issue of gender differences in speech styles has attracted attention from a broader range of disciplines than the topics of verbal ability and voice. A number of researchers (e.g. Aries, 1996; Cameron, 1997; Crawford, 1995) have noted that investigation into gender and speech is a multidisciplinary enterprise to which linguists as well as anthropologists, sociologists, psychologists, cultural/semiotic theorists and philosophers have contributed. The topic area is one that raises important psychological issues. As Lakoff pointed out, 'gender related differences have a strong psychological component: they are intimately related to the judgements of members of a culture about how to be and think like a good woman or man' (1990, p. 202).

Despite the multidisciplinary nature of research on gender and speech styles, much of the work reflects the general pattern, discussed in Chapter 2, of sex difference research found in psychology. That is, speech styles are polarised as being typical of either a woman's or a man's communication style; there is an absence of definitive evidence on what the exact differences in speech are; and differences are used either overtly (e.g. women's style is deficient), or more subtly (e.g. a woman's 'no' to men means 'yes'), to disadvantage women. In this chapter I will continue to consider why definitive answers to questions of differences are so elusive, whether questions about differences should be asked, and how the notion of women's speech styles has effectively been used to disadvantage women.

The next section briefly discusses some of the more explicit instances of gender differences in speech as deficits in women. Then some of the research engaging with the gender differences in speech styles debate will briefly be examined. The two major theoretical frameworks that have polarised the gender and language field will also be discussed. The first of these is the 'dominance' approach, which explains women's language as a consequence of the relatively powerless position of women compared to men. The second framework, the 'difference' or 'cultural' approach, considers the speech of women and men to be an alignment to a particular set of cultural values. According to this approach, women's speech style is orientated to values of connection and affiliation while men's style reflects their concern with status.

Differences as deficits in women

Numerous examples of language differences as deficits in women's speech can be found in popular beliefs about language. In the Western world, for example, there are widely held stereotypes about how talkative women are, and how trivial their talk is. Sources of information on cultural beliefs about women's speech include literature (see Graddol and Swann, 1989), proverbs (see Coates, 1986; Kramarae, 1982) and advice books (see Kramarae, 1982; Swann, 1992). Written records of proverbs about women's speech deal not only with their supposed garrulousness (e.g. 'a woman's tongue wags like a lamb's tail'; 'the North Sea will sooner be found wanting in water than a woman at a loss for a word') but also with their proclivity to gossip (e.g. 'tell nothing to a woman unless you would have the world know'). A striking example of the tendency for women's speech to be derogated was a newspaper article that interpreted an anthropological claim that Neander-thals may have had the capacity of speech as showing that women have been nagging for 400,000 years (*The Dominion*, NZ, 14/05/98).

In addition to revealing various (negative) cultural beliefs about women's speech (e.g. 'where there's women and geese there is noise'), proverbs and other language forms that reflect social beliefs may also function to dis-courage straying from cultural prescriptions about speech (e.g. 'crowing louder than a cock'). Certainly Shakespeare was not backward in com-municating how he thought women should speak. For example, in *King Lear* he wrote: 'Her voice was ever soft, gentle, and low – an excellent thing in woman.' Advice books have also been forthright in declaring the appro-priate way of speaking for women. Different surveys of prescriptive sources have investigated courtesy books of the Middle Ages through to con-temporary self-training manuals. Such sources include advice for women not to gossip, to avoid stating an opinion and to keep their voices low, soft and agreeable (see Kramarae, 1982; Swann, 1992). The advice for women and girls on how they should speak is evidence of the social rules that Cameron (1995) referred to as contributing to norms of 'verbal hygiene'.

The perpetuation of stereotypical beliefs about gender-appropriate speech is not just confined to popular media, literature and self-training books. Academic work has played an important role in legitimising beliefs about women's supposed deficits as speakers. For example, Jespersen (1922) wrote that women had a more limited vocabulary than men, that they used simpler sentence structures and were prone to speaking without thinking, resulting in the frequent use of incomplete sentences. Some fifty years later, Lakoff's (1973, 1975) 'Language and Woman's Place' also described a distinctive woman's speech style that conveyed weakness, uncertainty and unimportance. In her analysis Lakoff clearly considered women's language to be inferior to men's language, which she described as direct, clear and succinct.

Lakoff's (1973, 1975) work followed the general pattern established in the gender and language literature of giving whatever linguistic behaviour was associated with women a negative evaluation. However, her approach was recognised as innovative and controversial because it departed from previous research on gender and language in at least two respects (see Bucholtz and Hall, 1995). Her work was different from anthropological linguistics research conducted at that time because she focused on women's and men's speech in American English, rather than documenting the phenomenon of sex-specific language in 'exotic' cultures (see Bodine, 1975 and Key, 1975 for reviews of this kind of work). Her work also differed from that of English language scholars such as Jespersen (1922) in that she interpreted differences in women's and men's speech as reflecting their status differences in society, rather than being an inevitable consequence of their natures.

As already mentioned, Lakoff interpreted the style of speech that she thought characterised women's language as hesitant, ingratiating and weak. Her explanation of this style was that women are socialised to hedge meaning, in order to avoid offending men. However, regardless of the originality of Lakoff's thesis on gender and language, her work followed what was identified in the last chapter as an established pattern of sex difference research. Lakoff's assumption was that sex differences in language use existed, and she interpreted those differences as being deficits in women.

Lakoff's (1973, 1975) work inspired a huge programme of research on gender and language in linguistics, anthropology, sociology and psychology as well as in other fields. One of the most frequent criticisms of the work by psychologists was that her claims were based on intuition and subjective experience rather than on empirical evidence. Thus, a goal of much psychological research was to provide an empirical basis to support Lakoff's suggestion that women and men use language in different ways. Following the pattern of sex difference research in general, there has been a belief that good empirical research will identify the 'real' features of women's language. However, despite numerous investigations, straightforward demonstrations of Lakoff's claims have not emerged. Nevertheless, in a more recent work, Lakoff (1990) maintained that there are clusters of linguistic traits that reliably identify women's speech in Anglo-American culture.

The empirical avalanche on gender differences in speech

Lakoff (1973, p. 47) admitted that she considered her thesis less the final word on the topic of gender and language and more 'as a goad to further research'. The provocative claim that she made was that characteristics of women's language were evident in all levels of the English language. At the lexical level she suggested that women use more precise colour descriptors (e.g. mauve, beige, lavender), more 'empty' adjectives (e.g. divine, lovely), and weaker expletives (e.g. dear me, oh fudge) than men. At the syntactic level she suggested that women use more tag questions (e.g. John is here *isn't he?*) and hedges (e.g. sort of, you know) than men, signalling uncertainty. Lakoff also noted that the expression of uncertainty defining women's language was also characterised by a rising intonation pattern which has the effect of transforming a declarative statement into a question. Other aspects of women's language that Lakoff identified were features such as indirect request forms (e.g. will you please close the door) and precise grammar (e.g. 'I will not' instead of 'ain't'), which made them seem more polite.

Lakoff was hugely successful in so far as she achieved her aim of provoking further research. In a citation search of her 'Language and woman's place', between 1976 and 1992, Crawford (1995) found that, on average, there were over twenty-four references per year to her work in scholarly journals. Of course, citations of her work are only one indication of the interest that Lakoff inspired. Reviews of research investigating issues other than those raised by her suggest that the vast majority of work was conducted after 'Language and woman's place' was published. For example, James and Drakich (1993) reviewed research findings on gender differences in amount of talk. Of the sixty-three studies they examined only eight were conducted prior to 1973. Thus another offshoot of Lakoff's work has been research that has investigated the validity of cultural stereotypes about women's speech. In the case of verbosity, research indicates that it is frequently men and not women who talk more (James and Drakich, 1993). The rather wry explanation Spender offered for the gap between the myth and reality of women's talk was that 'The talkativeness of women hasn't been gauged in comparison with men but with silence' (1980, p. 42). Spender went on to suggest that when silence is the desired state for women, then any time a woman talks it will be considered too much!

So, Lakoff's work was like a seed and, partly because it was planted during the fertile social context of the second wave of feminism, it inspired a hugely productive field of research. In addition to studies that explicitly set out to test Lakoff's claims, was work that extended her idea of gender differences in language to include features of speech that she had not addressed. In 1995, some twenty years after 'Language and woman's place' was published, Fitzpatrick, Mulac and Dindia (1995) compiled a list of over thirty language features that had been investigated as possible predictors of speaker gender. The increase in the number of features that may be potentially gender-linked has served to highlight the non-resolution of questions about gender differences in language use.

Reviews of the literature in the area of gender and speech styles acknowledge the non-resolution of questions about gender and speech. Simkins-Bullock and Wildman suggested, 'Perhaps the most fundamental inconsistency is the lack of agreement about whether males and females use language differently' (1991, p. 149). Crawford (1995) also emphasised the lack of closure on the question of women's language. She cited major research figures in the gender and language field as making different statements about whether the evidence showed that sex differences are reliable and important or whether they are minimal and trivial. Some researchers (e.g. Hill, 1986; Zhan, 1989) have taken the view that the inconsistency in results means that more and better research is required. Other researchers choose to ignore the controversy altogether and motivate their research on the basis of 'substantial evidence of gender differences in face-to-face communication' (Thomson and Murachver, 2001, p. 193).

An extremely comprehensive recent review of the empirical literature on gender differences in language and communication is Elizabeth Aries's (1996) *Men and women in interaction. Reconsidering the differences.* In her book she critically examines a broad range of research that had investigated women's and men's verbal interactions. Topics that she covered included the content of conversations, language use, conversational management and the use of interruptions. On the basis of her review, she concluded that, counter to the dominant assumption underlying the research, women's and men's speech styles are more similar than they are different. Moreover, when specifically asked to position herself on the question of whether men and women speak differently, Aries (1997) responded with a resounding 'no'.

What exactly is it about gender in general, but gender and language use in particular, that makes the search for definitive answers about differences between women and men so popular and yet so futile? A simple reason for the popularity of the issue is that it reinforces gender differences over gender similarities and facilitates sex stereotypes that maintain rather than challenge women's position in society (Crawford, 1995). However, from within gender and language research, there are two widely discussed explanations for the lack of definitive answers to questions of difference. These explanations – the form–function problem and the problem of context – will be examined next.

The form–function problem

One explanation that has been offered for the contradictory results about whether women or men use more of a particular linguistic feature is that there are few direct relationships between a linguistic form and its communicative function (Cameron, McAlinden and O'Leary, 1989). The issue of the relationship between form and function was initially raised when researchers tried to understand the conflicting results reported in studies on gender differences and tag questions. Tag questions (e.g. that was a good movie *wasn't it*?) were one of the first features identified by Lakoff (1973, 1975) that attracted empirical research. According to Lakoff, tag questions were associated with a desire for confirmation or approval which signals a lack of self-confidence in the speaker. Thus speakers (i.e. women) who use tag questions will be perceived as weak, unassertive and lacking in authority. An unstated assumption was that the tag question was a linguistic form that was directly linked to weak and unassertive communication.

McMillan, Clifton, McGrath and Gale (1977) were amongst the first investigators to publish a study that sought to test Lakoff's hypothesis of gender differences in the use of tag questions. The study will be described in some detail because it highlights the kind of naïve faith in the ability of experimental research to establish the 'real' facts about women's and men's speech. Their study is also an example of where the assumption of a direct form–function relationship was unquestioned. McMillan *et al.*'s study (1977) was typical of what was considered to be a better and more scientific style of research than the anecdotal observation used by Lakoff. The importance placed on the design and careful execution of the study is evident in the description of the research. For example, subjects were randomly assigned to discussion groups of similar sizes which were either same-sex or mixed-sex; the makes and models of the recording equipment were described in detail; the length of time for discussion was kept constant. In addition, lest knowledge about the purpose of the study contaminate subjects' behaviour, the participants were deceived into thinking that the research was investigating problem solving.

The carefully orchestrated groups were recorded as they completed the task of solving a murder mystery. The discussions were video-recorded and treated as data for a content analysis. A content analysis involves identifying and then counting the number of times a particular feature (e.g. a tag question) appears in the data. McMillan *et al.* (1977) took great care to ensure that the identification and counting of the language feature were reliable. Reliability was established by using two independent coders whose coding was compared to ensure a high level of agreement between them. Another precaution to ensure that the experiment was free from bias was to establish that differences between groups in the amount of talking time did not render comparisons meaningless. Having followed the necessary steps to be considered a rigorous empirical study, McMillan *et al.* reported that on average the women in their study used tag questions twice as often as men did. The authors used that finding to support Lakoff's claims about women's deferential speech style.

In another study, conducted by researchers who were rather less enamoured of Lakoff's hypothesis than McMillan *et al.*, Dubois and

Crouch (1974) also set out to test Lakoff's claim about tag questions empirically. However, instead of using an experimental approach, Dubois and Crouch tape-recorded interactions at a small academic conference. Both men and women attended the conference, but Dubois and Crouch found that more tag questions were spoken by men than by women.

How can the discrepancy in the results of the two studies just described be accounted for? Of course there are significant differences in the settings (orchestrated vs. naturalistic), the status of the participants (students vs. academics) and the purpose of the discussion (solving a mystery vs. dissemination of information). Given this complex array of factors defining the situational context, the differing results suggest, at least, that there is no straightforward answer to the question of whether women or men use more tag questions. The use of tag questions by men and women may vary from situation to situation. The problem of context is discussed in more detail in the next section.

An assumption common to McMillan *et al.* (1977) and Dubois and Crouch (1974) was that, linguistically, tag questions simply and straightforwardly signal tentativeness. However, in a qualitative analysis of the function of tag questions in conversation, Holmes (1984) distinguished between two types of tag questions. One type she found and labelled was 'modal tags', which request confirmation of information of which the speaker is uncertain. These were the types of tags that Lakoff (1973, 1975) was referring to in her work. The other type Holmes defined as 'affective tags', which did not signal uncertainty but indicated concern for the addressee.

Holmes (1984) argued that affective tags are facilitative because they are largely concerned with saving the face of the addressee (e.g. you don't look too good today do you?), or with encouraging the addressee to take a turn at speaking (e.g. her pictures are quite static in comparison, aren't they?). From an examination of a large New Zealand linguistic corpus, Holmes coded and counted the number of times men and women used modal and affective tags. In her data, affective tags were used predominantly by women and modal tags were used predominantly by men. Holmes concluded that women's use of tag questions did not signal uncertainty; rather they were typical of a co-operative speech style that reflected women's competence as conversationalists. As well as drawing attention to the fact that a single linguistic form can have a number of difference functions, Holmes's work was important because she resisted Lakoff's assumption of the deficiency of women's language style. The way women used language was reinterpreted in a more positive light – a re-visioning that has typically led to a cultural explanation of gender differences in speech styles.

The form vs. function problem is one reason why investigations into whether women or men use more of a particular linguistic form can be understood as pursuing the wrong kind of question. Not only is there no one-to-one relationship of a form (e.g. a tag question) to a function (e.g. modal or affective), but a single form may be multifunctional. For example, 'you haven't done your homework, have you?' has an element of a softener, but also calls for confirmation (see Cameron *et al.*, 1989). Hence it is not possible to categorise linguistic forms as having invariant functions. Because of this, research that claims to have shown that women use more or less of some conversational feature than men, and goes on to interpret this as evidence signalling a single meaning such as 'assertiveness' or 'lacking in authority', must, at best, be treated with suspicion.

The problem of context

The lack of a one-to-one relationship between linguistic forms and their communicative function is one reason why straightforward answers to the questions of gender differences in language have not been found. Another explanation is that the way language is used and understood varies depending on when, where and under what circumstances an interaction is taking place. Aries (1996) suggested, for example, that definitive gender differences in language use have not been found because research has not paid sufficient attention to how women's and men's language use varies with the situational context of interactions. She defined situational context as including the characteristics of the participants (age, class, ethnicity, sexual orientation and so on), their relationship to one another, the length of the encounter, the task, and the interaction setting. Aries went on to urge researchers to pay attention to the features of interactants and their encounter that may create or mitigate the appearance of gender differences.

Outside gender and language research there has also been an increased awareness of the interdependence of language and context (e.g. Giles and Coupland, 1991). What this has meant for an experimental style of research is an ever-increasing array of variables to be identified and investigated or controlled for – a guaranteed lifetime research programme! The assumption is that, by reducing 'context' to its constituent elements, the effect that each variable has can be understood. This type of research is typical of a traditional social psychology that maintains the superiority of reductionism, quantification, experimental methods and hypothesis testing.

An example of the kind of conventional positivist paradigm being used to address the issue of context in gender differences and speech styles is a series of studies conducted by Antony Mulac and his colleagues (e.g. Mulac and Bradac, 1995; Mulac and Lundell, 1986; Mulac, Lundell and Bradac, 1986). The abstract of one of these studies illustrates how the issue of context gets reduced down to a single variable – in this case familiarity with interaction partners:

> Research on sex differences in the communication practices of men and women often ignores the contexts in which communication takes place. By comparing women and men as they interact with both strangers and spouses, the authors present a more nuanced view of gender differences in social interaction.
>
> (Fitzpatrick *et al.*, 1995, p. 18)

Fitzpatrick *et al.*'s study employed a design that they claimed allowed them to calculate how much 'gender preferential language' (a weighted combination of thirty-two linguistic and non-verbal forms) was due to the three 'independent' variables: the gender of the speaker, the gender of their conversational partner, and the type of relationship (stranger or spouse). The reported results were interpreted as showing that men's and women's language did differ and that 'gender preferential' language was influenced both by the type of relationship and the gender of the communicators. The findings were used to caution future researchers to be wary of the influence of these two contextual factors.

While Fitzpatrick *et al.*'s (1995) study can be commended for its experimental sophistication, it assumes that context can be reduced to a finite number of variables that will affect language use in predictable ways. Language, it is assumed, reflects the context in which it is being used. The authors of the study fail to demonstrate an appreciation that language use is not just dependent on context, but that language and context are interdependent. Any linguistic form gains different meanings and has different effects within different contexts, and these meanings can also be changed.

Silence is a good example of the interdependence of meaning and context. In early feminist analyses such as Ardener's (1975) muted group theory, women's silence was taken to mean passivity and powerlessness – those who are barred from public speaking cannot influence the powerful institutions in society. However, in other settings, such as job interviews, oral exams, police interviews or therapy sessions, it is the silent listener who has the power. Silence can be used as a weapon of power. For example, Sattel (1983) suggested that, in a domestic context, American men use silences as an intentional manipulation of a situation that threatens their position as 'king of the castle'. However, silence can also be used as a form of resistance, as is the case in 'silent' political marches, or the right to remain silent which can be exercised by the accused in some legal systems.

The example of silence shows us that context is indeed crucial to understanding language use but its impact is not reducible to a set of clearly identifiable independent variables. Thus even the most carefully designed and exhaustive programme of research will not be able to isolate the contextual features that invariably 'cause' women or men to speak (or not to speak) in particular ways. That the language used by women and men cannot be reduced to the effect of a particular set of contextual variables, however, is not to deny that both theoretically and practically an understanding of context can lead to important insights into gender and language variation.

An alternative to thinking of context as the sum or product of a set of situational variables is to think of it as a place where social practices get articulated. Eckert and McConnell-Ginet (1992) develop a notion of 'communities of practice' to encourage a view that connects gender and language with the social practices of particular local communities. A community of practice is defined as 'an aggregate of people who come together around mutual engagement in an endeavour' (p. 464). In the course of this mutual endeavour (e.g. a religious ceremony, a game of cricket, a chat with friends), rules, norms, beliefs, values, power relations and so on emerge.

Using the concept of a community of practice, speech styles are not simply a reflection of the gender of the communicators in a particular situational context. Instead, the language used in any interaction emerges from the social practices of a community in combination with the linguistic patterns that speakers develop as they act in their other linguistic communities. Thus the relationship of gender to linguistic behaviour can only be determined by careful study of the communities of practice in which it occurs. A community of practice approach shows that language should not be studied separately from other social practices, and gender cannot be isolated from the influence of other social variables. Thus Eckert and McConnell-Ginet (1992) advise researchers to 'think practically and look locally'.

Developing the community of practice notion, Cameron (1992) proposed that questions should not focus on gender differences but on the difference that gender makes in any community of practice. The strength of this kind of approach is that it side-steps some of the pitfalls that have plagued many experimental studies on gender and speech styles. A community of practice approach to gender identity will be discussed further in Chapter 6.

Explanations of difference: the dominance approach

The lack of definitive answers to questions about gender differences in language aside, two explanations for alleged differences have typically polarised the field – dominance approaches and difference approaches (see also Stokoe and Smithson, 2001; Weatherall, 1998). Although dominance approaches vary in their focus, they are unified in their emphasis on power or social status as the primary factor in explaining gender differences in speech styles. As already mentioned, Lakoff (1973, 1975) was the pioneer of a dominance approach to understanding 'woman's language'. According to Lakoff, women are socialised into using linguistic features that connote tentativeness, deference and a lack of authority, because women occupy a marginal and powerless social position. Hence, the way women are expected to speak is a direct reflection of women's subordinate status. Of course, not all women have low status and not all men have high status. Thus, like other work that has focused on gender difference, Lakoff's work tended to over-generalise the characteristics associated with women and men.

An explanation that acknowledged the possible status similarities between women and men emerged from research conducted in a courtroom. O'Barr and Atkins (1980) suggested that the idea of 'woman's language' was a misnomer and that the cluster of features identified as women's language was not a function of gender at all but a function of power. O'Barr and Atkins explicitly expressed their explanation in the title of their paper, '"Women's language" or "powerless language"?' They found that many of the linguistic features identified by Lakoff were only used in the speech of low-status persons in the courtroom, irrespective of gender. High-status women tended to avoid those same features in a judicial context.

The idea that gender and power get confused in some situations has been identified as one of the reasons why research on gender differences in speech styles has produced such contradictory results. Where women are in powerful positions they may not use a powerless speech style, and low-status men may use the characteristics associated with women's language. An illustration of how gender and power are often confounded was a study conducted by Eakins and Eakins (1978) on interruptions in a staff meeting at a university. Interruptions have typically been understood as a conversational strategy that signals power. Consistent with Lakoff's hypothesis, men interrupted more than women in the meeting. However, on closer inspection of the data, Eakins and Eakins found that the pattern of interruptions was almost perfectly correlated with a hierarchy of status based on rank and length of time in the department. The woman who was interrupted most frequently was the most junior staff member, with the next two lowest-ranking women being the next most interrupted.

Experimental laboratory studies have confirmed that gender and status are factors that interact with each other. For example, Leet-Pellegrini (1979) brought together, for the purpose of her study, same-sex or mixed-sex pairs to discuss television programming. In half of the pairs both partners were equally informed. However, for the rest of the pairs one partner became expert by having been given relevant information before the discussions began. The results showed that expertise and not gender increased the use of linguistic features associated with dominance. In addition, Leet-Pellegrini found that men, but not women, changed their speech style when given the extra information. Thus powerful language was not based just on expertise or gender alone, but on a subtle interplay between the two.

In a more recent study described by Aries (1997), the results were even more clear-cut than in Leet-Pellegrini's (1979) work. In a laboratory setting where gender of conversational partner was systematically varied, it was found that when men and women were given the same formal legitimate authority there were no gender differences in their use of 'powerless' linguistic features. However, both men and women used more of these features when they were placed in a subordinate role. After reviewing a host of studies, Aries (1996) suggested that the pervasive tendency people have to focus on gender difference in speech styles is an example of what social psychologists have called the 'fundamental attribution error'. That is, people overwhelmingly attribute the cause of behaviour to personal characteristics rather than to the situational context. People are more likely to think that the way people speak in a particular situation is due to their gender rather than the context or social role that they are in. On that basis Aries (1996, 1997) concluded that, although we may perceive many differences between men and women, gender may not account for the differences. Instead the differences may result from differences in power and social roles held by men and women. However, even when power and social roles are held constant, results about gender differences in language use are not consistent.

Regardless of how gender and power are related, it is interesting to consider what practical impact the dominance approach to understanding gender differences and speech styles has had. It seems that the refocusing from gender differences to 'powerless' language functioned in two ways – both, as we have come to expect from work focusing on difference, ultimately function to disadvantage women. First, a focus on power serves to divert attention away from gender and other important social categories. In some language research, gender has disappeared from the research agenda and has been replaced with issues of power. Furthermore the contribution made by feminist researchers in the field becomes obscured. For example, Ng and Bradac (1993) claimed that the issue of power in language emerged from the work of O'Barr and his colleague, without giving more than a token acknowledgement that O'Barr's work was inspired by Lakoff (1973, 1975).

The second outcome related to the dominance approach to gender difference can be seen outside the academic realm. In practice, the assumptions underlying the dominance view have informed an assertiveness training movement (Crawford, 1995). Women's low status and poor performance in business have been understood as a consequence of not asserting themselves. Assertiveness is operationalised as a communication style where talking for success is equated with talking like men. A presupposition is that it is women's communicative style (their inability to talk correctly – like men) that is responsible for their lack of success or the reason why they fail to be understood clearly (see also Frith and Kitzinger, 1997).

The dominance approach to gender differences is limited in so far as the effects of power cannot wholly explain why women in some situations appear to use a different speech style from men. In addition, despite intentions to the contrary, the dominance approach has negative spin-offs. It draws attention away from gender as an important issue in language research, and it has encouraged a practice where women are trained to speak like men. An additional criticism of the dominance approach is that it has tended to ignore how gender interacts with other social groupings such as ethnicity, class, age and sexual orientation (see Henley and Kramarae, 1991; Kramarae, 1990). However, despite the limitations of the dominance approach, it has been useful for highlighting that links between language and power exist. The links between language and power and how they can be used to understand 'the androcentric rule' will be considered in more detail in the following discussion.

Language and power

Lakoff's (1973, 1975) version of the dominance approach was to argue that language provided evidence of the social inequity in society 'between the roles of men and women' (1973, p. 46). Social inequity, however, is far broader and more complex than simply the social roles that people occupy. Since the publication of 'Language and woman's place' there has been considerable theoretical attention given to developing systematic theories of gender and power (e.g. Connell, 1987; Walby, 1990). What this work shows is that, as already mentioned, the reproduction of gender inequality (and resistance to it) is extremely complex. Gender relations are constantly being negotiated and renegotiated in different ways at different 'sites' of society. The sites include the structure of labour (e.g. paid work, house-work), powerful social institutions (e.g. political, military) and education. A 'gender order' operates at work, in the family and on the street (Connell, 1987). Language provides important indicators of the various ways in which gender and power are implicated in different levels of social life. The heterogeneous nature of gender relations and the diverse ways they manifest in language are another reason why simple answers to questions of gender differences in speech styles will not be found.

At an institutional level, for example, gender relations are reflected in language by who gets to speak and who gets heard. The world's parliaments and economic institutions are overwhelmingly dominated by men (French, 1992). Thus, by a simple process of exclusion, men's voices get heard and powerful language is spoken by men. In contrast, men's silence can be used as an instrument of power within domestic spheres (Sattel,

1983). Within an educational context, male dominance is reflected and maintained in a slightly different way. For example, Spender (1980) found that, in classrooms, teachers spent more of their time talking to boys than to girls. In a broader study, Swann (1992) not only considered gender differences in classroom interactions but also the images of gender and beliefs about language in books and other teaching materials. Swann's analysis highlighted the variety of ways in which language in education can be understood as contributing to gender inequality.

Other researchers using a dominance approach have focused on how gender relations are maintained in the private sphere. Conversational patterns within the family have been interpreted as reflecting gender inequality. One example of how patterns of male dominance get reproduced in everyday familial interactions was Fishman's (1977) study of hetero-sexual couples talking. In the conversations she collected, women appeared to be doing the active maintenance and support work. The women tended, for example, to initiate conversation, ask questions and use minimal responses such as 'mms'. Men, on the other hand, defined what they talked about by only developing their own remarks and failing to indicate any interest in or engagement with what their spouses were saying. The rather provocative label conversational 'shitwork' was given, by Fishman, to what she perceived to be women's domestic role in conversations.

Another example of research that has investigated how men's power is exercised in heterosexual relationships is Zimmerman and West's (1975) study of interruptions and silences in conversation. Zimmerman and West recorded couples' conversations from coffee shops, supermarkets and other public places. In these conversations it was found that men made the overwhelming majority of interruptions. The result was interpreted as showing that interruption was a strategy used by men to keep control of discussions and prevent women from talking. However, as already discussed, there is no simple relationship between form (e.g. interruptions) and conversational power. Interruptions may have a co-operative con-versational function and be part of a speech style showing interest and enthusiasm (see James and Clarke, 1993). Noting that interruptions can have multiple functions is not to deny, however, that interruptions may be used more by some men some of the time as a strategy to gain the conversational floor.

In his sociological analysis of gender and power, Connell (1987) suggested that the street could be considered alongside the family and schools as an institution where gender relations are ordered. Consistent with that analysis have been studies on gender and language that have examined verbal harassment in the street. Kissling (1991) suggested that verbal harassment – from seemingly innocent remarks like 'hello baby' to vulgar suggestions or outright threats – occurs throughout the world. Although the more innocent remarks can be depicted as complimentary or a bit of fun, they can also be interpreted as unwanted invasions of privacy and therefore a form of sexual harassment. Gardner (1980) pointed out that even when a street remark is positive it violates a general social norm of inattention between strangers in public places. That breach by men implies that women are of a lower status because the general behavioural norm does not need to be applied to them. Kissling went further and argued that verbal comments from men to women in the street can be understood as a tool of sexual terrorism. Men's public comments to women with whom they are unacquainted, whether complimentary or not, function to intimidate women and encourage them to monitor their behaviour.

A dominance approach is useful for interpreting gender relations and language use across a wide range of contexts. The strengths of a dominance view were succinctly captured by Henley and Kramarae when they noted:

> Hierarchies determine whose version of the communication situation will prevail; whose speech style will be seen as normal; who will be required to learn the communication style and interpret the meaning of the other; whose language style will be seen as deviant, irrational, and inferior; and who will be required to imitate the other's style in order to fit into the society. Yet the situation of sex difference is not totally parallel; sex status intercuts and sometimes contrasts with other statuses; and no other two social groups are so closely interwoven as men and women.
>
> (1991, pp. 19–20)

The dominance approach stresses the hierarchical nature of gender relations. Some theorists, however, disliked the implication that women's linguistic behaviour could simply be attributed to their subordination. Also there is a tendency, clearly illustrated in Lakoff's (1973, 1975) work, for the dominance approach to be confounded with a deficit position. The 'standard' or the 'norm' is not a truly neutral standard, but a male norm. Therefore women's speech and not men's tends to be seen as a deviation from what is desirable. West (1995), for example, noted how the dominance approach tends to misrepresent women's conversational skills. West argued for the importance of evaluating women's conversational competence in interaction, not in comparison to men, but with reference to what counts as meeting the demands of conversation *per se*. The tendency for the dominance approach to construct women's speech as a subordinated style prompted a reassessment of the literature on gender and language and the development of an alternative view. Instead of gender differences in speech styles being interpreted as evidence of a hierarchy, they were considered to reflect women's and men's development within different sociolinguistic subcultures. This cultural approach to gender differences in speech styles will be considered next.

Explanations of difference: the cultural approach

The cultural approach to gender differences in speech styles is based on a sociolinguistic framework that was developed for understanding problems in interethnic communication (Gumperz, 1982). When members of different cultures communicate they bring their own assumptions and rules of conversation with them to understand the interaction. Differences in assumptions about what is going on can result in misunderstandings. An example of such cross-cultural communication would be if a native American's quiet non-committal responses were misidentified as apathy or animosity instead of being correctly interpreted as a request for further information (see McNabb, 1986). Maltz and Borker (1982) in their influential paper 'A cultural approach to male–female miscommunication' were the first to suggest that cross-gender communication problems could be understood as an example of the larger phenomenon of cultural difference and miscommunication. The suggestion that boys and girls develop in separate and different cultures has also been referred to as the 'separate worlds hypothesis' (see Kyratzis and Guo, 1996).

Miscommunication theory is based on the idea that women and men have to communicate across a cultural divide. This idea was aired to the public in Deborah Tannen's (1986) *That's not what I meant* and popularised through her best-selling text *You just don't understand* (1990). John Gray (1992) joined the miscommunication theory bandwagon with his *Men are from Mars, women are from Venus*. In this book the cultural gender gap has become a chasm, overstated to the degree that men and women are described as coming 'from different planets, speaking different languages and needing different nourishment' (Gray, 1992, p. 5). Of course, the implication of the cultural approach and miscommunication theory is that women and men may experience frustration and misunderstanding when they try to talk to one another.

An example that Maltz and Borker (1982) gave to illustrate cross-gender miscommunication was minimal responses. Nods and comments like 'yes' and 'mm hmm' typify minimal responses. Maltz and Borker claimed that such responses have different meanings for men and women. Women allegedly use minimal responses to indicate that they are listening and wish the speaker to continue. In contrast, it is thought that men understand minimal responses as signalling agreement with what is being said. Given these understandings it is easy to imagine minimal responses as a cause of misunderstanding. When receiving minimal responses, a man is likely to think that a woman is agreeing with him, when she may simply be indicating that she is listening. In comparison, a lack of minimal responses by a man could be interpreted by a woman as a signal that he is not listening. Thus minimal responses are an example of where there may be a different set of rules for men and women for conversational maintenance, which may conflict and cause miscommunication.

According to the cultural approach, gender differences in speech styles develop as a result of early communication patterns. Girls and boys are thought to play predominantly in single-sex groups and, as a result, gender-specific cultures are thought to evolve with unique communication patterns (Maltz and Borker, 1982). According to this view, a female sub-culture creates and maintains relationships of closeness and equality. Hence criticism is couched in socially acceptable ways and females can interpret accurately and sensitively the speech of others. Thus women develop a co-operative style of communication. Males, on the other hand, come from a playground culture where they have learnt to assert a position of dominance, to attract and maintain an audience, and where they must assert themselves by interrupting when another person has the floor. Thus their style of communication is predominantly competitive. Tannen (1990, 1997) has summarised women's and men's styles in terms of rapport or co-operative talk and report or competitive talk.

The focus on positive aspects of women's speech is consistent with a maximalist position, identified in Chapter 2 on the sex differences debate. The case of tag questions, discussed earlier, was a more specific illustration of how a maximalist or feminist cultural perspective developed in gender and language research. First, tag questions were evaluated as a negative feature of women's language. Later the function of the tag question in women's speech was reinterpreted in a positive light as having an affiliative function. Research, such as that done on tag questions, using a cultural rather than a dominance framework, has suggested that women's speech is far from being deferential, confused and uncertain, but can be confident, facilitating and supportive.

While avoiding viewing women's language style negatively, the cultural approach still polarises gender. Like any approach that focuses on gender differences there is a danger that similarities get downplayed and contrasts are exaggerated. Thorne (1990) critically reviewed research that had documented the separate worlds of boys and girls. She concluded that gender separation was not as total as the work of researchers such as Maltz and Borker (1982) suggested. The amount of separation varied with the situation. For example, there was more cross-gender play in neighbour-hoods and in families than in school playgrounds. Ironically in the school context it was often the teachers who promoted gender separation by dividing children into groups along gender lines. Thorne's conclusion was that a focus on difference does nothing more than maintain and perpetuate sex-stereotypical thinking. Instead she suggested that researchers focus on the relevance of gender (or the difference gender makes) in different facets of social life.

In addition to encouraging stereotyping, the pattern established in sex differences research suggests that, once gender is polarised, differences in women are interpreted as female deficits. Does the androcentric rule apply to the cultural approach? What possible ideological function could be served by arguing that men's talk is competitive and women's talk is co-operative? Crawford (1995) argued that, like dominance in the asser-tiveness training movement, the cultural explanation of sex differences in language has become the mass-market metaphor for problems in com-munication. A popular understanding of interactional problems between men and women is that they result from speaking different languages. Of course it is women's supposedly indirect and hesitant speech style that makes effective communication difficult.

The concept that women's speech style is co-operative and men's speech style is competitive can be understood as simply extending sex-role stereo-types to linguistic behaviour. Thus it is not very useful for challenging and redressing social inequities. A greater concern is that not only does it polarise and stereotype the sexes, but the cultural explanation has also filtered through to public consciousness and is being used as an effective excuse for ignoring what a woman says. An example of this misappro-priation of the cultural explanation is Crawford's (1995) study which analysed discussions of date rape. The concept of different languages was used in the discussions that Crawford examined to account for the fact that some men can't understand that when a woman says 'no' to sexual advances, she means no.

The concept of different but equal conversational styles promoted by the cultural approach is consistent with the idea that men and women have different definitions or ways of expressing consent. From this perspective, date rape is deemed understandable and defensible because men don't understand that the way a woman says no actually means no and not yes. The problem lies with women's language because it is the woman who has failed to make herself understood. Thus, once more, we see the andro-centric rule in action. Men's misunderstanding of women's meaning is justified through the popular appropriation of scholarly explanations of sex differences in speech styles. A cultural explanation, despite intentions otherwise, can be understood as complying with the androcentric rule.

Acknowledging the danger of the separate world view, Henley and Kramarae made the point that 'the construction of miscommunication between the sexes emerges as a powerful tool, maybe even a necessity, to maintain the structure of male supremacy' (1991, p. 42). Many other researchers make a similar point, that the cultural approach fails to acknowledge that cross-gender interactions occur within a wider context of social inequality (e.g. Freed and Greenwood, 1996; Uchida, 1992). As

Aries noted, the two-cultures approach to understanding gender differences in speech styles can be quite compelling but:

> it fails to recognise the importance of sexual inequalities at a societal level. The two-cultures approach postulates that problems arise when men and women talk together 'as equals' in casual conversation. An implicit assumption is made here that men and women are equals, but men are accorded greater power, status and privilege in society than women are . . . the two-cultures approach does not recognise that many of the differences between the styles of men and women are associated with power-differences. Gender differences cannot be understood without putting them in the context of gender inequalities in society.
>
> (1996, p. 195)

In summary then, the cultural approach to speech styles treats gender differences as cultural differences that complicate and frustrate communications. The differences stem from the alleged separation of boys and girls in the peer groups of childhood and adolescence. The differently organised groups engaging in different kinds of activities give rise to them being different in their preferred communication style. In contrast, the dominance approaches focus on how speech styles can be understood as emerging from the differential status associated with men and women in society. From the dominance perspective the cultural approach pays insufficient attention to power and overstates the degree to which women and men are segregated in society.

Chapter summary

The theme of difference has been pervasive in gender and language research. This chapter has examined the issue of gender differences in speech styles. Research on gender differences in speech mirrors that on sex differences outside the gender and language field. Despite a huge amount of research on nearly every aspect of language use and speech, no features of language have been found that are exclusively used by women or only used by men. Not only have no stable and enduring differences been found, but alleged differences are interpreted as deficits in women. In addition, theoretical explanations for difference (the dominance approach and the cultural approach) can also be understood as functioning to disadvantage women.

There have been two suggestions offered to explain the lack of closure on the question of what features of language differentiate the speech styles of women and men. One is the form–function problem, which refers to the realisation that there is no simple one-to-one mapping of linguistic form (e.g. tag question) on to communicative function (e.g. uncertainty). A recognition of this problem has not meant abandoning the search for difference. Instead the kind of differences sought have shifted from individual linguistic variables to the rather more nebulous concept of 'communicative style'.

A second explanation offered for the lack of answers to questions of gender differences in speech is the effect of context. Of course, language use varies across contexts. One suggestion has been that stable and enduring gender differences in language have not been found because not enough attention has been paid to context. The underlying assumption of this is that, once the effects of context are controlled for, the real gender differences in speech will emerge. This second explanation, like the form–function one, has not discouraged sex differences research. Instead it is assumed that more and better research will provide clearer insights into gender differences in speech.

Methodological problems aside, two theoretical explanations for (alleged) gender difference have typically polarised the field. These are the dominance approach and the cultural approach. Cameron (1997) suggested that, despite the differences between the dominance and cultural approaches, they are similar in so far as they both assume that there is some kind of unproblematic category of 'women' and of 'men' that pre-exists 'language'. That is, both approaches are essentialist because they assume that there is something that can be identified as a women's or a men's speech style. In addition, both rely on the notion of 'socialisation' to account for the development of that style. An alternative suggestion is that 'women's language' as a category does not have to be understood as deriving from a person's social identity; rather 'women's language' can be understood as a symbolic cultural construct that is potentially constitutive of a feminine identity (e.g. Gal, 1995). A social constructionist view is that being a 'woman' or being a 'man' can be considered a matter, amongst other things, of talking like one. The significance that a shift from an essentialist to a social constructionist view has on the kind of questions and problems typically associated with gender and language research will be discussed in the next chapter. Important aspects of a social constructionist approach for the gender and language field are that it provides an alternative explanation for the lack of closure in sex difference research and it can be used to support calls to abandon research questions that ask about gender difference in speech.

4

THE DISCURSIVE TURN

Introduction

In the past, there has been a sharp division between studying the way women and men use language and studying their representation in language (i.e. sexist language). However, the two areas are not necessarily mutually exclusive. In a review of the gender and language literature, Cameron (1998a) described the inter-relationships between language use by and language about women and men, in the following way:

> When a researcher studies women and men speaking she is looking, as it were, at the linguistic construction of gender in the first- and second-person forms (the construction of I and you); when she turns to the representation of gender in, say, advertisements or literary texts she is looking at the same thing in the third person ('she' and 'he'). In many cases it is neither possible nor useful to keep these aspects apart, since the 'I-you-she/he' is relevant to the analysis of every linguistic act or text.
>
> (Cameron, 1998a, p. 957)

A realisation that the boundaries typically dividing gender and language research are artificial has had a significant influence on the field. Consistent with Cameron's (1998a) insight, more recent work on gender and language has shifted focus so that the distinction between the two areas has become less marked. One consequence of the breaking down of old question boundaries is that the focus of research has shifted to discourse rather than language *per se* as the main locus for the construction (and contesting) of gendered and sexist meanings. At a discursive level, language about women (and men) and women (and men) speaking are both aspects of one process – the social construction of gender.

A shift in thinking from essentialist to constructionist approaches for understanding gender is part of a more general 'turn' to language in the humanities and social sciences (Burman and Parker, 1993). That turn has been brought about by the influence of poststructuralist ideas that stress the thoroughly discursive and textual nature of social life. In her review essay Cameron (1998a) attributed the renewed vigour of language and gender research from the mid-1990s to this change in thinking which gives language a more constitutive role.

So, one of the most profound changes to be brought about by the discursive turn has been the way in which gender as a social category has been conceptualised. Instead of gender being viewed as an essential characteristic of an individual's psyche, it is understood as a thoroughly social construct, one that is produced by language and discourse. The shift from an essentialist to a constructionist view of gender has resulted in new explanations of key problematic issues that have emerged from some aspects of gender and language research. Those problems include the lack of definitive answers to questions of what the gender differences in speech are, and how those differences disadvantage women. This chapter will discuss the fresh insights and research that a social constructionist perspective brings to the field of gender and language.

From language to discourse

The term discourse is variously used in the gender and language field. It may be used in a linguistic sense to refer to language beyond that of words. Or it may be used in a poststructural sense to refer to broad systems of meaning. The different uses of the term discourse embrace two senses of gender as a social construction. On the one hand, gender is constructed in the ways it is described in talk and texts. On the other hand, gender as a concept is itself constructed – a social meaning system that structures the way we see and understand the world.

Research has moved from language to discourse (in the first sense of the term mentioned above) by considering how language in use reflects and perpetuates gender stereotypes. So while early gender and language work documented how individual words could be considered sexist (see Chapter 1), later work examined how texts were constructed in sexist ways. A wide range of different areas of language use has been examined for sexism, including comic strips (Thaler, 1987), children's literature (Cooper, 1987), birthday cards (Brabandt and Mooney, 1989), Japanese women's magazines (Hayashi, 1997), American popular songs (Butruille and Taylor, 1987) and political speeches (Jansen and Sabo, 1994). The constructionist lesson to be gleaned from this research is that sexist language is not just a matter of negative words for women, but of how language, in a variety of everyday contexts, constructs gender in stereotyped ways that ultimately disadvantage or demean women.

A context where sexist discourse is rife is in linguistic representations of women in the media. Studies of sports and wildlife programmes have analysed those genres and found evidence of explicit sexism. For example, an American study by Messner, Duncan and Jansen (1993) analysed the verbal context of televised coverage of women's and men's athletic events. They found that female athletes and Black American male athletes were more often referred to by their first names than white male athletes. All female athletes and Black American male athletes were referred to as girls and boys respectively. In addition, the achievements of female athletes were interpreted in terms of luck more than the achievement of males.

Crowther and Leith (1995) analysed how the script and narrative of wildlife programmes used a patriarchal set of values to describe the behaviour of animals (e.g. Mrs Badger cleans out the bedding; the leader of the pack has a harem). Crowther and Leith argued that the underlying set of assumptions upon which the content of the voice-overs was based functioned to reproduce dominant cultural beliefs about gender and sexuality in both human and animal worlds.

In contrast to the sports and wildlife television genres, soap opera is understood to be a genre aimed at, and watched largely by, women (Geraghty, 1991). The roles played by women in soap opera are contra-dictory. On the one hand, female characters are stereotyped in so far as they are portrayed within the domestic sphere as being concerned with family life and interpersonal relations. On the other hand, females are not depicted as being weak and dependent; rather they are strong and central to the social action. Allen (1985) went so far as to argue that soap opera is feminist because it addresses women's issues such as motherhood and female relationships which are not dealt with in other genres. Consistent with the idea that soap opera can be understood as feminist, I found that scripts of a British soap opera, *Coronation Street*, provided virtually no evidence of a pervasive bias against women in language. Nevertheless, in particular scenes language was used in a way that assumed women's secondary status in society (Weatherall, 1996).

The ideas associated with the discursive turn influenced my motivation to use *Coronation Street* as a context for examining sexist language. Up until the time of that study, psychological research on sexist language had focused primarily on the mental processes involved in the production and comprehension of language. Furthermore, studies had largely been laboratory-based, using experimental methods and 'made-up' examples of language (e.g. the use of vignettes). By examining language use in *Coronation Street* I was taking an initial step away from the idea of words as stable units of meaning and moving towards an interest in the construction of gender in discourse.

The meaning of the term discourse is not restricted to spoken language but also refers to written language. Some discourse analytic work has examined the construction of gender in written media. For example, Stirling (1987) examined the linguistic treatment of women and men in a large corpus of Australian newspapers. She explored the range of expressions and techniques – including the use of metaphor, metonymy, punning, passivisation and syntactic parallelism – that served either to exclude women or to define them narrowly and negatively. In a similar type of analysis Hawes and Thomas (1995) compared language bias against women in British and Malaysian newspapers. They found that sexist language in the Malaysian press was less explicit than in the British press, but even in the Malaysian papers there was a bias towards males as the topic of serious news stories.

Arguably, the most important type of language use for the production and reproduction of gender is mundane conversation. However, there are relatively few studies of how gender is reproduced in everyday interactions. In an early, rare study of 'real'-life language use, Wolfson and Manes (1981) documented how the differential forms of address in interactions constitute sexism. Their study investigated how women and men were addressed in public service encounters in the north-east and south of the United States. The results showed that, despite regional variation in the specific form used, men were consistently addressed using respect forms, such as sir. Women, matched for the men's age and status, were addressed using familiar terms, such as honey, love or dear. The authors suggested that women can find familiar forms of address irritating because they imply that the addressee is subordinate to the speaker (see also Brouwer, 1982).

In a more recent study, Mott and Petrie (1995) examined telephone conversations in the workplace between recruitment consultants, their employees and their clients. They didn't mention the patterns of address used but they did find that both the gender and status of the addressee affected the conversational style of the consultants. Women and lower-status conversational partners were given less co-operative responses and were interrupted more than men and high-status conversational partners. What this study shows is that gender is constructed not only by linguistic representations but also by the process of conversational interaction.

Some discourse analytic work not only examines linguistic constructions of gender but also considers how they operate to reproduce the dominant social order. For example, Lees (1983) discussed how the threat of remarks works to control women's behaviour. Lees found that young British women were very careful of how they behaved towards young men for fear of being labelled a slag. Referring to verbal sexual abuse, Lees (1997) argued:

> Therefore language (or the discourse of female reputation in particular) acts as a material discourse with its own determinate effects, acting as a form of control over their emotions and passions and steering girls into subordinate relationships with men.
>
> (Lees, 1997, p. 4)

The idea that discourses about gender have material consequences is key to understanding why the notion of gender differences tends to function practically to disadvantage women. The use of the term discourse in this sense acknowledges the power in language to shape thoughts and guide behaviour. Lees refers to the discourse of female reputation having material effects on girls. The following section introduces the idea that gender differences in language are not so much a description of how women and men speak but more a discourse that has material consequences.

Discourse as power/knowledge

A substantive problem that has emerged from research on gender and language use is that ideas about 'women's language' and gender differences in speech have so easily been used in anti-feminist ways. In Chapters 2 and 3, I detailed how work on sex difference in language has been used practically to reinforce sex stereotypes and justify discrimination against women (see also Weatherall, 1998). So, what light can the idea of language as discourse in a more social constructionist sense throw on why research to date has largely failed to develop understandings of gender and language that are useful and congenial to social changes that would benefit women?

Crawford (1995) suggested that an important insight from social constructionism is that the production of research findings invariably has a political agenda, whether or not that is deliberate or acknowledged explicitly. A similar point has been made by feminist philosophers of science for a long time – the impossibility of impartiality in knowledge production (e.g. Harding, 1986). In poststructural terms, power and knowledge are a system of discourses where what counts as truth is no more than an effect of the cultural order, an idea represented by 'power/knowledge'. According to this view, knowledge about women's and men's speech styles may not be objective, absolute truths about gender and language but rather an effect of a society where men and maleness are valued over women and femaleness. Thus the term discourse can be used to refer to the ways in which social and political relations are embedded in the ways of thinking and talking about the world. As we shall see below, when gender differences in language are viewed as a discourse that is imbued with social power, it becomes clearer why there has been a tendency for gender and language research to be used in ways that are counter-productive for improving women's status in society.

Power is a pivotal concept for understanding gender relations within a social and political context. Conventionally in gender and language research, the differential social status of men and women has been important in interpretations of issues that are raised. For example, the interactional styles of women and men as co-operative and competitive, respectively, have also been viewed as reflecting men's powerful social position relative to women. Being polite and co-operative is likely to be most effective at promoting positive interactions for those who hold little power. On the issue of language about women, the existence of sexist language has been attributed to the power that men have had in making language rules. The notion of power common to all these explanations of gender differences and sexist language is that it is a commodity that some people 'have' and others don't. A social constructionist perspective on language and discourse offers a conception of power that is fundamentally different.

For social constructionist perspectives, especially those that are influenced by Foucault's ideas, power is not a commodity. Instead of power being understood as an entity that may be possessed by an individual or a social group, it is an *effect* of discourse (see Halperin, 1995). Thus the very notion of women's speech as different from men's speech can be understood as an effect of a cultural order organised around gender differences and men's dominance. Power is not something that can be owned but, according to Foucault, a 'force relation' exercised through discourse (Weedon, 1987). When power is viewed as relational, and as an effect of discourse, then fresh explanations emerge as to why knowledge about women's (and men's) speech has so easily been turned to anti-feminist ends. Knowledge about the way women and men speak is inextricably bound to gender relations.

Gender discourses, beliefs and ways of talking about gender can be thought of as producing power relations between men and women. The institutionalisation of those power relations through, amongst other things, education, the law and the division of labour reproduces the patterns of advantage and disadvantage evident in society. Discourses of gender difference may be considered as part and parcel of knowledge/power complexes that function to disadvantage women. A realisation that questions of gender differences support and recreate women's disadvantage in society has resulted in the recommendation by many feminist researchers to abandon 'difference' as a worthwhile question and to approach sex difference research very critically.

Gender as discourse

An aspect of the discursive turn is that it moves away from the idea of language as simply a system of representation, towards the notion of language as discourse, where discourse is used in a constructionist sense: the categories in language don't reflect the world but constitute it. Thus gender is not just reflected in language but the concept of gender is itself constituted by the language used to refer to it. In this section the concepts of sex and gender are re-examined in order to consider in what sense they can be understood as constructed rather than natural concepts.

Since around the 1960s an important distinction has been drawn between sex as biological and gender as social. This distinction was, and continues to be, important in challenging arguments that use biology to rationalise and police people's lives. For example, men's 'natural' rationality and women's natural emotionality can (and have) been used to justify their relative roles – for example, in public and private life. From the perspective of biological determinism, any man or woman defying the natural order of things is deviant or just plain mad. However, when roles such as housewife or breadwinner are viewed as the result of social learning rather than biology, there are more possibilities for change. Women can be engineers, doctors and politicians; men can be nurses, secretaries and homemakers. It is not biology but social learning that limits what women and men think they can do. Thus gender has been construed as the social 'trimmings' of sex and it has been assumed that the social is more malleable and less foundational than the biological.

A social constructionist sense of gender as discourse offers a radical critique not only of biological determinism but also of the sex/gender distinction. Instead of viewing sex as primary and biological while gender is secondary and social, the order is reversed and the boundaries made less distinct. A constructionist view is that social and cultural beliefs are primary and cannot be separated from biological 'knowledge'. The meanings associated with the two gender categories unavoidably cloud every aspect of thought, perception and behaviour.

A good example of how gender can influence understandings of sex is Martin's (1991) study of scientists' descriptions of fertilisation. Observations about the behaviour of the ovum and the sperm were interpreted as being gender-stereotyped. For example, sperm have been described as being active and as competing against the odds to penetrate the egg, which is viewed as rather more docile and placid. However, subsequent tests have shown that very little forward momentum is achieved despite the sperm's wriggling. Furthermore, the egg is now seen as having far more control in the fertilisation process. The important point here is that biology is not separate from or outside the social context. Rather, an understanding of biology is contained and constrained by beliefs about gender. Given the inseparability of the biological from the social, the traditional distinction between sex and gender cannot be maintained. Shifting emphasis from the biological to the social is not to deny the materiality of bodies. People have skin, bones and so forth. Also people have various combinations of chromosomes, hormones, and primary and secondary sexual characteristics that make them more or less able to reproduce if certain sexual activities are practised at the appropriate times. What a social constructionist approach does is to change the focus from the biological to the discursive as the prime site for understanding individuals, social groups and society. Discourses are an integral part of social life, and a central activity of social life is, of course, language and talk.

Gender can be understood as a discourse because it is an integral part of social life that is produced through everyday language and talk. An issue that a social constructionist approach to gender raises is to question the necessity and desirability of understanding gender as comprising two and only two gender categories (i.e. male/boy/man and female/girl/woman). Those taking a poststructural approach have argued that a belief in two and only two genders supports a system where heterosexuality is viewed as normal and homosexuality is seen as unusual and/or deviant (see Butler, 1990b, 1993).

For people who take gender for granted as a natural and inevitable consequence of biology, the social contructionist idea that sex/gender could be something other than the two-category system may seem rather strange. However, the idea of two and only two sexes is actually a relatively recent idea. Thomas Laqueur (1990), a cultural historian, documented that, prior to the nineteenth century, a one-sex model of sexual difference dominated – women were merely imperfect versions of men. Evidence of the one-sex view is the medical terms that were used for sex organs. When the one-sex view was dominant the same words were used to refer to female ovaries as to male testes, with the context clarifying which was being referred to. Laqueur used sketches from early anatomists as another form of evidence to show that, prior to the nineteenth century, female sex organs were believed to be mere inversions of male sex organs. It was not until the late eighteenth century/early nineteenth century that the one-sex model gave way to the two-sex view: women and men were of different kinds. The shift in understanding was paralleled by the development of a vast array of terms to distinguish male from female sex organs.

The simple belief in two and only two sexes can be understood, not as a biological given but as a normative social construction, a product of gender discourses. A case that starkly illustrates the primacy of the social in constructions of sex/gender is the experience of people who are born intersex. It has been estimated that as many as 5 per cent of infants are born ambiguously sexed; however, nearly all are assigned as 'male' or 'female' (see Kessler, 1998). Thus, despite the biological variation in gender, people are categorised as one of two genders. Anne Fausto-Sterling, a biologist and geneticist, suggested that at least five gender categories were required to fully capture the biological variation in sexual characteristics (Fausto-Sterling, 1993). Commenting more specifically on language, Bing and Bergvall (1998) noted that because the terms female and male insufficiently categorise our experience, English also includes tomboy, sissy, bisexual, gay, lesbian, hermaphrodite, androgyne, transvestite, transsexual, transgendered, etc. The negative connotations often associated with these words

suggest that, although multiplicity exists, these are aberrations and depart-
ures from a basic dichotomy of female and male.

A social practice that is particularly revealing of sex as a social construction is the logic of decisions justifying genital surgery with infants (see
Kessler, 1998). There are tables that provide doctors with guidelines about
the 'normal' size range of an appendage that should be considered a penis
or a clitoris. If a penis is small or missing, then, regardless of chromosomal
make-up, the infant is defined as a girl. A medical definition of a penis is
that it must have the potential to get erect and penetrate a vagina. A viable
vagina is one that can accommodate an erect penis. These norms and
definitions are not biological givens but socially determined. They reflect
and reproduce a value system where a phallus symbolises male, and
normative sex is penile–vagina penetration. Furthermore, genital surgery is
not straightforward. It generally results in the deadening of any sexual
sensation, which has led queer rights activists to suggest that genital
surgery is genital mutilation. Making an infant's sex fit into social gender
categories is given priority over the future sexual health of the child.

Beliefs about what men and women are get used in ambiguous cases,
such as intersex individuals, as prescriptions for how people should be. The
idea that to be a man you have to have a penis, capable of erection and
vagina penetration, is a social, not a biological, definition. Cases of intersex highlight how cultural beliefs are used to make biology 'fit' into social
categories. They also illustrate the need for greater flexibility and increased
acceptability in relation to variations that fall outside common-sense
experience. Haraway (1991) suggested that a cyborg metaphor of gender
may promote a greater tolerance of gender and sexual diversity. People as
gender cyborgs would have some body bits of men and others of women, a
combination that makes them both male and female in the same way that a
cyborg is both human and machine. The coining of expressions such as
gender-bending, uni-sex, virtual gender, and queerspeak may be a glimpse
of the possibility of another paradigm shift in the way sex/gender is
understood. In the late eighteenth century there was a shift from a one-sex
to a two-sex view. Now there may be another change that challenges the
pervasiveness of the present two-category system. A current idea is that
challenging the naturalness and inevitableness of two and only two genders
is an important step in challenging sexual inequality (e.g. Livia and Hall,
1997; Butler, 1990b, 1993).

Social constructionism and gendered speech styles as discourse

A social learning explanation sometimes gets confused with social constructionism (Bohan, 1992). However, the two approaches are fundamentally different. In social learning approaches, gender (norms, roles, speech
styles, etc.) is acquired and becomes part of the internal psychological

make-up of an individual. For instance, Maltz and Borker took a social learning approach when they suggested that women's and men's speech styles are a result of 'having learned to do different things with words in a conversation' (1982, p. 200). Of course, what is learnt may vary across cultures and with time, but a social learning explanation evokes an essentialist theoretical approach because gender is viewed as being part of the individual. For social constructionism, gender is not just acquired; it is something that is done. Gender does not reside in the psychological make-up of the individual but is produced by a complex, contradictory and fluctuating set of social norms.

Articulating a social constructionist critique of gender essentialism in language research, Gal wrote:

> What is missing in such work is the understanding that the categories of *women's speech*, *men's speech*, and *prestigious* or *powerful speech* are not just indexically derived from the identities of speakers. Indeed, sometimes a speaker's utterances create her or his identity. These categories, along with broader ones such as *feminine* and *masculine*, are culturally constructed within social groups; they change through history and are systematically related to other areas of cultural discourse such as the nature of persons, of power, and of a desirable moral order.
>
> (Gal, 1995, p. 171)

The assumption that language reflects the nature of gender identity is common to much theory and research that is polarised on other issues, such as the origin or explanation of gender differences. Cameron (1997) made this point when she used Mathieu's (1989, cited in Cameron) three-paradigm typology of the relationship between sex and gender to re-examine theoretical debates in feminist linguistics. Cameron highlighted the similarities in different theories when she wrote:

> In much recent discussion, Lakoff and Tannen have been made to stand for diametrically opposed views of the relationship between language, gender and power – in shorthand, the 'dominance' and 'difference' approaches. Yet while the differences between them are significant, from the point of view adopted here they are really more similar than different. Both exemplify Mathieu's 'analogy' paradigm; both assume that 'women's language' is, in essence, the language characteristically used by women. A presupposition here is that 'women' pre-exist the 'language'. 'Women's language' is the language of subjects who are already, definitively, women. Which brings us back to Simone de Beauvoir's question . . . [are there women really?].
>
> (Cameron, 1997, p. 27)

From a social constructionist perspective language and discourse are the meaning systems that produce (rather than reflect) gender as an important and salient social category. A social constructionist approach to gender views it as an ideological-symbolic aspect of language and talk that potentially constitutes identity. Thus gender is not a stable set of traits residing within an individual psyche and reflected in behaviour. Gender has no fixed or stable meaning. Rather gender is a social process; it is created and renegotiated in interpersonal relationships and encouraged and maintained through social structures. Gender is something that is done in social interaction. So, from a social constructionist approach, women's (or men's) speech styles are no longer seen to be derived from the social identity of those who use them, but are treated as a discursive or ideological-symbolic concept available to construct one's self as a man or a woman. Thus being a woman or a man is a matter, among other things, of talking like one.

An example of a study that was informed by a social constructionist approach to gender was Hall's (1995) investigation of speech styles and telephone-sex work. Hall examined the instructions of training manuals and the language used (by women) in pre-recorded telephone-sex messages. Telephone-sex workers (also referred to as fantasy makers or call-doers) were also interviewed on the techniques they used to communicate the kind of feminine, sexy persona that there was a demand for in the industry. Across the material examined there was evidence that the notion of a feminine interactive style was used as a resource to construct an identity that customers would want to buy. For example, training manuals suggested strategies consistent with what has been defined as a (feminine) co-operative style – showing interest by asking questions, using back-channels, not interrupting and so forth. The pre-recorded messages used a dynamic voice shifting from high to low pitch depending on the level of sexual innuendo. The sex-workers themselves reported using linguistic strategies reminiscent of Lakoff's (1973, 1975) 'woman's language' during their calls.

Throughout the telephone-sex industry that Hall (1995) studied, cultural prescriptions of gender were used as resources to construct a feminine identity that would attract and satisfy male customers. Interestingly, one of the telephone workers was a man who posed as a female heterosexual for callers. As with the women in the study, he reported that his callers were most pleased when he used the speech characteristics typically associated with femininity. The behaviour of the telephone-sex workers points to the non-essential nature of gender behaviour. The call-doers' speech style was not a reflection of their gender identity. Rather their speech behaviour reflected and perpetuated conventional cultural norms of femininity. Thus, in Gal's (1995) terms, the utterances created the telephone workers' gender identity. The resources used in that construction were stereotypes about women's speech.

The idea that gender-typed behaviours are performances is not new and will be discussed in more detail in the next chapter. The important point here is that when gender is construed as a socially constructed category, the question of stable, enduring gender differences makes little sense. Thus the complete lack of consensus in the results of empirical studies of gender differences is unremarkable – it is merely the consequence of the mistaken assumption that gender is located inside the individual as a stable set of characteristics. Research that seeks to pin down the exact nature of those differences is thus misguided because the meanings of femininity or masculinity are not fixed, measurable entities but plural and contradictory notions that shift and change in the ongoing business of social life. So for a social constructionist, questions of gender difference in language are misleading because they are based on a concept of gender that is wrong – that being a man or being a woman is an essential aspect of the self.

To say that research that asks questions about gender difference in language is misguided is not to say that men and women do not talk or communicate differently. Of course they do. Men and women differ in their opportunities to make political speeches, they differ in their access to communication technologies, and they often differ in the degree of risk they take if they are rude and obnoxious. If there were no differences between men and women, gender as a social construct would be meaningless. The important point is not that men and women differ but that it is not possible to be definitive about the exact nature of those differences, because what it means to 'do being a man' or to 'do being a woman' is dynamic and variable. For example, a high pitch may be used to mark femininity but a high pitch is not necessarily feminine – it may just be nervousness.

Ochs (1992) developed the concept of 'gender indexes' to clarify the constitutive relationship between language and gender. The analytic notion of indexing is important in language and gender research that follows a social constructionist theoretical perspective. Ochs pointed out that there are only a very few features of language that directly and exclusively index gender. Examples of direct gender indexes include sex-specific pronouns (e.g. he and she) and nouns (e.g. woman, man), although even gender pronouns and nouns can be 'inverted'. For example, Bunzl (2000) found that in conversations between gay men feminine pronouns were sometimes used to index a male referent. Bunzl interpreted the inverted use of gender pronouns as a strategic attempt by the men to subvert the binary sex/gender system.

With direct gender indexes, the gender of the speaker (e.g. in Japanese the pragmatic particles *ze* and *wa* generally presuppose that the speaker is male or female respectively) or the gender of the referent (e.g. son, daughter) is transparent from the linguistic form. The exclusivity of gender indexes refers to whether a linguistic form is used only by one sex. Ochs

86

(1992) used tag questions to illustrate the non-exclusive relation of linguistic features to gender. Tag questions in English are associated not only with female speakers but also with hesitancy and utterances that seek confirmation. Thus both men and women use tag questions.

Indirect indexes of gender are far more frequent than direct ones. The indirect nature of gender indexes is because linguistic features tend to index social meanings other than gender. For instance, the speech act of an imperative form is a directive – that is, it is an order for the addressee to do something. Men, more often than women, are in a position to issue imperatives. Thus directives are an indirect and non-exclusive index of gender. The use of imperatives forms part of the pool of linguistic resources for constructing oneself as masculine and/or powerful.

The notion of indexicality is useful for understanding the complex constitutive relationships between language, discourse and speaker identity. As Gal (1995) pointed out, the indirect and non-exclusive relation of gender and language means that the categories 'women's language' and 'men's language' are not the empirical reality of the language used by women and the language used by men (respectively). Instead, women's language and men's language should be viewed as *symbolic* rather than *descriptive* categories. The notion of gender-specific speech styles is a cultural resource for producing and negotiating gender in interactions, rather than a description of how women and men actually speak.

Apart from Hall's (1995) study of telephone-sex workers, another study that has successfully maintained the distinction between ideologies of gender and language and actual linguistic practices was Okamoto's (1994, 1995) work on the language used by Japanese women. As already mentioned, Japanese, more than English, has forms that have traditionally been understood as being direct indexes of speaker gender. As a consequence of the direct indexes, Japanese has been characterised as having distinct female and male speech registers. Thus linguistic differences between Japanese women and men can be extensive. However, Okamoto argued that even in Japanese, where direct indexes of gender are more common than in other languages, the categories of women's language and men's language represent sex stereotypes rather than the actual language practices of women and men. In a series of studies Okamoto found that strongly feminine linguistic forms were used predominantly by older and more middle-class female speakers. In comparison, younger women and career women were more likely to use fewer feminine and more masculine forms – especially during informal conversations with friends.

Okamoto (1994, 1995) argued that the language used by her female participants, which included a high frequency of masculine forms, supported Gal's (1995) proposal that sex-specific language styles were more a symbolic-ideological construct than a reflection of how women and men actually speak. The construct of Japanese women's language is ideological

87

in so far as the linguistic features that are associated with it signify ideal femininity (politeness, social sensitivity and formality). The same characteristics may also reflect lower status and powerlessness. The notion of women's language is symbolic because it functions as a norm against which women's actual language use gets judged. The avoidance of strongly feminine forms and the use of more forms most commonly associated with being masculine, by younger women and professional women, Okamoto interpreted as being an expression of resistance to that traditional ideal. Thus, in the sample of Japanese women Okamoto studied, the cultural stereotypes about women's and men's language became resources for women who wished to signal their resistance to (or support of) traditional beliefs about appropriate gender roles.

Gender and language in discursive psychology

Alongside some strands of feminist social psychology one of the few other areas of psychology that embraces social constructionist ideas is discursive psychology. The sub-field of discursive psychology has developed the philosophical ideas associated with the 'turn to language' into its theoretical and analytical orientation to understanding social behaviour, including that relevant to gender. Historically, social psychologists have been interested in language only for what it can reveal about 'underlying' cognitive structures and processes. For example, sexist language research has used memory for words to demonstrate how masculine generic terms are stored and retrieved during cognitive processing (Ng, 1990). In contrast, for discursive psychology, language itself is the object of enquiry because, consistent with social constructionism, language is understood as constructing, limiting and guiding people's understanding of their worlds and themselves. Furthermore, it is through language that the business of living is conducted.

Discursive psychology has been developing within its parent discipline in conjunction with critiques of conventional research practices, such as experimentation, quantification, and a questioning of the dominant epistemological assumptions of realism and positivism. Many of the shortcomings associated with traditional psychology that have been highlighted by discursive critiques had already been well established by feminist psychologists (see Gavey, 1989). For example, both discursive and feminist theories in psychology have rejected the possibilities of absolute truth and objectively-established knowledge. The postmodern point made by both critiques is that, far from being neutral, widely accepted conceptions of the material and social world tend to be consistent with the values associated with the dominant moral order. The idea that gender difference in speech styles is a discourse rather than a 'true' reflection of the ways women and men do speak is consistent with a postmodern view of knowledge about the world.

Discursive and feminist psychology share scepticism about psychology's supposed objectivism and its belief in establishing enduring facts about human behaviour. That scepticism, combined with the long history of feminist interest in language, has meant that gender issues have emerged as a focus of many discourse-analytic studies in psychology. The prominence of gender issues in discursive psychology research has meant that discourse analysis has been understood, in psychology at least, as synonymous with feminist research. However, as Wilkinson and Kitzinger (1995) pointed out, despite some theoretical similarities, there is nothing distinctively or inherently feminist about discourse analysis. Indeed, some feminists have been quite sceptical about the use of discourse theory in the pursuit of feminist goals (see Gill, 1995; Hepburn, 1999).

Despite debates about the compatibility of feminism with discursive psychology, discourse analysis has featured prominently in feminist psychology since the early 1990s. An integral aspect of feminist discursive psychology is a focus on gender and language. However, the questions asked by feminist discursive psychologists are very different from those typically associated with the gender and language field. Consequently the theoretical insights and methodological advances emanating from feminist discursive work have had little impact on the area – a situation that I hope this book will go some way to rectify.

Just as it is possible to identify different feminist approaches to research in psychology (see Morawski, 1990), it is possible to distinguish between different styles of discourse analysis within discursive psychology. At a general level, the different kinds of discursive psychology are all more or less influenced by linguistic philosophy and pragmatics, ethnomethodology, conversation analysis and poststructuralism (see Potter, 1996). The particular style varies depending on theoretical emphasis. For example, Widdicombe (1995) differentiated discursive psychology into two broad strands – that which is more informed by poststructuralist ideas, and that which is more informed by ethnomethodology and the philosophy of language. Others (e.g. Wetherell, 1998) have argued for a more synthetic approach that weaves together a range of influences. What follows is a brief description of the style of discourse analysis that places more emphasis on the broader meaning systems invoked in talk and less importance on the structural features of their articulation. Then some examples of research that has investigated issues relevant to the gender and language field will be presented. Research following what has been identified as a more ethnomethodological/conversation analytic style of discourse analysis will be discussed in the next chapter.

In the discourse analytic studies that will be discussed in the remainder of this chapter, the concepts of action, construction and variation are key analytic tools. An important focus of the research is what is being achieved (i.e. social action or function) in any interaction. Often an analysis concentrates on the management of an *issue* or *dilemma* – for example, presenting something as factual (e.g. sex differences) when there is a personal stake involved (to justify discriminatory practices). The term *ideological dilemma* has been coined to refer to the contradictory beliefs and ideas that constitute our common-sense understanding of the world (Billig, Condor, Edwards, Gane, Middleton and Radley, 1988). For example, when referring to many people working together on a task we may say 'many hands make light work' or 'too many cooks spoil the broth'. The version that will be promoted depends, of course, on what we are doing with the idea (e.g. recruiting or discouraging volunteers).

An example of a feminist discursive psychology investigation using the concept of an ideological dilemma was Kitzinger and Thomas's (1995) study on the way sexual harassment was constructed by participants who volunteered to be interviewed on the topic. A particular focus of the analysis was how particular incidents or experiences were included or excluded as examples of sexual harassment. Kitzinger and Thomas found that the ways in which sexual harassment was construed functioned, rather paradoxically, to discourage experiences of harassment being defined as such. For example, many of the women in their study resisted labelling their experiences as incidences of sexual harassment because they did not want to cast themselves as victims. Further dilemmas that emerged from the analysis related to incidence frequency and definitions of sexual harassment. For example, some participants reported that incidents occurred frequently, while others suggested that sexual harassment was an unusual and rare occurrence. However, if sexualised interactions happen all the time between women and men, then it cannot be harassment – it is just a normal part of life. In contrast, if they only happen rarely, then it cannot be that important. Furthermore incidents were described as being about power and not about sex, but if it is more about power then why is it called 'sexual' harassment? Kitzinger and Thomas argued that the various constructions and dilemmas associated with labelling behaviours as sexual harassment functioned to render sexual harassment less visible and more difficult to challenge in practice.

Aside from ideological dilemmas, a further characteristic of this type of discourse analytic approach is that it aims to identify the linguistic and rhetorical resources that are used by a speaker to construct behaviour or social action as reasonable and rational. The identification of broader patterns of language use, sometimes referred to as *interpretative repertoires*, *practical ideologies*, or *discourses*, is often an aim of the research. What is meant by interpretative repertoires, practical ideologies or discourses is the 'often contradictory and fragmentary notions, norms and models which guide conduct and allow for its justification and rationalisation' (Wetherell,

Stiven and Potter, 1987, p. 60). The use of the term 'ideology' in ideological dilemmas and practical ideologies suggests the critical nature of many discursive studies. The term ideology is used here in a sense that is similar to some uses of 'discourse' – that is, to refer to the systems of beliefs or thoughts that contribute to the maintenance of asymmetrical power relations and social inequalities between groups. For example, the belief that women are 'naturally' more nurturing than men contributes to women having to shoulder the major burden of childcare and eldercare.

One of the earliest published discourse analytic studies in psychology to utilise the concepts of interpretative repertoires and practical ideologies was Wetherell *et al.*'s (1987) study of the accounts that university students gave of employment opportunities for women. The interpretative repertoires that emerged from the analysis were called 'individualism' and 'practical consideration' talk. These two repertoires functioned in the students' accounts to naturalise and justify sexual inequality in employment. On the one hand it was up to individuals to show they had the knowledge, experience and skills worthy of employment. On the other, there are practical considerations (e.g. lack of adequate childcare) making the employment of women a problem (see also Gough, 1998). Wetherell *et al.* suggested that the repertoires of individualism and practical considerations allowed speakers to endorse the concept of equal opportunities, thus presenting themselves as liberal and open-minded. However, at the same time as endorsing the notion of equal employment opportunities, they were denying the possibility that bias against women in employment existed. The simultaneous endorsement of equity and denial of bias constructs a discursive context that discourages actions that would encourage women into employment. Wetherell *et al.*'s study illustrates the point that negative attitudes towards women are not necessarily the whole explanation for discriminatory employment practices. Rather, the discursive articulation of inequality masquerades as positive attitudes while functioning to discourage affirmative action.

The two discourse studies just described are examples of the methodological approach that has developed as a result of the shift in emphasis from language to discourse and from essentialist to constructionist notions of identity and other social objects. These shifts have meant that the boundaries imposed by the concerns traditionally organising the gender and language field have been removed. No longer does research in the area have to be confined to questions about sex bias or sex differences in language use. Instead investigations into gender and language include any research that examines the discursive construction of gender or the discursive articulation of any issues that are relevant to gender or the experiences of women and men.

A collection of discourse analytic research presented in Wilkinson and Kitzinger's (1995) volume *Feminism and discourse* showcases the kind of

91

work that, as a consequence of the discursive turn, can now be considered as research on gender and language (see also Burman and Parker, 1993). A comprehensive discussion of research on the discursive articulation of gender and/or issues relevant to gender is beyond the scope of this chapter. Indeed it is a topic that can be the sole focus of a book (see, for example, Edley and Wetherell, 1995; Wodak, 1997). However, some discourse analytic studies have touched on issues directly relevant to concerns that are most typical of gender and language research, and it is to these studies that I now turn.

Already discussed in Chapter 3 is the tendency for any linguistic characteristic associated with women to be evaluated negatively. In the area of broadcasting this has had a profound impact on the gender profile of people employed as presenters. Typically there are far fewer women than men employed as presenters. When women have been employed, they have tended to be allocated shifts at airtimes that attract the smallest audiences. Of course, one justification given for not employing women as presenters is that their voices are not suited to broadcasting as much as men's (lower-pitched) voices are. Using a discourse analytic approach, Gill (1993) investigated how men who were currently working at radio stations explained the lack of female disc jockeys (DJs). The data consisted of interviews with the men which were subsequently transcribed. On examination of the interview material Gill found four broad accounts that were used by the broadcasters.

The first and most prevalent type of explanation given by the radio station workers was that women just didn't apply for jobs when there were vacancies advertised. The typical reason given for women's non-application was that women were not interested in doing that kind of work. Gill (1993) suggested that one of the functions of this kind of explanation is that it deflects any possible charges of sexism away from the radio stations. The implication is that there is no purposeful discrimination against women. Rather, responsibility for the lack of female DJs lies with women themselves because of their lack of interest in the job. Women's non-application is a compelling explanation for the lack of female DJs. However, a characteristic of discourse analytic studies is not to endorse the 'truth' of any one explanation. Rather, one of the aims is to identify the different accounts given (sometimes by the same person) and to consider any inherent contradictions, thus highlighting the discursive nature of the problem.

A contradiction in the accounts was highlighted when the second type of explanation for the lack of female DJs was considered. A second reason Gill (1993) found in her interviews (and sometimes both explanations were used within the same interview) focused on the audience's alleged negative reaction to female presenters and their preference for men's voices. The interesting thing to note here is the inherent inconsistency between the two explanations of women's non-application and of audience's preference for men. In the light of the latter explanation, the lack of women in broadcasting looks less like the result of non-application and more like a deliberate policy not to employ women because of audience preference for men's voices. Aside from the inherent inconsistency, a feature common to the explanations is that they both deflect the attribution of blame away from the radio station.

The third type of explanation given invoked the notion of gender differences. Women supposedly lacked the kind of qualities and skills necessary to be a radio presenter. This explanation, like the one that referred to the audience's supposed preference for male presenters, contradicts the first explanation. So the lack of female DJs is justified by their lack of skills – a deliberate decision rather than a consequence of their non-application. Even if they did apply they would not have the required skills. With the gender difference explanation, Gill (1993) paid close attention to the exact nature of the skills that the men interviewed listed as being necessary for the job. A noteworthy finding was that the interviewees tended to avoid being explicit about the skills required, but when they were, the skills mentioned (e.g. being dextrous and having a personality) did not seem to fit more readily with masculine than with feminine stereotypes. Thus Gill's work illustrates the point that the *notion* rather than the 'reality' of difference is sufficient to justify sexual inequality.

The other type of explanation that Gill (1993) identified revolved around the supposed unsuitability of women's voices. As might be expected, women's voices were not described in positive terms. Rather, adjectives like 'shrill' or 'grating' were used. Gill found a 'catch-22' situation in the way women's voices were described by the broadcasters. On the one hand, if women sounded 'grating and shrill' they turned listeners off – justifying not employing women as presenters. On the other hand, the duskiness and sexiness of some women's voices may switch audiences on – thus justifying limiting female DJs to unpopular night shifts. The important point here is that however women's voices were described, it supported discriminating against them in broadcasting jobs. Furthermore, despite the contradictions and inconsistencies between and within the four broad types of explanations, they formed a compelling set of discourses that could be used to undermine accusations of sexism and weaken the justification for affirmative action campaigns. Thus the sexual inequality evident in broadcasting may be seen as an effect of the discourses about the lack of female DJs. In contrast, an essentialist approach would assume that negative attitudes towards women are *reflected* in the language and that those attitudes are the cause of sexual inequality.

Another discursive study relevant to the concerns of gender and language was a study conducted by a postgraduate student and me on how people made sense of cultural naming practices (Bähr and Weatherall, 1999). As discussed in Chapter 1, the sexism inherent in Western naming practices has been criticised and challenged by feminists for a long time. Given a widespread awareness of the criticisms levelled at the practice of a woman taking her husband's surname on marriage, we (Bähr and Weatherall) were interested in the explanations used to justify conventional as well as alternative naming practices. In our analysis of interviews with women and men about their experiences and choices of personal names we identified four interpretative repertoires. These were called: names as labels, naming practices as tradition, names as identity, and names as social markers. The interpretative repertoires functioned in three different ways: to normalise the use of names and naming in general; to dismiss any allegations that naming practices are sexist; and to challenge the perceived sexism of naming conventions. An important point was that the repertoires were not alternative accounts espoused by individual participants. Rather the interviewees drew upon and combined the repertoires when constructing their accounts of how they understood names and name-changing.

Names as identity is one of the repertoires that has been associated most with a feminist position – names being considered an important aspect of personal identity that should not be lost. However, despite the association of particular repertoires with feminist or traditional positions about name-changing on marriage, we found that no one repertoire appeared to be exclusively 'feminist' or 'conservative'. So, the names as identity repertoire was used to argue *for* women changing their name on marriage in order to promote a strong sense of family identity among parents and children. The repertoire that was used consistently but not exclusively to counter the feminist argument that naming conventions are patriarchal was the names as labels repertoire. This repertoire constructed naming practices as a value-free system necessary to maintain social order. The idea of names as 'just' labels was used to dismiss the claim that naming practices reflect cultural beliefs and values. More subversively, however, the names as label repertoire was also used to counter the argument that name-keeping is necessarily a feminist political practice. Women who keep their names are not necessarily feminist – they are 'just' using the system to keep their lives orderly. The discursive approach to naming that we took highlights that a single or simple explanation of naming and naming practices, while compelling, may be inadequate for promoting social change. Instead an understanding of the discursive fabric of the issue may be an important step in constructing convincing arguments to support social changes that benefit women.

Chapter summary

This chapter has discussed the impact of what has been called the discursive turn on the field of gender and language research. Typically two concerns have preoccupied research in the field – gender bias in language and gender differences in language use. However, the realisation that language about women and men and the way men and women speak are both aspects of the social construction of gender blurs the distinction between the two concerns. A shift from an essentialist to a constructionist theory of gender has resulted in new insights into problems that arose from research on gender differences in speech. Those problems were the lack of closure on the question of what exactly the differences between women's speech and men's are, and that research on gender differences in speech has so readily been turned to reinforce rather than challenge bias against women.

According to a social constructionist perspective, the failure to establish what are the true and enduring differences between women's language and men's language is predictable. Gender is not a stable and enduring feature of the individual which is reliably and transparently reflected in language use. Rather, gender can be viewed as a set of discourses or ideological/symbolic constructs. In the case of speech, being a woman or being a man is, among other things, a matter of talking like one. Few speech features directly and exclusively mark gender. Instead, most speech features, such as tag questions, back-channels and verbosity, have social meanings other than gender. Thus the notion of 'women's language' must be considered as separate from but related to the language that women actually use when they speak. The way women and men speak may or may not map on to the cultural beliefs about language styles. Speech style may be one form of behaviour that can be used to resist or challenge conventional sex stereotypes.

The suggestion that questions about gender differences in language use are based on false assumptions is not to say that gender differences in speech do not occur. Of course women's use of language may differ from men's. From a social constructionist perspective what is interesting is how beliefs about gender and language are created and challenged in social life. An important point is that cultural beliefs and values about women's and men's speech must be treated as something distinct from, but influential on, the language used by women and men during interaction. Stable and enduring differences between the individuals who belong to the general categories of 'women' and 'men' do not exist. Instead there are only depictions of masculine and feminine speech behaviours that form what will be discussed in Chapter 5 as a 'schedule for the portrayal of gender'. These schedules are fluid and variable. Furthermore, such behaviours may or may not be manifest in an individual's behaviour in any single interaction.

A further insight associated with a social constructionist theoretical perspective is the impossibility of complete impartiality in knowledge production. Thus the very notions of women's and men's speech can be understood as an effect of a cultural order organised around gender difference and valuing men and maleness over women and femaleness. Hence one reason why research on gender difference in language has failed to develop the anticipated social critique to end discrimination against women is that knowledge about gender difference in speech styles and the gendered social order are like two sides of a piece of paper. The realisation that the notion of difference is tied to women's disadvantage has led many feminist scholars, including myself, to argue that questions about gender difference are rarely useful ones to pursue.

Another consequence of the discursive turn has been a methodological shift in research practice. Feminist research in discursive psychology is a good example of how the theoretical changes associated with social constructionism have resulted in a change in methodological approach. One feature of discourse analysis is that the object of study is language use itself. This contrasts with more conventional social psychological approaches where language is treated as reflecting some kind of underlying cognitive reality about attitudes, identity or whatever. The types of questions asked about gender differ between discursive and essentialist approaches. For example, a discursive study is interested in how the notion of gender difference is mobilised to justify and rationalise discrimination against women. Discursive research has begun documenting the discursive patterning of bias (see Gill, 1993; Gough, 1998; Wetherell *et al.*, 1987). Research has found, for example, that arguments about women's disadvantage can be constructed in a way that simultaneously endorses the ideal of equity while denying the existence of bias and the need for social change.

Feminist research taking a discursive approach asks different kinds of questions from the concerns that have typically organised the gender and language field. As a consequence new and exciting insights are emerging about the nature of gender, of gender bias and of their relationship to language. The discursive turn has renewed the vigour of gender and language research, which had been in danger of being stuck on the same tired old debates (i.e. is sexist language significant and what are the gender differences in speech?). Now an important aspect of gender and language research is the examination of everyday, spontaneous language use. What ordinary language use can reveal about gender is a question that conversation analysts might ask, and it is the contribution that conversation analysis can make to gender and language research that will be the focus of the next chapter.

5

GENDER AND LANGUAGE IN ETHNOMETHODOLOGY AND CONVERSATION ANALYSIS

Introduction

The influence of the discursive turn has meant that, increasingly, there has been a shift away from studying how language reflects (and helps to perpetuate) women's disadvantage. Instead, there is a greater emphasis placed on the constitutive role of language in relation to social reality. Instead of viewing gender as something separate from, but related to, the study of language, it is increasingly treated as a socially constructed category. Language does not merely mirror social beliefs about gender and reflect the nature of gender identity. Rather, it is through language (and discourse) that gender is produced and gains its significance as a social category. Thus, the study of texts and talk in interaction become prime sites for examining gender.

Discursive psychology was described in Chapter 4 as one approach that has developed for examining the social construction of gender. The type of discourse analysis described in that chapter has been identified as a poststructuralist style of discursive psychology (e.g. Nikander, 1995; Widdicombe, 1995). Although a refreshing new direction for the study of gender and language, the poststructuralist strand of discursive psychology is not without criticism. For example, Widdicombe (1995, 1998) suggested that by prioritising the identification of interpretative repertoires and by considering their political significance, not enough attention has been paid to demonstrating what exactly characterises their existence in talk (see also Widdicombe and Wooffitt, 1995).

Kitzinger (2000b) related the problem of ignoring the micro-structural details of talk directly to a dilemma of feminist discursive research where analyses may construe speakers as merely parroting cultural discourses, thereby colluding in their own oppression (see also Weatherall, Gavey and Potts, in press). This issue is similar to one identified in sexist language work where feminist theories about linguistic bias stressed women's alienation in language. Ironically, early theories about women's silence and

97

negative definition in language made women feel passive and silent (Cameron, 1985; see also Weatherall, 1998).

Schegloff (1997) identified a separate but related problem with post-structuralist styles of discursive psychology. This style of research tends to focus on power issues. The critical element of the empirical work means that the focus lies on the political implications of discourses rather than on how they are articulated. When this happens, researchers are open to the accusation of merely imposing their own political view or analytic concerns on to the data. Schegloff alluded to this as a problem in gender and language research, where feminists have interpreted patterns of language use, such as men interrupting, as showing social concepts such as 'dominance'. Given that a speaker has multiple social identities (e.g. as a woman, an academic, middle-aged), it seems reasonable that a scholarly analysis wishing to invoke one of these (e.g. gender) demonstrates that it is relevant to the interaction being analysed. In Schegloff's words:

> The reservation I wish to feature here is that such analyses [interpreting an interaction along gender lines] make no room for the overtly displayed concerns of the participants themselves, the terms in which they related to one another, the relevancies to which they show themselves to be oriented. Such analyses insist instead on characterisations of the parties, the relevancies, and the context, to which the *analyst* is oriented.
>
> (Schegloff, 1997, p. 174, emphasis in the original)

A conversation analytic style of discursive psychology can be identified as a second broad strand of discursive psychology. It overcomes some of the problems identified with the poststructuralist style by placing a greater emphasis on what people say and exactly how they say it in an ongoing interaction. A distinctive feature of this approach is that the analysis is limited to what the participants themselves demonstrate is relevant to them in an interaction. A conversation analyst would not invoke gender as a category, a priori, to explain patterns of language use found in conversations. Rather, gender would be seen as pertinent to an analysis only when there was evidence that the participants in the conversation were using gender as a relevant feature of the interaction. Similarly, words would not be predefined as sexist but would only be identified as sexist if they were demonstrably viewed as such from the speaker's perspective. Researchers who have used this approach to investigate gender issues promote its potential for feminist language research (e.g. Kitzinger and Frith, 1999; Stokoe, 1998).

A theoretical foundation common to different strands of discursive psychology is the ideas associated with ethnomethodology (see Potter and Wetherell, 1987). Both ethnomethodology and conversation analysis stress the importance of paying close attention to the kinds of socially organised inferential processes, or general assumptions, that people use to structure the ongoing business of everyday life. These shared assumptions promote common understandings and help co-ordinate social action. For example, I, like other members of Anglo-American cultures, infer that the question 'how are you?', during the initial moments of an interaction, is not a question that I am required to answer. Rather, I treat the question as the first part of a greeting. I can comfortably respond with 'hi there'. However, I know that if at a later stage of an interaction I said 'hi there' to the question 'how are you?', that would seem rather strange and be something I might have to explain.

The ethnomethodological influence on discursive psychology is particularly pertinent to the field of gender and language because one of the earliest social constructionist approaches to gender was developed from an ethnomethodological perspective (Kessler and McKenna, 1978). The first part of this chapter will describe the ethnomethodological approach to gender and language. Conversation analysis is an analytic approach to examining talk that developed from ethnomethodology. The second section of this chapter will describe in greater detail some of the organisational sequences that have been identified by conversation analysts as structuring social interaction. This description has a double purpose: to readers unfamiliar with conversation analysis it will provide an introduction; it will also provide the necessary background to understand the feminist conversation analytic studies that will be discussed. Finally in this chapter, I will briefly consider a debate about the extent to which a conversation analytic mentality is useful for gender and language research.

Gender as an everyday accomplishment

Ethnomethodology is the study of the mundane activities, referred to as 'methods', that 'members' (people) use to make sense of everyday life and accomplish actions (Garfinkel, 1967). So, an ethnomethodological approach to gender examines the methods that members use so that gender structures interactions and seems such an unremarkable aspect of the ongoing business of everyday life. Ethnomethodologists interested in gender have asked:

> How in any interaction, is a sense of the reality of a world of two and only two genders constructed? How do we 'do' gender attributions? That is, what kinds of rules do we apply to what kinds of displays, such that in every concrete instance we produce a sense that there are *only* men and women, and that this is an objective fact, not dependent on the particular instance.
> (Kessler and McKenna, 1978, pp. 5–6)

For most people, being accepted as a member of one's assigned gender category requires little effort. Furthermore, assigning others to a gender category is generally a seamless part of interactions. Being a man or being a woman (and seeing others as belonging to one of those two gender categories) is so much part of the ongoing, mundane activity of everyday life that it appears to be nothing other than a natural and inevitable consequence of one's sex and of social learning. It is precisely the ordinariness and taken-for-granted aspects of gender that make it of interest to the ethnomethodologist. How does the ordinariness and taken-for-grantedness of gender get achieved during the ongoing activities of social life? The idea that gender is an accomplishment rather than something that women and men 'just are' is one that has been missing from the widely accepted (essentialist) psychological theories of gender.

In contrast to conventional psychological theories, an ethnomethodological approach highlights the constructed nature of gender: it is something that gets done during interaction. Garfinkel's (1967) ethnomethodological study of a transsexual individual ('Agnes') is compelling evidence that one's gender identity is more than a reflection of biology or an internalisation of social norms. Agnes, unlike most people, had to consciously work at achieving and securing her sex status. Agnes was identified as a male at birth because of her normal-appearing male genitals. Consequentially, she was raised as a boy. However, at puberty, Agnes developed female secondary sex characteristics, and at 17 years old she decided to live as a woman. Garfinkel met with Agnes on a number of occasions to discuss her experiences. Garfinkel's analysis of those discussions identified the strategies that Agnes employed to establish and maintain a legitimate gender status. Agnes had learnt to 'pass' as a woman by presenting herself appropriately and behaving in a manner consistent with conventional conceptions of femininity in different social situations.

Garfinkel (1967) referred to Agnes as a practical methodologist of gender. Being a practical methodologist, Agnes was a person who made 'observable *that* and *how* normal sexuality is accomplished' (Garfinkel, 1967, p. 180, emphasis in the original). According to Garfinkel, intersexed individuals and transsexuals like Agnes 'had as resources their remarkable awareness and un-commonsense knowledge of the organisation and operation of social structures that were for those that are able to take their sexual status for granted routinized, "seen but unnoticed" backgrounds of their everyday affairs' (p. 118). Of course, important elements in the accomplishment of gender are speech and communication style. It is not surprising, then, that Garfinkel made explicit reference to Agnes's voice and the way she talked as part of the devices that she used to pass as a woman. He reported that 'her voice was pitched alto level, and her delivery has the occasional lisp similar to that affected by feminine appearing male homosexuals' (p. 119). He also commented on her use of euphemisms, a

100

stereotypical feature of women's speech, which Agnes used strategically to avoid disclosing detailed information about her past that may have revealed an absence of a girlish childhood.

Cases of intersexuality and transsexuality provided kinds of 'real life' examples of what Garfinkel (cited in Heritage, 1984) engineered in his 'breaching experiments'. These experiments followed the same general pattern. A confederate and a naïve participant would be involved in some activity, such as playing a game. The confederate would violate one of the established rules of the activity, or game, and the participant's reactions to those violations were noted. Participants' responses to the rule violations led to the general conclusion that people are motivated to normalise discrepancies. For example, in a game of noughts and crosses, when confederates rubbed out their opponents' marks, participants tended to assume that a new game was being played. Either that or the participants got very upset and annoyed.

Effectively what the breaching experiments did was to highlight strategies that people use to achieve a sense of understanding about their world. The breaching experiments revealed members' motivation to normalise behaviours that were counter to the framework of meaning they were applying to the situation. Garfinkel (1967) understood Agnes, in part, as someone who breached the social rules about gender. Thus she highlighted to him the types of beliefs that constituted people's framework for understanding of gender. That is, Agnes made more explicit the usually implicit cultural norms and rules about gender. Garfinkel referred to these norms and rules of gender as members' 'natural attitudes' towards gender. Garfinkel argued that the accomplishment of gender rests on members' shared natural attitudes towards the 'facts' about gender, even though cases like that of Agnes are evidence that these facts are not always true. Kessler and McKenna summarised Garfinkel's description of members' natural attitudes towards gender as consisting of the following eight rules:

1 Female and male are the two and only two genders.
2 Gender is stable and enduring. That is, you always are, you always have been and you always will be the gender assigned to you at birth (or before).
3 An essential aspect of gender is one's genitals. Females have a vagina and males have a penis.
4 Anyone who does not clearly belong to one of the two gender categories is a joke or abnormal.
5 There are no transfers from one gender to another with the exception of pretences (e.g. 'drag' parties).
6 Everyone belongs to one of the two gender categories – there is no such thing as someone without a gender.

7 Two and only two gender categories is a 'naturally' occurring fact.
8 Membership in one of the two gender categories is 'natural' and inevitable.

(1978, pp. 113–114)

Cases of intersexuality and transsexuality are violations of the normative rules about gender. Thus, the studies of those cases make it easier to see how gender is a social accomplishment, rather than a natural fact. Indeed, the study of transsexuality has been useful for developing a theory of gender that does not just reproduce common-sense notions of gender (see Kessler, 1998). The ethnomethodologically inspired studies of gender have provided insights that challenge essentialist (and common-sense) views of gender as a 'natural fact'. Gender is not just a natural and inevitable consequence of one's sex. Nor is it just an essential feature of an individual's personal and social identity. A key aspect of gender is that it is part of the routine, ongoing work of everyday, mundane, social interaction. This ethnomethodological insight further highlights one of the messages of the previous chapter. That is, that it is more constructive to treat 'women's language' and 'men's language' as ideological, symbolic notions than as reflections of how women and men actually speak.

Garfinkel's (1967) contention of gender as an achievement was developed by Goffman (1976) in his work on gender displays. Goffman used the term 'gender display' to refer to the kind of ritualistic, conventionalised acts of interpersonal interaction that members (for non-transsexuals unconsciously and for transsexuals consciously) perform to portray the cultural indicators of gender. Hairstyle, clothing and tone of voice were considered by Goffman to be 'early warning' displays of gender, with more subtle and indirect behavioural displays, such as politeness features, varying in different interpersonal and social contexts. Goffman, like Garfinkel, believed that what characterised a person as a man or a woman was not an expression of biological sex or learned gender. Instead what characterised an individual as being a man or a woman was their willingness to sustain, and competence at sustaining, the appropriate schedule of gender displays.

Among other things, Goffman (1977, in Lemert and Branam, 1997) was interested in how gender displays become ritualised through institutionalised features of gender organisation. He noted, for example, how women and men are more similar than different in the production of bodily waste products and their elimination. However, the social environment is largely organised with two sets of toilet facilities. Such organisation, according to Goffman, encourages the development and honouring of subcultural gender differences. Entering the 'ladies' or 'gents' is part of many people's everyday lives. Toilet segregation is generally understood as a natural consequence of the difference between women and men. However, Goffman suggested that sex-segregated public facilities effectively function to honour and to reproduce beliefs about gender differences.

Goffman (1976) understood gender expressions (such as using separate toilet facilities) to be a mere show, but a show that constituted a considerable substance of society. Articulating what I would now label a social constructionist approach to gender, Goffman stated:

> What the human nature of males and females really consists of, then, is a capacity to learn to provide and to read depictions of masculinity and femininity and a willingness to adhere to a schedule for presenting these pictures, and this capacity they have by virtue of being persons, not females or males. One might just as well say there is no gender identity. There is only a schedule for the portrayal of gender.
>
> (Goffman, 1976, p. 224)

Kessler and McKenna's (1978) ethnomethodological approach to gender shared Garfinkel's (1967) view that gender is omnirelevant in everyday interactions, and Goffman's (1976) notion of gender as a display. However, an additional insight of Kessler and McKenna was that gender 'work' is not only required of the person displaying gender. While the 'displayer' creates the initial gender attribution through their appearance or talk, that attribution is maintained by perceivers' natural attitude towards gender. That is, once an initial gender attribution is made, the perceiver is unlikely to change it, because of, amongst other things, a belief about the invariant nature of gender. Thus for Kessler and McKenna, passing as a man or a woman is not only an ongoing practice for the displayer but also for the perceiver – so gender is a joint achievement in interaction. The idea that the construction of social reality is a joint activity is central to conversation analytic approaches, discussed later in this chapter.

West and Zimmerman (1987) were amongst the first to advance an ethnomethodological approach in the gender and language field. Like Kessler and McKenna (1978), West and Zimmerman wanted to emphasise gender as an *omnipresent activity* embedded in *all* everyday interactions – a routine, methodical, reoccurring achievement integral to every social interaction. They contended that:

> the 'doing' of gender is undertaken by women and men whose competence as members of society is hostage to its production. Doing gender involves a complex of socially guided perceptual, interaction and micro-political activities that cast particular pursuits as expressions of masculine and feminine 'natures'.
>
> (West and Zimmerman, 1987, p. 126)

Essentialist theories fail to capture the idea of gender as a set of inter-actional activities. In contrast, an ethnomethodological approach to gender has highlighted gender as an activity that people engage in during inter-action. As West and Zimmerman (1987) noted, competence at doing those gender activities is necessary in order to be accepted as a 'normal' member of society. A somewhat paradoxical feature of doing gender, which was also noted by West and Zimmerman in the cited quotation, is that doing gender is so pervasive, so everyday and so mundane that gender gets seen to be something that it is not – a reflection of gender identity.

A social constructionist position on gender and language, discussed in Chapter 4, is that beliefs about the speech of women and men are a separate issue from the way individual women and men actually do use language. This position is consistent with the ethnomethodologically inspired idea of doing gender. The distinction between beliefs about gender and gendered behaviour is central to explaining the inconsistent and contradictory evidence about gender differences in speech. At any one instant an individual may, to a greater or lesser extent, exhibit the speech characteristics that people believe are typical of their gender. Furthermore, individuals may use a feature considered typical of the other gender but that feature may not be a gender display. A man may use a plethora of flowery and 'empty' adjectives – speech features typically associated with women's language (Lakoff, 1973, 1975). However, the excessive use of adjectives is not necessarily a display of femininity. The fellow may, for example, be displaying a performance consistent with his role as an expert in wine. Thus, beliefs about the way women and men speak are a separate, albeit related, issue from how individual women and men actually do speak.

Gender performativity

The idea that we 'do being a woman' or 'do being a man' is not confined to ethnomethodologically inspired approaches to gender. Judith Butler, feminist philosopher and queer theorist, used Austin's (1962) notion of performativity to demonstrate the discursive constitution of gender (Butler, 1990a). The Austinian legacy is that he distinguished between two types of utterances: those that are descriptively true or false (e.g. all trees are plants), and those that do things (e.g. I now pronounce you husband and wife). The latter kind of utterances Austin called performatives because by their pronunciation an act is performed. The pronunciation of 'husband and wife', by the appropriate celebrant, does not describe marriage; rather, the statement constitutes an entry into that institutional state. Butler suggested that the identification of an infant's sex before or at birth is not so much a description as a performative act, 'one that initiates the process by which a certain girling is compelled' (Butler, 1993, p. 232).

Performatives only function as acts when they fulfil appropriate rules and norms. Thus pronouncements of marriage only work when certain conditions are followed. Similarly declarations of gender work because they set into motion a series of social norms that guide the behaviour of a person and influence others' interactions with them. Gender is an act in the sense that it is 'a reenactment and reexperiencing of a set of meanings already socially established; it is the mundane and ritualised form of their legitimation' (Butler, 1990b, p. 277).

Individuals may have particular styles of 'doing their gender' which, to differing degrees, support or challenge cultural norms. Gay women may mark their sexual identity by using some of the speech characteristics typically associated with men, because the features associated with 'women's language' carry implications of heterosexuality. In a rare study of the nuances of language used by lesbians, Livia (1995) described how lesbians identifying as butch or femme appropriated particular elements of language stereotypically associated with men or women. So, language can be used to transgress gender and/or sexuality norms by challenging a 'natural attitude'. Ironically transgressions of social expectations about gender, sexuality and speech are dependent upon those expectations and thereby function to reinforce the very stereotypes that they are seeking to challenge.

The following quote from Butler captures (in a reasonably succinct way) the usefulness of performativity as a way of thinking about gender as discursively constituted:

> Gender reality is performative which means, quite simply, that it is real only to the extent that it is performed. It seems fair to say that certain kinds of acts are usually interpreted as expressive of a gender core identity, and that these acts either conform to an expected gender identity or contest that expectation in some way. . . . [If] gender attributes, however, are not expressive but performative, then these attributes effectively constitute the identity they are said to express or reveal. . . . [That] gender reality is created through sustained social performances means that the very notions of an essential sex, a true or abiding masculinity or femininity, are also constituted as part of the strategy by which the performative aspect of gender is concealed.
>
> (Butler, 1990b, pp. 278–279)

Conversation analysis (CA)

It has already been mentioned that conversation analysis (CA) as an analytic approach developed from ethnomethodology. CA's specific focus on investigating language and social interaction distinguishes it from ethnomethodology's more general examination of how people understand their social worlds. For CA, 'the core analytic objective is to illuminate how actions, events, objects, etc., are produced and understood' (Pomerantz and Fehr, 1997, p. 65). Of course, the production of gender is one of a range of activities that may be a focus of conversation analytic research. Typically, conversation analysts focus on mundane conversation because, as Heritage put it:

> The social world is a pervasively conversational one in which an overwhelming proportion of the world's business is conducted through the medium of social interaction.
>
> (Heritage, 1984, p. 239)

The development of CA was influenced by the ethnomethodological insight that everyday behaviour is not random or accidental but structured by a set of stable, underlying organisational features (Garfinkel, 1967). An important assumption of CA is that the organisational features of everyday interaction are structures in their own right and are social in character. They are independent of the psychological or other characteristics of particular speakers (see Heritage, 1984). Meaningful social conduct is produced and understood because culturally competent members share knowledge about how it is organised. For example, a strand of CA, membership categorisation device analysis (MCDA), investigates how fragments of texts are interpreted in the same way by 'members'. The sentences '*The baby cried. The mother picked it up*' are uniformly understood as referring to the baby's mother (Sacks, 1972, cited in Titscher *et al.*, 2000). In this example, members make category-based inferences about family to achieve common understandings about meaning.

CA is based fundamentally on the model of communication as a joint activity. In the case of written texts it is joint in the sense that people share knowledge about how to interpret them. In interaction, CA is concerned with how participants produce joint achievements such as conversational openings and closings, requests, storytelling, medical diagnoses and so on. Gender is one of the many joint achievements of texts and talk.

In the strand of CA concerned more with talk-in-interaction, sequences are an important focus because each utterance (or gesture) is understood as a contribution to the joint activity. Thus an important focus of sequential CA is on how interaction unfolds across sequences of actions by different participants. Common to all strands of CA is that the significance of a sentence, utterance or gesture is indexical. That is, it is highly dependent on the situational conditions of its production. In conversation, the unfolding of an interaction depends on the interpretation of a current speaker's utterance by the next or a subsequent speaker; and to show that they are engaged in a joint activity they need to display their interpretation of that utterance in some way. Even if the next speaker's interpretation is 'wrong' from the original speaker's point of view, it is open to the original speaker to offer a correction. In general, any utterance can be interpreted in numerous ways by analysts; for CA it is important to find evidence in the interaction of which of these possible interpretations have been taken by the participants (see Stubbe, Lane, Hilder, Vine, Vine, Holmes, Marra and Weatherall, 1999, in press).

For CA, participants' actions in interaction are, in general, locally occasioned. What this means is that any conversational action is viewed, for example, as responsive to a prior utterance, or as relevant to a current non-linguistic activity. Thus utterances are viewed as fitting into whatever current sequence of actions is relevant to the interaction. Spontaneous interaction thus has an improvised character. Functional categories of utterances are not based on analysts attempting to read speakers' intentions, but rather on their responsiveness to earlier actions and on the actual or potential following actions.

An example of how the unfolding of action depends on the participants' displayed orientation to the interaction is illustrated in the extract presented below. The extract was taken from an interaction that was used by a discourse analysis research group, to which I belong, to explore the utility of different discourse analytic approaches (Stubbe *et al.*, 1999, in press). The extract is from a workplace interaction where CT has asked TR why she wasn't approached to act in a management role:

#59: TR: so the issue in terms of + acting you into the role + is [drawls]: probably: one that um + you could address directly with joseph
#60: CT: right
#61: TR: 'cause i've given you my reasons why i did it
#62: TR: //abso\lutely nothing + sinister or any other agenda other than that
#63: CT: /right\\
#64: CT: no i'm not looking for that

At #62 there is a spontaneous denial of bias by TR, which displays his understanding of CT's request for an explanation as a complaint, maybe about discrimination. However, CT appears to deny this in #64. Thus, what can be said at this point is that TR's orientation to the interaction is that TR is dealing with a complaint whereas for CT it is about a request for information.

The notion of normative rules is another feature of a conversation analytic approach. In CA, 'rules' (e.g. for turn-taking, for how sequences can unfold) are not invariant descriptive rules in the linguistic sense, or statistical generalisations, but rather normative and interpretative. That is, normative rules provide reference points for participants to treat actions as unremarkable or as deviant. The rules allow participants to justify actions or complain about violations. An example of a normative rule being occasioned is displayed in the following extract:

```
#7:   TR:   can i just grab th- just grab that phone
#8:   TR:   sorry about that
#9:   CT:   that's okay
```

(Stubbe *et al.*, 1999, in press)

On the basis of their wordings, lines #7, #8, and #9 look like a request, an apology and an acceptance respectively. The apology is indicative that TR's answering the phone violates some rule. On the basis of this example it can be inferred that a rule that TR and CT are following is that an interaction once started should be continued (through to a negotiated close) rather than abruptly stopped to start another interaction.

Stringer and Hopper (1998) examined the normative rules governing the use of masculine generics in conversation. In their corpus of 1970s American speech they found that the default assumption was that referents of 'he' were male. Only when that assumption was false (i.e. the referent was female) would a speaker be corrected. On the basis of their analysis Stringer and Hopper concluded that there was no evidence of 'true' masculine generics being used in conversation. Rather, speakers' use of 'he' functioned as a pseudo-generic, biased only to the extent of the assumption of a male referent. In contrast to Stringer and Hopper's findings, I have witnessed conversations where the assumption of a male referent does get challenged, even when there is no specific referent (e.g. using 'he' to reference an unspecified doctor). Thus, at least in my speech community, normative assumptions of maleness are being challenged more fundamentally than was evident in Stringer and Hopper's corpus.

Conversational organisation

Heritage (1984) details a body of conversation analytic work that has established some of the structural features and norms organising social actions such as requests. That work will be summarised here because it provides the background needed to understand Kitzinger and Frith's (1999) work which illustrates the usefulness of CA to feminist work on an issue of concern to the field of gender and language. Kitzinger and Frith's work is interesting because it develops a further critique of miscommunication theory – the idea that men and women speak different languages, which leads to misunderstandings in cross-gender interactions, which, in turn, cause confusion, frustration and tension (see Crawford, 1995; Ehrlich, 1998, 1999; Frith and Kitzinger, 1997).

An important CA finding is that many conversational actions occur in pairs. Greetings are an example of a conversational action having two parts. More complicated patterns of paired actions include questions, which get followed by answers; requests, which are followed by consents or rejections; and invitations, which are accepted or declined. The technical term for these kinds of actions in conversation is an 'adjacency pair'. One of the norms that structure the use of adjacency pairs and thus organise interaction is that a first part (e.g. a question) requires a second part (e.g. an answer). This does not mean that a question is always followed by an answer. Instead, the adjacency pair structure is seen as normative. So, for example, if a greeting is not followed by a greeting in response, then it seems as though something is amiss. One might think that the person had not heard or that an insult was intended. Similarly, a norm is breached if a question fails to invoke an answer (even if it is 'I don't know').

One form of evidence used to support the claim that adjacency pairs have a normative structure is that nearly every case found conforms to the rule. The first part of an adjacency pair is, in the majority of instances that have been examined, followed by an appropriate second part. However, the strongest empirical evidence that adjacency pairs have a normative structure is from 'deviant cases' – instances where the adjacency pair structure is not followed fully or is in some way problematic. The examination of deviant cases in CA follows the ethnomethodological technique, described earlier, where violations or breaches of norms are examined to shed light on the nature of norms.

Heritage (1984) used cases where initial questions failed to elicit responses, to illustrate the normative character of the adjacency pair structure. In two cases, reproduced below, Heritage noted that when the initial question failed to elicit any response the questioner repeated the question; then, because a response was still not forthcoming, re-repeated it until an answer was finally provided. The relatively long pauses between the utterances containing the initial question and those containing the prompts are a further indication that a response was expected.

A: Is there something bothering you or not
    (1.0)
A: Yes or no
    (1.5)
A: Eh?
B: No

Ch: Have to cut the:se Mummy.
    (1.3)
Ch: Won't we Mummy
    (1.5)

Ch: Won't we
M: Yes.

(Atkinson and Drew, 1979, cited in Heritage, 1984, p. 248)

In the next cases, reproduced below, Heritage noted that although responses were given to the questions, those responses were not treated as answers. Instead the second speakers offer explanations for the lack of an adequate response to the question. The explanation is an indication that not being able to provide an answer goes against a norm.

M: what happened at (.) <u>w</u>ork. At <u>Bull</u>ock's this evening=
P: =.<u>hhhh</u> Well I don'<u>kno</u>:::w::.

J: But the <u>trai</u>:n goes. Does th'train go o:n th'boa:t?
M: .h .h Ooh I've no idea:. She ha:sn't said.

(Heritage, 1984, pp. 249–250)

Heritage also discussed other cases where a question is responded to not with an answer, but with another question. In these cases, the second question is treated as an 'insertion sequence'. The second question asks for some kind of clarification of the first question (e.g. the question of 'would you like an ice-cream?' being responded to with the question 'what flavours are there?'). However, an important point illustrated by extended sequences of questions and answers is that each utterance is locally occasioned and related to the previous one. So, although the answer to the question may not be given in the adjacent utterance, the sequence proceeds under the expectation that the first part of the question will ultimately receive its answer.

Preference structure

Questions have just been discussed as one kind of conversational action that has an adjacency pair structure. Both the producers and recipients of questions display their expectation that questions are the first part in a sequence that requires a second part. It was previously mentioned that an explanation or account was offered when an answer to a question could not be provided. Also mentioned was that, for many adjacency pairs, there are alternative responses for the second part. For example, a request can be granted or denied; an invitation can be accepted or rejected. Conversation analysts have found that the different responses typically follow one of two patterns. The generic term for those patterns is preference structure, with the two patterns being referred to as preferred actions and dis-preferred actions.

110

The structure of a preferred action is straightforward. The reply is simple and made with no hesitation. In the case of an invitation, the preferred response is an acceptance. Below is an example of an invitation followed by an acceptance.

B: Why don't you come and see me some [times
A: [I would like to
(Heritage, 1984, p. 263)

In contrast, dis-preferred responses have a far more complicated structure. They may be characterised by pauses or hesitations before a response is given, or by the use of appreciations and apologies; an explanation may be offered and there will also be an indirect or qualified declination component. In the following extract an invitation is declined. It shows the kind of structure typical of a dis-preferred response – it begins with a filler (hehh), then there is an appreciation (that's awfully sweet of you), the mitigated declination (I don't think I can make it this morning), and an account of why the invitation is declined.

B: Uh if you'd care to come over and visit a little while this morning I'll give you a cup of <u>cof</u>fee.
A: hehh Well that's awfully sweet of you, I don't think I can make it this morning .hh uhm I'm running an ad in the paper and-and uh I have to stay near the phone
(Heritage, 1984, p. 266)

An important point is that preferred responses are not merely agreements or acceptances and dis-preferred responses are not always dis-agreements or declinations. In the case of self-depreciatory comments, preferred responses are disagreements and dis-preferred responses are agreements. Similarly, in the case of accusations the preferred response is a denial and the dis-preferred response is an admission of guilt. An interesting social psychological aspect of the dis-preferred response structure is that it is inherently affiliative. That is, the normative structure of a response shows sensitivity to the other speaker. Thus, the normative structure of preferred and dis-preferred responses promotes a sense of social solidarity. This is one illustration of how conversational organisation and social processes are intricately linked.

Conversation analysis and gender and language

Conversational actions within the concerns of the gender and language field are those of request and refusal. Managing responses to requests for favours (including sexual ones) has been the focus of assertiveness training

111

programmes, many of which are primarily aimed at women. A type of assertiveness skills training, which achieved widespread awareness, was the feminist anti-rape campaign. The slogan promoting that campaign was 'no means no'. There are at least two related ideas captured by the 'no means no' slogan. One message is that women should feel free to say no to unwanted sexual advances. The other idea is that saying no clearly and directly is the best way of doing refusals to sexual invitations. So, despite its explicit feminist orientation, the 'no means no' campaign carries the implicit assumption that simple and direct speech (features commonly associated with men's speech) is the best form of communication. The flip side of the implicit assumption is that saying no in a hesitant and indirect manner (features typically associated with women's language) is inadequate for communicating a refusal.

On the basis of the kind of knowledge about CA just presented, Kitzinger and Frith (1999) developed a critique of the 'no means no' anti-rape campaigns. They suggested that programmes that advocate the strategy of refusing requests by 'just saying no' are fundamentally problematic. Not only are they based on assumptions of women as inadequate communicators but they also promote the idea that 'just saying no' is the best way of doing refusals. However, CA has demonstrated that saying no in a simple and straightforward manner is not how refusals are done in everyday conversational interaction. Instead, refusals are typically hesitant, indirect and mitigated. Culturally competent members have shared knowledge about how to go about refusing a request. Thus Kitzinger and Frith suggest that claims made by men about not understanding refusals should be viewed, not as a reflection of real mis-understanding, but as self-interested justifications for coercive behaviour.

The critique made by Kitzinger and Frith (1999), of programmes that recommended refusing a request by 'just saying no', was based on the CA notion of preference structure. Their work also analysed the content of focus group discussions conducted with female school and university students, where the issue of women saying no to sex was talked about (see Frith and Kitzinger, 1997). Consistent with CA work on refusals, Kitzinger and Frith found that the young women commonly reported finding it difficult to refuse requests for sex. The difficulty associated with saying no is, as already mentioned, evidenced by the organisational structure of dis-preferred actions. That is, declining a request or an invitation, even when it is of a non-sexual nature, typically involves being indirect and hesitant. Thus Kitzinger and Frith argued that crafting a refusal is a relatively complex and difficult task – an action that with careful management can avoid giving offence to the person who has made the offer. However, the social skill involved in making refusals, highlighted by CA research, goes unrecognised in the advice given in assertiveness training, where a simple and direct refusal style is promoted.

CA has demonstrated that a simple and straightforward response is, under normal circumstances, how invitations are accepted and requests granted. Thus, it is possible to argue that if 'no' is said simply and straightforwardly without hesitations, pauses or explanation, then, if there is an absence of malice, ill-feeling or frustration, 'no' may in fact be meant as 'yes'. Under normal circumstances then, advice to 'just say no' can be construed as misguided. Furthermore, CA has shown that hesitations and indirectness when declining requests or refusing invitations are the socially accepted form of those speech acts. There is no evidence from a CA perspective that indirect, hesitant speech is in any way inferior to direct straightforward speech.

In sum, Kitzinger and Frith (1999) considered the CA literature on refusals in combination with young women's self-reports about how diffi-cult, on the whole, they found turning down unwanted sexual advances. They developed an argument about women's difficulties in refusing, and men's difficulty in understanding those refusals, that did not rely on notions of gender differences in language use or miscommunication theory, approaches emerging from the gender and language field that are prob-lematic. Instead, they endorsed the communication competence of both women and men, arguing that speakers have a sophisticated ability to convey and comprehend refusals as refusals, even when they are hesitant and indirect. If one accepts that women and men have a shared knowledge about how social actions (such as refusals) are done in conversation, then the assumption of miscommunication theory, that men and women speak different languages, seems unlikely. Instead, claims to mis-understanding can be interpreted as compelling but questionable justifications for coercive behaviour.

Gender as context in conversation analysis

In many of the approaches to gender and language discussed so far in this book, gender has been regarded as one of the characteristics of the speakers that contributes to the features of the interactional context that may influence language use. For example, whether conversation is held between same-sex or mixed-sex groups is viewed as a variable that has an important influence on the speech style used (for example, see Aries, 1996, 1997). CA takes an approach to understanding context that differentiates it from other perspectives. Context is not seen as given prior to interaction. Social and contextual factors such as participants' gender, age and ethnicity are not analysed as independently specifiable causes of behaviour, but rather as resources that can be invoked as relevant in a normative/interpretative way. Context is viewed as being constituted by the inter-action itself, as the following examples illustrate.

#1:   CT: yeah um yeah i want to talk to you about um oh it's a personal issue um + well i- the decision to make um jared acting manager while joseph is away

(Stubbe *et al.*, 1999, in press)

In #1, CT's formulation 'it's a personal issue' paradoxically indicates that this is an institutional interaction of some kind because it implies that it is relevant to make a distinction between personal and non-personal issues.

#5:   CT: well i've been overlooked quite a few times but i wanted to find out specifically how what i could do to help myself be considered next time

(Stubbe *et al.*, 1999, in press)

In #5, CT's apparent request for advice implies an advising or mentoring role for TR, the other person in the conversation, and an advisee role for CT. Later, at #81 TR suggests that CT goes to J, 'because he's your immediate controlling officer'. In this instance TR is invoking a particular contextual factor, namely the workplace hierarchy, in order to accomplish a particular situated action, i.e. redirecting CT's request for advice to J. So, CA has a unique position on context – the interaction is the context. Analysts do not need to look outside the interaction unless some 'external' factor is invoked in the interaction. Furthermore, it is assumed that participants display to each other their mutual understanding of what aspects of context are relevant for them. The notion of 'noticing' has been developed in CA to refer to moments when participants display their orientation to something as relevant to the interaction. Gender noticing is moments in an interaction when gender is invoked as relevant to the interaction.

Gender noticing

The concept of gender noticing provides a solution to a problem that is raised by a constructionist approach to gender and language. How does one differentiate between those aspects of speech that are 'doing gender' and those that are not, without linking language use to the (gender) identity of the speaker and without relying on gender stereotypes. A conversation analytic approach to context resolves this issue by advocating that social categories such as gender, age and ethnicity should only be used in an analysis when speakers make it explicit that that is a relevant feature of the conversational interaction (Schegloff, 1997). What this means is that analysts avoid seeking the influence of predetermined categories on interaction (such as 'gender' or 'power' or 'sexist language'), but instead only analyse what the speakers or members explicitly orient to as relevant to the interaction.

114

Stokoe (1998) suggested that the analytic mentality of CA may provide a way of escaping the historical tendency of work, in the gender and language field, to perpetuate and endorse stereotyped beliefs about the ways women and men speak. Using a CA approach, the study of gender is restricted to interactions where participants demonstrably orientate to it as something relevant and pertinent to the interaction they are participating in. However, a current problem is to explicate what 'counts' as a display that gender is being oriented to.

The study by Hopper and LeBaron (1998), working from within the field of CA rather than gender and language, is amongst the few studies to date that have strictly followed the CA line in their empirical analyses of gender and talk-in-interaction. Hopper and LeBaron operationalised gender relevance by restricting their analysis to where explicit reference to gender was made. Thus, in Ochian terms, their analysis was limited to examining the use of direct gender indexes – where gender was directly and explicitly referred to (see Ochs, 1992). Another characteristic of Hopper and LeBaron's research is that it is typical of sequential CA in so far as they were interested in structural features of interactions where gender emerged as relevant to the conversation. The aim of their work was to document how gender was achieved as a joint activity.

After examining numerous interactions that contained direct gender indexes, Hopper and LeBaron (1998) proposed that gender relevance, like other conversational actions, was achieved through a sequence of utterances, which they referred to as a noticing series. They suggested that the sequence through which gender as a conversational action is achieved has three phases: it begins with a peripheral gendered activity, then is followed by a gender noticing, which, in turn, occasions the possibility of gender's relevance being extended. The following interaction illustrates the three phases of the noticing series where gender becomes a relevant aspect of the conversational action.

#1: Mary: Look in: (0.6) it's at the very top of one a those ba:re *hhh
             bushes there.
#2: Cissy: ^O::h
             ((*long pause*))
#3: Mary: (I)'ve lost him
#4: Cissy: Pardon?
#5: Mary: I've lost the one that [was singing
#6: Cissy: [He was- (0.2) he was so pla:in, *hh
             wasn't he (1.8) I'm saying he, it might be a she, huh huh
             huh=
#7: Mary: =If it sings it's a he.
#8: Cissy: Oh is it really?

#9:   Mary: There are very few female birds that sing, which is one of those *hhh sa:d things.
#10 Cissy: Oh I didn't notice that?
         (Hopper and LeBaron, 1998, pp. 65, 68 – line numbering added)

In the above example, the peripheral gendered activity occurs in lines #1 to #5. Mary uses three different reference terms (it, him and one) for the same bird in lines #1, #3 and #5 (respectively). Following Mary at #6, Cissy also refers to the bird using a masculine pronoun. The second step in the sequence, the gender noticing, occurs later in #6 when Cissy explicitly refers to her use of a masculine pronoun and acknowledges that she does not actually know the gender of the bird that she has seen. The extension phase is evident in the interaction at #7 to #10 where there is discussion about the sex of birds that sing.

The turn by turn increasing salience of gender illustrated by the example above was also evident in other extracts discussed by Hopper and LeBaron (1998). On the basis of the examples they analysed, they claimed that their findings began to answer the ethnomethodogically flavoured question of how gender is made to seem so natural as it is routinely performed in talk. Hopper and LeBaron suggested that gender's omnirelevance in everyday interaction is facilitated by the immense array of language resources (e.g. personal names, and terms of address and reference) for indexing gender in talk. Furthermore, they suggested that the gender noticing series – the peripheral orientation, the noticing of gender and the extension of its relevance – results in gender creeping into talk, rather than it being introduced by a speaker as an explicit issue.

Discursive psychology, conversation analysis and gender

Mentioned at the beginning of this chapter was that a conversation analytic strand has been identified as a second broad strand of discursive psychology. Proponents of this approach (e.g. Antaki and Widdicombe, 1998; Edwards, 1998; Widdicombe, 1995) endorse the CA line that analysts should focus their attention on what participants, at any moment in an interaction, make relevant and orientate to as consequential to their ongoing interaction (Schegloff, 1997). Within psychology, discursive psychology has developed, in part, as a critique against cognitive approaches to social identity. A shift in emphasis from cognition to talk moves the analysts' attention away from representation to action. Thus, instead of worrying about how particular identities get 'switched on', analyses examine what people do with social categories (see Edwards, 1997 for a detailed critique of social cognitive approaches to identity). Debates between discursive and cognitive approaches to psychological phenomena aside, the important point is that just because someone is a woman, a New

Zealander, middle-class, or whatever, doesn't justify invoking those categories as a way of explaining how that person talks and interacts.

Mentioned earlier was that feminist sociolinguists have used aspects of CA in their research for some time. However, feminist sociolinguistic work tends not to follow the CA analytic mentality where data are considered, without imposing predetermined categories on to the analysis. Instead, this work tends to link conversational features (e.g. interruption, hedges, talk time and so on) with gender (as a fixed category). When patterns are found between the conversational feature and gender it is interpreted within standard dominance or difference theoretical frameworks. Examples include that men's use of interruptions was understood as evidence of men's conversational power (Zimmerman and West, 1975), and women's use of hedges was taken as showing their interpersonal orientation (Holmes, 1984). Gender is implicitly essentialised in these studies, which makes them theoretically inconsistent with the kind of analytic mentality advocated by CA.

Compared with feminist sociolinguistic work, attention to CA by feminist social psychologists has only been relatively recent. CA was influential in the development of discursive psychology (see Potter and Wetherell, 1987), and it is the CA emphasis that differentiates the two strands of discursive psychology (Nikander, 1995; Widdicombe, 1995, 1998). However, a feminist discursive psychology taking a stricter CA analytic approach has emerged (e.g. Frith and Kitzinger, 1997; Stokoe, 1998, 2000). Kitzinger (2000a) used a feminist conversation analytic approach in a study of lesbian and gay 'coming out' stories. In the conversations she examined, 'coming out' tended to occur in the middle of an extended turn. This conversational placement of the personal disclosure meant that it was less likely to attract comment because of the structural organisation of topic management in talk.

As well as demonstrating the analytic utility of CA, Kitzinger (2000a, 2000b) has also considered the theoretical parallels between CA and feminist research. She suggested that CA's treatment of speakers as people who actively accomplish social meaning through joint activity is compatible with feminist approaches where women are viewed as active agents, not merely victims of heteropatriarchal oppression. For example, in her analysis of women's talk about breast cancer, Kitzinger (2000b) found that speakers resisted the cultural idiom 'think positive' by slightly delaying their response when it was used, thus signalling a lack of affiliation with the speaker's utterance. Kitzinger suggested that a poststructuralist style of discourse analysis can miss the nuanced ways in which women mark their resistance by ignoring the micro-structural features of conversation.

Another aspect of CA that makes it compatible with feminist language research is that its emphasis of the everyday and mundane mirrors the importance placed by feminism on the lived experiences of women. Of course, a big advantage of a CA approach for gender and language research is that it avoids the tendency of other research approaches to essentialise and thus polarise and stereotype differences between women and men.

From within the gender and language field, Stokoe (1998, 2000) has been a strong advocate of a conversation analytic approach. Stokoe welcomes the constructionist shift for the study of gender and language but argues that some of the newer work confounds a constructionist position with gender essentialism. Stokoe argued that research like that of Coates's (1996) *Women talk* is problematic because it utilises the constructionist notion of 'doing' gender but continues to perpetuate an essentialist position where the way women talk is identified as 'doing' femininity. Describing 'doing' masculinity and 'doing' femininity rests on an assumption of two genders. Notions of what defines 'doing' femininity and masculinity stem from cultural norms and stereotypes about the sorts of things men and women talk about. Thus, Stokoe suggested that conversational data are only analysable as 'doing masculinity' or 'doing femininity' because researchers are culturally competent members and know what this talk may look like. Research that assumes that when women talk they are doing femininity and when men talk they are doing masculinity effectively perpetuates the notions of gender differences in speech, because any commentary that treats women and men as different categorical groups reinforces gender polarisation.

In contrast to work that makes a priori assumptions about what constitutes doing gender, Stokoe (1998, 2000) restricted her analysis of gender and language to those moments during an interaction when gender as a topic is raised. The data she examined were recordings of groups of young adults discussing the future, employment and family orientations. She found that participants' orientations to gender tended to be occasioned when the topics of employment and family were discussed. The notion of what Stokoe (2000) referred to as the 'generic mother' was used by some participants when arguing for better childcare facilities where women make up a majority of the workers. Other participants called attention to (i.e. 'noticed') the implicit assumption of women as caregivers. As described by Hopper and LeBaron (1998), these noticings occasioned extended discussions about the relative roles of women and men in childcare. Furthermore, Stokoe found that disclaimers of the kind 'I'm not sexist but . . .' or 'I'm not chauvinistic but . . .' were used to occasion a non-sexist identity for a speaker precisely at the moment when they were invoking sex stereotypes (e.g. associating wives with washing and ironing). Stokoe's finding that the articulation of sexist ideas occasioned claims of a non-sexist identity provides a glimpse of how sexist views get recycled under the guise of egalitarianism.

Discursive psychology's conversation analytic approach has only just begun to be utilised to interrogate issues that have traditionally concerned the gender and language field. On the issue of biased language, Speer and Potter (2000), for example, used a discursive approach to examine (hetero) sexism in language. Following a conversation analytic mentality they avoided assuming they knew what heterosexist language was and only interrogated what speakers oriented to as biased. Their analysis identified several rhetorical devices that had a dual function. These served to point to speakers' orientation to heterosexism as a relevant feature of the conversation, and they revealed how heterosexist utterances were managed by speakers to reproduce and challenge biases about sexual orientation.

I applied the conversation analytic mentality to an analysis that I conducted of children's conversations (Weatherall, 2000b). A conventional gender and language approach would involve coding the conversations for the use of particular linguistic features and testing for sex differences. However, using a conversation analytic mentality I selected only those conversations where gender was demonstrably relevant to the children. The selected conversations showed the kind of noticing series identified by Hopper and LeBaron (1998). In addition it seemed that whenever the children were noticing gender it was to (re)establish or contest gender norms. For instance, in the following extract the children are discussing where dolls should sit in a train. GEO asks GIS (an adult) where the train goes. ROS volunteers the front of the train as the appropriate position for the doll.

GEO: which one is this one go in?
GIS: any one that. <2>
ROS: front.
GEO: i can put it in <> he in the back if i want.
ROS: no it goes in the front cos he's the driver.
GEO: no [i can put it.]
ELF: [or the red one] could be the driver.
GEO: i can put which   [1ever] one. <>
ROS: [1yeh.]
ROS: but you have but <> you ha put the red one in cos <> um you can put any one.
GEO: it's a girl one the red one so that doesn't go there. <3>

(Weatherall, 2000b)

The above extract is interesting because we see the children negotiating gender norms. While ELF states that the red doll (wearing a dress) could be the train driver, GEO orients to the assumption that gender limits where the doll gets placed. By restricting my analysis to interactions where gender was noticed as relevant to the ongoing business of the interaction, I successfully avoided making the assumption that the children's speech was indexing their gender when they weren't demonstrating the relevance of

119

their gender. Instead I felt I had shown how gender was being re-enacted by the children.

It seems, from the research discussed, that a conversation analytic mentality has the potential to overcome the tendency of gender and language research to essentialise gender. A question that has been asked by some researchers is whether conversation analysis is sufficient for a complete analysis of gender. I have argued that it is not (Weatherall, 2000a). Gender is a pervasive social category. The identification of a person as belonging to one of two gender groups is a fundamental guide to how they are perceived, how their behaviour is interpreted and how they are responded to in every interaction and throughout the course of their life. Linguistic indexes of gender may occur at every level of language. So, even if gender is not explicitly privileged by participants as relevant to the conversation, it is an omnipresent feature of all interactions.

Compelling evidence that gender constitutes part of the 'argumentative texture' for meaning-making was Cameron's (1998b) analysis of a vignette 'Is there any ketchup, Vera?' The utterance, produced by Vera's husband, was used to illustrate how gender subtly influences communication and social interaction in a pragmatic sense. In this example, Vera understands that her husband is not enquiring as to the presence of ketchup in the house, but is requesting that she fetch it for him. The relevance of gender here is not marked by 'gender noticing' but through a consideration of the pragmatics of the exchange (i.e. a similar request from a daughter may have received a different response).

Gender is relevant to understanding the structure and meaning of any social interaction. Thus an ongoing problem for feminist language researchers is the issue of when, where and how to import cultural knowledge about gender in analyses of interaction. Stokoe and Smithson (2001) have begun to explore the potential of MCDA (membership categorisation device analysis) to provide empirical evidence of the relevance of cultural information not immediately oriented to as relevant to speakers. The failure of much gender and language research to produce knowledge congenial to social change for women demands critical reflection about our assumptions about gender and language and the relationship between the two. The work of feminist conversation analysts such as Kitzinger (2000a, 2000b) has shown that essentialist assumptions about gender are not necessary to feminist language research.

Chapter summary

In this chapter the contribution made by ethnomethodology and conversation analysis (CA) to issues concerning the gender and language field was considered. An ethnomethodological perspective is particularly pertinent to the field of gender and language because it was from that approach that Kessler and McKenna (1978) developed one of the earliest social constructionist analyses of gender – an approach that is becoming more dominant in research on gender and language. According to an ethnomethodological view, gender is not an essence but a form of activity, something that is an achievement of everyday interaction. In the gender and language field, ethnomethodological ideas were promulgated through West and Zimmerman's (1987) notion of 'doing gender' – the idea that gender is a routine and joint accomplishment of situated conversational activity. As with social constructionism, questions of gender differences are inappropriate from an ethnomethodological viewpoint.

A feature of CA that makes it distinctive from other analytic approaches is its stance on context. Unlike other approaches which take context to be a complex of features that influences how an interaction proceeds (e.g. characteristics of the speaker, physical location), for CA, context is not seen as prior to interaction. Context is viewed as being constituted by the interaction and is displayed by the speakers. Some styles of discursive psychology follow the CA stance on context. Advocates of these approaches argue that analysts should focus their attention on what speakers attend to as relevant aspects of context. Thus gender would be included in an analysis only when it was demonstrable that gender was relevant for the speakers of the interaction. Stokoe (1998, 2000) has suggested that it is only by taking a conversation analytic approach that gender and language research can avoid perpetuating essentialist notions of gender. However, the potential omnirelevance of gender means that limiting analyses to where gender is explicitly relevant may limit an understanding of the importance of gender as a category that structures people's lives and social interactions.

An issue that has been implicit in much of the work described in the book so far, and which cuts across the different theoretical approaches that have been discussed, is that of gender identity and language. Already mentioned is that, from an essentialist theoretical position, language and speech provide insights into identity. In contrast, a social constructionist view is that gender is not something that we are; rather it is something that we do. In the next chapter, the topic of gender identity and language will be addressed in more detail.

6

LANGUAGE, DISCOURSE AND GENDER IDENTITY

Introduction

The topic of gender identity and issues concerning its relationship to language and discourse have been mentioned at several points in this book so far. An important point was made in Chapter 4, when I described the discursive turn as being characterised by a theoretical shift in the conceptualisation of identity. That change was from a notion of gender identity as existing prior to language, to the idea of gender identity being discursively constituted. However, up until now I have discussed identity largely as it has been relevant to other issues, such as why definitive answers to questions of gender difference in language use have not been found, and the similarities amongst different explanations of 'women's language'. The purpose of this chapter is to explore more thoroughly the topic of language, discourse and gender identity.

This chapter will begin with a discussion of a more traditional strand of research based on essentialist and realist assumptions about gender identity – essentialist in the sense that gender identity is seen to be a property of individuals and society, and realist because it is assumed that there is some kind of correspondence between individuals' gender identities and the way gender is manifest in the organisation and structure of society. Following these assumptions, gender identity is understood as an internalisation (through socialisation and social learning) of the gendered organisation of society. Thus, conventionally within psychology, gender identity has been viewed as an internal, stable and coherent psychological characteristic of the individual that motivates, amongst other behaviours, speech style.

Research following a conventional psychological approach has investigated language use as a site where gender identity is expressed. A (questionable) distinction made by such research is between 'real' sex markers of speech (linguistic features that truly differentiate between women and men) and speech sex stereotypes (beliefs about the features associated with each gender regardless of actual use) (Smith, 1979). A key point here is that the conceptual distinction between 'real' and 'stereotyped' gender differences

122

in speech is problematic. Differences between women's and men's speech may well exist, but what differentiates women's speech from men's cannot be reduced to a set of simple (or even complex) features. To use the Ochian phrase, few features of language directly and exclusively index gender (Ochs, 1992).

An aspect of language use that has been strongly linked to social identity variables such as gender is phonological variation. Feminist sociolinguistic research on gender and language has moved from essentialising and universalising the relationship between gender identity and language to the view that gender is constructed through local communities of practice. A brief overview of this shift will be given. In contrast to social cognitive approaches and in line with recent developments in feminist social linguistics are discursive psychology approaches to identity, which argue that a sense of self is socially constructed. A conversation analytic style of discursive psychology investigates the local and occasioned nature of social identity categories, such as gender in talk. In a poststructuralist style of discursive psychology, an individual's identity is a result of both the cultural meaning systems available and the ongoing demands of any social interaction. A more eclectic strand of discursive psychology weaves together both the local and global discursive practices that function to produce gender in everyday talk (see Wetherell, 1998; Wetherell and Edley, 1998).

Identities in speech

Although the theoretical ideas about the relationship between gender identity and language are still being debated and developed, it is generally accepted that there is a relationship. For social psychologists taking an essentialist and realist approach to identity, the social significance of the expression of identity in speech and talk is at least twofold. On the one hand, it is assumed that people will have attitudes towards women's and men's speech that are consequential for evaluations of speakers. On the other hand, speech cues are thought to trigger attributions about the gender identity of the speaker (that is, how masculine or feminine they are). As already mentioned, underlying these kinds of concerns is the assumption that language is both a medium for expressing (an internal, stable, measurable) gender identity and a reflection of that identity. The essentialist and realist assumptions about gender identity and its existence 'outside' language are ideas that are questioned by other approaches discussed later in this chapter.

An early example of a study on beliefs about the language of women and men was Kramer's (1978) study on perceptions of women's and men's speech. Kramer found that a sample of American teenagers described men's and women's speech differently. In general, men's speech was seen as logical, concise and dealing with important topics, whereas women's speech was rated as emotional, flowery, confused and wordy. In a review of the research on the speech styles associated with men and women, Aries (1996) found that there was a broad general agreement in Anglo-American cultures in beliefs about how men and women talk. The styles of speech believed to identify men and women have been variously labelled as report and rapport talk (Tannen, 1990), competitive and co-operative communication styles (Maltz and Borker, 1982), and more popularly (and controversially) as like Martian and Venutian languages (Gray, 1992; but see Crawford, 1995; Potts, 1998).

Another line of social psychological research has investigated the degree of correspondence between people's self-reported gender identity on the one hand, and perceptions of that person as masculine or feminine on the other. Using an experimental approach, Smith (1985) tested whether speech-based attributions of masculinity and femininity bore any resemblance to speakers' self-assessed masculinity and femininity. The speakers' gender identities were measured by their degree of endorsement on items asking about sex stereotypes. A speaker of each sex was chosen with a relatively masculine identity, a relatively feminine identity, an androgynous identity (that is, had they endorsed both masculine and feminine characteristics as being like them) and an undifferentiated identity (that is, they had eschewed both masculine and feminine characteristics as being like them). The kind of approach to the measurement of gender identity used in this study has been the target of considerable critique (e.g. Skevington and Baker, 1989). Questions that can be raised about Smith's method for establishing gender identity include: do people's responses to the items reflect a stable, inner, gender identity? If so, how can we be sure that the responses will be the same at different times and in different places? Furthermore, what evidence is there that the 'gender identity' of the person explains the variation in speech?

Methodological problems with the measurement of psychological gender identity aside, the results of the study showed a high level of correspondence between the listener-judges' perceptions and the speakers' self-rated masculinity and femininity. Smith (1985) interpreted that finding as indicating that speech was quite a reliable marker of a person's gender identity – an explanation that does little more than to restate the assumptions of the research. In an additional experimental twist, Smith examined whether listeners' gender identities would affect their ratings. The results suggested that the stronger the gender identity of the listener-judges, the more likely they were to polarise the differences between women and men speakers and to exaggerate the similarities among same-gender speakers. Such a finding was consistent with the predications of social identity theory (discussed below).

In Smith's (1985) study, gender identity was treated as an essential (internal) and real aspect of an individual's psychology. Using similar assumptions, Cutler and Scott (1990) investigated the influence of speaker gender on listeners' judgements of speaker verbosity. In their research, identical dyadic dialogues taken from plays were recorded. Each person in the dialogue contributed equal amounts of speech to the conversation. The gender of the speakers in the conversation was systematically varied. When the dialogue was between a man and a woman, the woman was judged to be talking more than her conversation partner who was a man. When members of the same gender performed the dialogue, then each speaker was judged as contributing to the conversation equally. The study demonstrated that people reproduce cultural beliefs about gender and speech in experimental situations when asked to make simple, fixed judgements. However, this kind of study does little to enlighten us about the relevance and significance of cultural beliefs about speech in everyday interactions.

A persistently asked question that attracts the attention of conventional psychologists is the extent to which evaluations of women's and men's speech are influenced by actual differences in language style or stereotyped beliefs about the way men and women talk. The (dubious) presupposition here is that there are real and stable gender differences in speech. Most recently, the suggestion that evaluations of men's and women's speech may differ in the absence of linguistic sex differences was dubbed by Lawrence, Stucky and Hopper (1990) as the sex stereotype hypothesis. Evidence for the sex stereotype hypothesis comes from studies, such as Cutler and Scott's (1990) study described above, where the same speech is either attributed to or delivered by a man or a woman. Another example of this kind of research was a study by Duran and Carveth (1990), who asked participants to rate written scenarios describing communicative behaviours which had been attributed to 'Michael' or 'Valerie'. They found that the same communicative behaviour was rated more competent when the communicator was identified as Michael rather than Valerie.

In an attempt to finally resolve the relative importance of stereotypes about speech and actual speech differences for person perception, Lawrence et al. (1990) set out to test what they dubbed the sex stereotype hypothesis and the sex dialect hypothesis. As already described, the sex stereotype hypothesis asserts that speaker gender alone triggers differential evaluative responses in listeners. In contrast, the sex dialect hypothesis proposes that different evaluations of men and women are due to differences in their speech patterns. The experimental design used to test the two hypotheses was rather complicated. The conversations that were used in the study were based on short segments of a previously recorded naturally occurring conversation between a woman and a man. That naturally occurring segment was transcribed and then re-recorded. In one condition actors of the same gender as the original speakers reproduced the conversation. In the other condition the parts were reversed, so a woman took the man's part in the original conversation. The sex dialect hypothesis

125

would predict that listener-judges' ratings would be influenced by the original speaker gender, whereas the stereotype hypothesis would predict that listener-judges would be influenced by the attributed speaker gender.

Perhaps unsurprisingly the results of the study did not straightforwardly support the predictions made by the sex dialect hypothesis or the sex stereotype hypothesis. Rather, the results suggested that the listener-judges were being influenced both by the original speaker's gender and by the attributed speaker's gender. In addition, those influences varied depending on the particular conversational segment being listened to. Lawrence *et al.* (1990) concluded that the impact of gender difference in speech styles and gender stereotypes may be fluctuating and transitory in nature. They suggested that there was a need for descriptive research on how speakers produce and orient to social identities such as age, gender and social class in interactions – a conclusion remarkably consistent with the ideas promoted by discursive approaches. Despite this consistency, the social cognitive and discursive theoretical approaches to understanding gender identity and language are based on very different assumptions about the nature of identity and its relationship to language. However, before moving to alternative approaches, the kind of social cognitive explanations given for the development of gender identity and other social identities will be described.

Social identity theory

According to social identity theory, a person's sense of who they are is comprised of aspects of the self deriving from themselves as an individual and those that arise out of their membership of social groups (see Augoustinos and Walker, 1995 for a good overview). Social identity theory emphasises that the ways people think and behave depend partly on the social groups they belong to. Characteristics of group behaviour that have been associated with social identity include stereotyping and in-group favouritism. An important aspect of the theory is that it recognises that different social groups vary in terms of the power and status that they have in society – a recognition that is essential to a comprehensive understanding of women and men as social groups but one that tends to be ignored, or at least downplayed, in many studies that mobilise gender as a way of categorising people and explaining their behaviour.

Social identity theory is based on the assumption that people are motivated to view themselves in a favourable way. Some of the processes involved in achieving a positive self-concept require making social comparisons in order to evaluate the opinions and abilities of people who share, or don't share, your social group membership. If a group to which a person belongs has a low social status they may try to overcome any sense of inferiority stemming from that group membership through a number of identity maintenance mechanisms. One possible strategy, generally referred to as social mobility, may be to leave the group that has low social status – this is an individual strategy. For example, if the sports club you are a member of has a bad reputation, you may change the club you are affiliated with. If your membership of a social group is more fixed (as is the case with gender or ethnicity), other strategies, known collectively as social creativity and social competition, may be employed to achieve a positive self-esteem. A tactic to maintain a positive sense of identity may be to try to change the status of the group by, for example, redefining the negative characteristics associated with the group positively. Other identity maintenance strategies may be to compare your group to other, inferior groups or to create new dimensions for comparison.

Social identity theory was originally developed to explain the behavioural patterns (of reward allocation) of individuals in experiments when they were assigned to random groups. However, it was soon applied as a framework for understanding the influence of important social group memberships (e.g. ethnicity, religious affiliation) on cognition and behaviour. Williams and Giles (1978) argued that social identity theory could be used to demonstrate that the diverse actions and perspectives of women in a feminist era, far from being trivial and irrational, were coherent strategies for promoting social change. Their interpretation of social identity theory was not entirely congruent with later readings of it (see Augoustinos and Walker, 1995). However, despite inconsistencies, Williams and Giles's application of social identity theory to women is an example of a framework that can be used for understanding the relationship between gender identity and language. Particularly relevant is that some of the identity maintenance strategies described by Williams and Giles involved reference to language issues.

Williams and Giles (1978) suggested that prior to the women's liberation movement of the 1960s to 1970s, women had largely accepted their secondary status in society. Thus, according to Williams and Giles, prior to the second wave of feminism the majority of women would have achieved a positive social identity by individual means. For example, they suggested that individual women would have achieved a positive self-concept by comparing themselves with other women on dimensions such as performance of domestic duties, or by comparing the social status of their husbands with that of other women's husbands of lower social standing. Another strategy that individual women were understood to have employed was to psychologically disassociate from other women and use men as their reference group. In recent times, women who have excelled in politics (e.g. the first women prime ministers of Britain and New Zealand – Margaret Thatcher and Jenny Shipley, respectively) are often interpreted as using this strategy and to all intents and purposes 'becoming men'.

127

The feminism of the 1960s and 1970s led to a raised consciousness of the illegitimacy of women's secondary social status. In addition, the American Civil Rights movement meant that it was also an era where the possibility of social change was salient. Williams and Giles (1978) argued that it was precisely under such social conditions that social identity theory would predict a mobilisation of women in a political movement. Moreover, the theory was interpreted in a way that gave a coherent framework for understanding the social actions resulting from that political movement. Attempts to gain equality in employment, legal and political conditions with men were interpreted as being consistent with an assimilation or merger strategy outlined in social identity theory (c.f. Augoustinos and Walker, 1995). A limitation of an assimilation strategy is that it preserves the values and belief systems of the dominant group, and thus does not seriously challenge the status quo.

Of relevance to the issue of gender and language was that attacks on sexist language were seen as a strategy to achieve a positive identity, equivalent to the promotion of women's studies courses at universities, the emergence of women's art exhibitions, women's companies, the reassessment of women's contribution to history, and so on. All these activities were viewed as being consistent with a tactic outlined in social identity theory, where a low-status group will attempt to redefine their value on a set of pre-existing dimensions. According to Williams and Giles (1978), another strategy that members of a low-status group might use to improve their social identity was to create new dimensions for comparison with other groups. They suggested that feminists who promoted a co-operative and consensual style of managing groups could be understood as an example of creating new dimensions for comparing women with men.

Social identity theory has been influential in sociolinguistic accounts of language variation. For example, Coates (1986) suggested that, in terms of gender and language, an assimilation strategy was a widespread identity maintenance tactic being used by women to enhance their social identity. The linguistic evidence she cited of how women assimilate to men included their use of deeper voices, their increased swearing and use of taboo language, their adoption of falling rather than rising intonation patterns, and their increasing use of non-standard accents. For the strategy of redefining negative characteristics positively, Coates suggested that the linguistic correlate was the reappraisal by women of the relative merits of co-operative as opposed to competitive strategies in conversation. In addition there have been moves, particularly in feminist academic circles, to redefine features of women's language, such as gossip, positively.

Since Williams and Giles's (1978) study, there has been considerable criticism, especially from feminist psychologists, about the validity of treating women as a single, coherent social group. The limitations of social identity theory for understanding the multifaceted nature of womanhood in contemporary society have been well documented (see Skevington and Baker, 1989). Criticism also emerged from the feminist critique of sex differences research (see Chapters 1 and 2). The heterogeneous nature of what it means to be a woman or to be a man is also a problem for research based on essentialist and realist assumptions about gender identity and its relationship to language. Despite the considerable problems with social identity theory for understanding women's identities, it continues to be used, particularly in sociolinguistics (see later in this chapter), as a framework for understanding the relationship between identity and language.

Accommodation theories

The psychological concept of social identity in general, and gender identity in particular, appears in a slightly different guise in another influential theory called communication accommodation theory or CAT (Giles and Coupland, 1991). CAT was strongly influenced by social identity theory and is based upon the assumption that language is a fundamental marker of social identity. CAT, and its precursor, speech accommodation theory or SAT, has been used as a framework for understanding the relationship between social identity and language variation during interactions. It has also been used as an explanation for sex differences in language use.

According to a social identity approach, one of the fundamental processes of social identification is the categorisation of people into different groups. Of particular relevance to this chapter so far is that language has been understood as an important basis for social categorisation and a consequential marker of social identities. Hence, an important strand of the research on social identity and language is that a person's speech style may tag them as belonging to a particular social group (or groups). In addition, on hearing a speech style associated with a certain social group, identity maintenance processes may be triggered that will influence a listener's perceptual evaluation and linguistic response to a speaker using that style. For example, a high-pitched voice may be a linguistic identity marker of womanhood. High-pitched speech may trigger evaluations consistent with feminine stereotypes (she sounds nurturing, dependent, etc). Moreover, a person wanting to dissociate themselves from such evaluations may deepen their pitch.

The first theoretical framework proposed to consider the individual and social psychological processes influencing language use in any interaction was speech accommodation theory or SAT (see Giles and Smith, 1979). SAT integrated and applied four social psychological theories to language use. Influenced by similarity-attraction theory, SAT suggests that speech convergence (adjusting the way we speak to be more like the person we are speaking to) may be used to indicate that we like or want to be liked by the person that we are interacting with. For example, a boy wanting to signal his liking of a girl may reduce his 'normal' use of swearing and taboo language. A corollary of this pattern is that we may judge the speech of a person we like to be more similar to our own speech than that of a person we don't like.

Similarity-attraction theory emphasises the benefits of speech convergence – that is, an increase in attraction or approval. However, according to SAT, such convergence also has costs. So, for the boy using more polite speech, he may be losing language markers that identify him as masculine. Social exchange theory predicts that convergent speech acts would only occur when the potential advantages of that change outweigh the disadvantages. The possible dilemmas for women concerning the costs and benefits of using a particular language style were highlighted in a study by Carli (1990) on gender, language and influence. Carli found that women who used a more tentative speech style were more persuasive when talking to a man than when talking to a woman. However, a person with a more tentative speech style was rated by both women and men as less competent. These results can be interpreted as showing that the cost of using assertive language for women is not being persuasive, particularly to men, but the benefit for women of using such language is that they are perceived as more competent.

The third theoretical strand influencing SAT was used to explain how any speech shift would be evaluated. Causal attribution theory suggests that the way in which speech shifts are perceived and evaluated will depend on the motives and intentions that are attributed to the change. For example, if the boy reduces his swearing because the girl's mother is around, the girl may be less likely to attribute that change to the boy's attraction to her. The final theoretical influence on speech accommodation theory was social identity theory. Giles and Smith (1979) argued that in situations where group membership is a salient issue, speech divergence – or moving your language style to make it more dissimilar to that of the person you are interacting with – could be understood as a group identity maintenance process. A speech style shift could be understood as a strategy to mark yourself as distinct from other social groups. For example, a woman wanting to emphasise her femininity may exaggerate the features stereotypically associated with women's language.

CAT developed from SAT by acknowledging that a wider variety of speech features may be used to negotiate the interpersonal and intergroup dynamics of an interaction. SAT was largely used to explain accent shifts or code switching, whereas CAT noted that changes in features such as pitch, speech rate, syntax, vocabulary and topic may also be motivated by the social characteristics of the interaction. CAT also acknowledged a broader range of shifts that might be made by interactants. For example, some participants in a conversation might show more or less speech convergence or divergence than others (see Giles and Coupland, 1991). The comprehensive range of psychological and linguistic aspects of CAT makes it a sophisticated framework for understanding the influence of social identity on speech styles. However, while theoretically neat, technically, for research, it raises two considerable problems – what are the linguistic elements in a speech style that might change in identity maintenance processes, and how can these be measured. The indirect and non-exclusive relationship between linguistic variables and identity is a further problem for this approach.

In practice, social psychological research has largely avoided trying to identify and measure the aspects of a group's speech style that might be associated with the social identity of group members. In the case of gender identity, research using CAT has tended to rely on stereotyped notions of gender differences in speech. For example, Hannah and Murachver (1999) operationalised a (feminine) facilitative speech style as the higher use of minimal responses, fewer interruptions and not looking away during an interaction. They then looked for divergence from or convergence to the facilitative or non-facilitative style across two conversations between either same-sex or mixed-sex dyads. Their results showed no compelling patterns of change motivated by gender identity. Some sociolinguistic work, described later, has been more successful at identifying particular linguistic features that are mobilised to mark a gendered group identity (e.g. Eckert and McConnell-Ginet, 1995).

Social identity theory, SAT and CAT have been influential social psychological approaches for interpreting language behaviours. For example, social identity theory has been used to explain: why women in politics use lower pitch; feminist challenges to sexist language; and the promotion of a co-operative communication style in business. CAT provides a framework for understanding why speech style might shift during the course of any interaction, depending on the relative importance of interpersonal or intergroup dimensions in that interaction. An aspect of language use that has been linked strongly to social identity variables, such as gender, social class and ethnicity, but which has tended to fall outside the realm of social psychology, is phonological variation. Although some forms of linguistic variation have been considered in social psychological approaches such as SAT and CAT, phonological variation has largely fallen within the realm of sociolinguistics. Scholars involved with research on identity and phonological variation are also important players in the gender and language field (e.g. Cameron, 1985; Coates, 1986; Eckert, 2000; Eckert and McConnell-Ginet, 1992). In the next section I will briefly consider some threads in sociolinguistic work on identity and linguistic variation. A focus will be on how research in the area, particularly that using the community of practice (CofP) notion, has conceptualised gender identity and its relationship to language.

Identity and linguistic variation

Sociolinguistic research aims to examine the relationship between linguistic variation and other variables. Further, it considers the social meanings associated with different sounds and how those meanings influence patterns of language change. Some very striking findings emerged from early quantitative studies on sound and sound change in people's accents. One result was that phonological variation in speech communities shows clear social stratification. A classic pattern of social stratification of a stable linguistic variable is that, in any given speech style (e.g. reading, informal speech), a person from a higher social class will use proportionately more standard ('posher') forms and fewer vernacular ('local') forms than a person from a lower class. For example, the linguistic variable (ng), appearing in words with 'ing' endings has two variants: '-in' (vernacular form) or '-ing' (standard form). In a study of dialect variation in Norwich, people who were categorised as middle middle class (MMC) used more tokens of the '-ing' variant than the lower middle class (LMC), who used more than the upper working class (UWC), who used more than the middle working class (MWC). The lower working class (LWC) used the 'ing' variant least frequently (Trudgill, 1972).

A second classic pattern is for a linguistic variable undergoing change – that is, when a certain sound is starting to be used, or being dropped from use, within a speech community. For a stable linguistic variable, each social class is ordered hierarchically by the frequency with which the forms of that linguistic variable are used. However, for a linguistic variable that is changing there is a cross-over pattern, where LMC speakers use more tokens of the standard variant than speakers from higher social status groups (see Coates, 1986; Holmes, 1992). Labov's (1972, cited in Coates, 1986) study of the post-vocalic (r) in New York is considered a famous example of the pattern of a linguistic variable in the process of change. There are two variants of (r): it is pronounced or not pronounced in words like 'gore' and 'car'. In less formal styles only UMC speakers used the prestigious post-vocalic (r) with any consistency. However, in the more formal styles LMC speakers used more tokens of the prestigious (r) than UMC speakers. Labov argued that when there is a sound change occurring in an accent, LMC speakers, who are aware of their social position between the middle and lower classes, have greater sensitivity to the use of the new prestige variant. This heightened sensitivity is thought to motivate such speakers to make a conscious effort to speak 'properly', a pattern referred to as hypercorrection.

On the basis of various studies on sound change, it is thought that regular, systematic changes to dialects tend to enter through the speech of the lower-middle-class population and then move upwards through the socio-economic hierarchy. For sociolinguists, whose focus is on understanding language variation, social class is a useful structural social identity category for explaining sound differences within a dialect. For social psychologists interested in language, the findings of variation studies were interesting, not for language's sake but for what they implied about social identity. The sociolinguistic ideas of 'heightened sensitivity', 'hypercorrection', dialect maintenance and sound shift were easily recast in terms of psychological social identity (see Giles and Coupland, 1991). For example, the 'hypercorrection' of LMC speakers was understood as being motivated by a desire for a positive social identity. The higher frequency in the use of 'prestige' variants by UMC speakers was an attempt to maintain the linguistic distinctiveness of a high-status group. Furthermore, the persistence of low-prestige linguistic variants was viewed as a marker of group solidarity among lower social classes (Ryan, 1979).

An important additional characteristic of the classic patterns of social stratification in phonological variation is that they are differentiated by gender. Although there are some exceptions, generally within each class women's speech is characterised by the use of more standard and fewer vernacular forms than that of men from the same social class (see Coates, 1986). One explanation for women's more standard speech was similar to that given for the stratification of phonological variables by social class. It was suggested that women are more status-conscious than men because their social status is more precarious than men's. Feminist sociolinguists were quick to criticise this interpretation (see Cameron, 1985; Coates, 1986). The explanation was based on the rather sexist assumption that women were either housewives or mothers. Also, women's social class tended to be categorised on the basis of their husband's, which was also problematic. Furthermore, the concepts of 'linguistic sensitivity' and 'status consciousness' are rather subjective and circular in their definitions.

Speech communities

The considerable problems associated with ideas like 'status consciousness' meant that alternative explanations for gender differentiation in the use of standard speech were needed. A widely supported explanation for gender-differentiated linguistic variation used the concepts of social networks and speech communities (Cameron, 1985). Social networks may be relatively 'open' or 'closed'. In a closed social network, people all know each other, whereas in a more open network an individual's personal contacts tend not to know each other. Closed social networks tend to reinforce local, vernacular forms, whereas more open networks encourage linguistic change. In studies where LMC women were using more standard forms, the women tended to have more open networks (a range of different social contacts, particularly associated with paid work), whereas men had more closed, tightly-knit networks. Hence the use of more standard linguistic forms by women and the use of more vernacular linguistic forms by men could be attributed to the different patterns of social contact that women and men tend to have in any speech community (see Cameron, 1985; Coates, 1986).

The social network or speech community explanation does not rely on stereotyped ideas about what role women play in society. Gender differentiation in the use of standard speech can be explained by considering the different linguistic influences that people are exposed to. The speech community explanation of gender differences in phonological variation was a welcome development because it considered the influence of social contact on speech, but it too has been the subject of feminist critique (Bucholtz, 1999; Eckert and McConnell-Ginet, 1992). One problem with the speech community explanatory framework is that gender identity is effectively reduced to a position within a social structure. Being a 'woman' or being a 'man' is treated as a social address. However, sociolinguistic research has documented considerable variation within gender categories. The intra-gender group variation casts considerable doubt on the validity of treating gender identity as nothing more than a social position.

In a particularly lucid description of variation studies and their use of identity, Eckert and McConnell-Ginet noted:

> Variation studies have used correlation to determine the role of linguistic variables in social practice. Sociolinguistic variables are seen as passive 'markers' of the speaker's place in the social grid (particularly in the socio-economic hierarchy). . . . Speakers are seen as making strategic use of sociolinguistic markers in order to affirm their membership in their own social group, or to claim membership to other social groups to which they aspire . . . variables that women use more than men throughout different strata of a community signal female identity and men who rarely use those variables thereby signal their male identity. In all cases, identity, interpreted in terms of place in the social grid is seen as given, and manipulation of the linguistic repertoire is seen as making claims about these given identities.
>
> (1992, pp. 468–469)

As well as reducing gender identity to a social address, Eckert and McConnell-Ginet (1992) noted that analysts use statistical generalisations to make global statements about what typifies the speech of women and of men. The problem with those generalisations is that they homogenise both gender categories and marginalise and demonise individuals who don't fit into the generalisations. As noted in Chapters 2 and 3, claims about how men and women 'are' all too easily slip into claims about how men and women 'ought to be'.

Communities of practice (CofP)

Eckert and McConnell-Ginet (1992) suggested that the notion of communities of practice (CofP) be used instead of speech communities in order to avoid treating social identity as fixed and gender as a homogeneous identity category. A CofP is understood as a combination of people who meet round some kind of mutual engagement or project. A key distinction between a speech community and a CofP is that the former is defined by its membership only while the latter is defined by its membership and by the social practices that the membership shares. Shared social practices in a CofP mediate the relationship between identity and language. Holmes and Meyerhoff (1999) compared the notion of a CofP with other explanatory frameworks for linguistic variation. They suggested that the key dimensions of a CofP are: mutual engagement through regular interaction; a joint enterprise where there is mutual accountability; and a common pool of linguistic and discursive resources for making meaning.

Applying the CofP notion to the study of gender means abandoning the idea that gender can be isolated from other aspects of social identity and relations. Instead, there is a strong emphasis on the heterogeneity and dynamism of gender identities. For Eckert and McConnell-Ginet (1992), a CofP framework is a constructionist approach to the relationship between language and identity. They describe gendered practices as constructing members of a community 'as' women or 'as' men, and argue that this construction also involves constructing relations between and within each sex. Thus gender identity is accomplished through the activities of communities. Despite Eckert and McConnell-Ginet's insistence that the CofP approach to identity and language is constructionist, research utilising the concept tends to slip into conceptualising identity in essentialist (albeit dynamic) terms, as the following examples will illustrate.

One example of the conflation of essentialist with constructionist notions of identity is Bucholtz's (1996, 1999) otherwise innovative study of a nerd identity. Bucholtz argued that the structural notion of identity, typically used to explain linguistic variation, was insufficient to explain identification as a nerd in the students that she studied. Bucholtz found that students identifying as nerds had to negotiate their identity through a complex and dynamic set of practices. These practices involved distinguishing themselves from the dominant 'cool' (clothing) styles of other students while creating other practices (such as using formal language, complex vocabulary) as unique signifiers of their identity. Thus, while it was clear that identification as a nerd was constructed within and in response to other identity practices, Bucholtz seemed to maintain the assumption that identity exists prior to language.

The CofP notion of identities as mediated through social practices is more consistent with contemporary feminist views where gender identities are not predetermined, stable or unified. Rather, people may engage or disengage with identity practices across times and places. One consequence of the parallels between feminist theories of identity and the CofP approach is that the CofP framework has had considerable influence on sociolinguists researching gender and language (see Holmes, 1999). One of the most substantive examples of research on linguistic variation and identity using a CofP framework is a study of the identity practices of students in an American high school (Eckert, 1988, 2000; Eckert and McConnell-Ginet, 1995). However, as the following description of that study will illustrate, essentialist assumptions are still present in research using the CofP approach.

Eckert (2000) suggested that the school life of the students whom she studied was ordered around two dominant social identity categories: 'jocks' and 'burnouts'. Jocks were effectively an adolescent version of the corporate middle class, where students' visibility was achieved through their commitment and success in school-related activities. The prototypical jock was the accomplished male athlete. In contrast, burnouts tended to embrace norms more associated with working-class ideals. Their lives were based more in their local neighbourhoods than in school. Eckert suggested that the distinctiveness of the jock and burnout social groups was marked not only by their different involvement in and commitment to school activities, but also at the phonological level of language.

The geographical location of the school fell within an area where a change in accent, known as the Northern Cities Chain Shift (NCCS), had been documented (see Eckert, 2000). Eckert and McConnell-Ginet (1995) showed that the linguistic variables involved in the NCCS were a social symbolic resource for the students to construct their gendered social identities as jocks or burnouts. The use of the more innovative form of the vowels was more highly correlated with girls and students who identified as burnouts. Thus phonological variation functioned alongside involvement in other activities (e.g. sport, taking drugs) to mark the students' identities which were simultaneously gendered and classed.

Eckert (2000) emphasised that the social meaning associated with the phonological variation should not be understood just as a reflection of the students' group membership. She also argued that it should not be viewed as a way of claiming membership to either the jock or burnout group. Nevertheless, Eckert tended to describe the social categories as pre-existing within the social structure. Students had the relatively stable identities of jocks or burnouts, and those identities were expressed by (the creative use of) phonological variants in their accents. Despite describing jocks and burnouts as somewhat stable and pre-existing social identities, Eckert maintained a strong constructionist thread in her perspective. Eckert viewed social identification as meaning-making. She argued that the meanings associated with identities are constructed in use, and linguistic variation is one resource available for constructing meaning. Local variations and the meanings that become associated with them, in turn, contribute to the construction of broader social categories such as gender and class.

The CofP framework encourages researchers to focus attention on the local linguistic accomplishment of identity. Studies tend to consider specific speech communities and to focus on how gendered social identities are accomplished through the activities and practices of those communities. The advantage of attending to the local and practical accomplishment of identity is that it avoids treating women and men as presupposed monolithic categories. It also discourages universalising claims about gender. However, what focusing on the particular misses is the power of broader meaning systems to shape local practices. That is, a CofP framework fails to attend to the wider ideological influences on linguistic identity practices.

The failure to take into account the broader discursive context of speakers was demonstrated by Ehrlich's (1998, 1999) research on gender identity and language in a sexual assault tribunal. Ehrlich argued that if the CofP framework is adequate to explain the relationship between identity and language then it should provide insights into the differences in the linguistic behaviour of women in a university tribunal hearing of a rape case. Ehrlich's analysis showed that the tribunal members, one of whom was a woman, constructed the female complainant's acts of resistance as minimal, thus implying consensual sex. Tribunal members and complainants can be construed as belonging to different communities of practice – the former concerned with upholding institutional values, the latter withholding personal ones. Thus the women involved in the tribunal had different goals in their construction of events.

Ehrlich (1999) suggested that a problem with the CofP framework arose when she considered how gender difference was strategically invoked during the tribunal proceedings. Gender difference was invoked both by the woman tribunal member and the defendant's representative. The defendant invoked the woman tribunal member's gender as a way of suggesting that she was biased towards the complainant. In contrast, the woman tribunal member invoked her gender as a way of warding off charges that her line of questioning was biased. Ehrlich argued that the CofP perspective on social identities arising out of participation in practices fails to explain how gender identity assumed an importance in the hearing beyond the speech communities of the participants. Thus, invoking gender identity is a powerful and pervasive social practice in its own right. It is precisely these moments when social identity is taken up or imposed upon others for strategic purposes that are analysed by discursive psychological approaches to identity.

Discursive psychology and identities

Conventional social psychological research on gender identity and language has viewed language as some kind of medium that is related to, but exists independently of, identity. It is assumed that, when salient, people express their internal, fixed gender identity through language and that it is in language and interaction that a reflection of gender identity can be found. In stark contrast is the view taken by discursive psychology, where identities are produced and negotiated in the ongoing business of social interaction. In this view identities do not have predefined, essential characteristics. Rather, identities emerge from the actions of local conversations and are limited to the kinds of subject positions available to an individual. Thus identity is not viewed in essentialist terms as something that people 'are'. Rather, identities are progressively and dynamically achieved through the discursive practices that individuals engage in. So, in discursive psychology the emphasis is on talk and not cognition as the most important site for studying identity (see, for example, Edwards, 1997).

One style of discursive psychology places more emphasis on how identities as social categories are invoked, made relevant and managed in order to do things in interaction. This kind of discursive work tends to follow a more ethnomethodological and conversation analytic approach to the analysis of interactions. Another form of discursive psychology considers the broader meaning systems that form the background upon which people can position themselves. For example, within a medical discourse various identities as having particular illnesses are available. This kind of discourse analysis tends to align itself along poststructural or Foucauldian lines where the primary concern is to consider the relationships between discourses, power and subjectification. These two different discursive approaches to the study of gender identity and language will be discussed separately below. Despite the different emphases of the two styles of discursive psychology, Wetherell (1998) has suggested that the most productive approach for the study of identity is a stance that weaves both together. Wetherell and Edley (1998) develop the notion of gender practices to embrace the concerns of the different styles of discursive psychology.

Social categories in talk

The issue of context was mentioned in the last chapter in order to contrast more traditional approaches to gender with a conversation analytic one. Typically, gender and language research has treated social categories such as gender as one of the features of the interactional context 'outside' the conversation that may influence language use. Thus, whether a conversation is held in a mixed-sex group or a same-sex group would be considered an important influence on language use. The conversation analysis (CA) perspective on context is markedly different. Context is not seen as some kind of combination of situational and social variables that define the nature of the interaction in advance. Rather, context is viewed as being constituted by the interaction itself. The context of an emergency telephone call, for example, is not necessarily fixed in advance but is constituted by participants' orientation to such things as the identities of 'call taker' and 'call maker' (see Zimmerman, 1992).

One style of discursive psychology follows quite closely the conversation analytic mentality about context in the study of identity. Antaki and Widdicombe's (1998) edited volume *Identities in talk* is an excellent showcase of this kind of theoretical and empirical approach to the study of identity. According to this perspective the important question is:

> not therefore whether someone can be described in a particular way, but to show *that* and *how* this identity is made relevant or ascribed to self or others. . . . If there is one defining principle displayed in this kind of analytic approach, it is the ethno-methodological one that identity is to be treated as a resource for the participant rather than the analyst.
>
> (Widdicombe, 1998, p. 191)

Absolutely counter to the ethnomethodological principle is the practice followed by conventional social psychological research where social identity categories are invoked at the discretion of the analyst. For instance, the research discussed earlier in this chapter treated gender identities as taken-for-granted facts about people, which have predictable consequences. Social psychological experiments on gender and speech simply assumed that the participants had an internalised gender identity. In some studies the 'strength' of identity is measured, but in others it is taken to be the same as the gender category that the participant belongs to. It is then assumed that people's speech, or responses to speech, are somehow causally related to their gender identity. This research practice has been criticised by conversation analysts as an act of intellectual hegemony, where the researcher imposes their concerns, over what is demonstrably relevant to the participants, on to the analysis (Schegloff, 1997).

One way of avoiding the imposition of a researcher's concerns is to take the approach that Widdicombe (1998) alludes to in the above quote. A conversation analytic style of discursive psychology argues against treating identities as a kind of demographic or psychological reality, whose relevance to behaviour can simply be assumed. Instead of asking about the strength of gender identity or the kind of contexts where that identity is salient, the focus is on whether, when and how identities are used. Thus, in CA terminology, the concern is with the relevance of identities at a

139

particular moment in a conversation and how they are consequential for the ongoing business of that interaction. What this means is that the existence and relevance of any feature of the interaction are introduced into an analysis only when the participants have demonstrated their orientation to that feature as relevant.

Treating identities as a participant's concern avoids the difficulties associated with specifying what gender identity is (e.g. a pattern of responses to sex-stereotypical traits or assigned gender category). It also avoids the problems associated with the ontological status of gender categories – that is, the difficulty in defining what are the experiences and social characteristics that all women or all men share. Another important advantage of a discourse conversation analytic approach is that it avoids making the assumption that identity is always guiding behaviour. Instead, the relevance of gender identity is grounded in the interaction itself rather than in the more abstract and vague assumptions made by conventional social psychological approaches. Avoiding these assumptions is important for gender and language research. When gender identity is treated as something that women (and men) really are, and language is seen as expressing and reflecting that identity, then questions tend to focus on gender differences in speech, which ultimately function to disadvantage women.

Edwards's (1998) study is a good example of a discursive study influenced by a conversation analytic approach to gender identity (but see also Stokoe, 1998, 2000). The data for the study were transcripts of a family's counselling sessions. The analysis focuses on a particular session with a couple, Connie and Jimmy. Early in the first session with this couple the counsellor asks a series of questions in order to 'make some sense' of the couple's 'rich and complicated lives' (Edwards, 1998, pp. 20–21). Those enquiries offered up various kinds of identity categories (e.g. age, marital status, parenthood) that presumably had some relevance to understanding Connie and Jimmy's relationship problems. However, following a CA approach the task is to examine what it is, if anything, that the participants in the sessions *do* with these kinds of social categorisations.

In his analysis Edwards (1998) focused on the terms 'girl' and 'woman' to investigate the rhetorical subtleties of gender, as it was mobilised as a relevant category in the counselling session. Edwards was interested in how these words, with their different connotations of age, marital status and potential sexual availability, were applied to highlight the relevant thing about the person being referred to. One instance where gender identity categorisations were being made during the counselling session was when the topic of their relationship difficulties arose. The matter that arose was how Jimmy had left Connie with the children. Connie attributed Jimmy's walking out to an extra-marital relationship, whereas Jimmy blamed his leaving on various aspects of Connie's social activities.

During the discussion of Jimmy's walking out, Edwards (1998) noted that the terms girl and woman were used variably for the same referent. For example, Connie referred to the other person in the extra-marital affair as 'this girl', which seemed to downgrade her status as someone worthy of bothering about. In contrast, Jimmy denied leaving Connie for another 'woman' and reformulated what Connie referred to as an 'affair' as a 'fling'. Edwards argued that Jimmy's vocabulary choice functioned to downgrade the status of the extra-marital relationship and helped to counter Connie's claim that it was a serious and long-term threat to their marriage.

Edwards (1998) found a similar kind of rhetorical variation in the use of gender identity terms in descriptions of Connie's social activities. Jimmy's objection to Connie's going out was her flirtatiousness. However, Connie claimed she wanted the freedom to go out with her 'friends' for a 'girls' night out'. Edwards argued that the categories of 'friends' and 'girls' worked together to define going out as unthreatening and harmless. Jimmy maintains his objection to the way Connie behaves 'out with company'. A bit later Connie reformulates the relevant identities of her friends from 'girls' to 'married women'. This reformulation attends to Jimmy's complaint about her going out as being an opportunity for unfaithfulness.

The substantive point illustrated by Edwards (1998) is that identity categories such as 'girls', 'married women' and 'the other woman' do not get used merely because that is what the people being referred to *are* or even because that is how those people *think* of themselves. Instead the social identity categories of girls and women get used to attend to the local, rhetorically important business of the interaction at hand. An analysis of what people *do* with identity categories in interactions avoids the idealisations of gender categories and assumptions about their effects that are made by more traditional approaches to gender identity and language. As Edwards, amongst others, has pointed out, social identity categories are also verbal categories. The analysis of how these verbal categories are locally constructed, occasioned and rhetorically managed to refer to the self and others as gendered offers an approach that is yet to be widely used by gender and language researchers.

Subject positions

Conventional social psychological perspectives view individuals as unified rational subjects who have a core self that dons social roles. Alternatively, subjectivity (a sense of self) can be theorised as multiple, not purely rational and potentially contradictory. This latter view of identity and of subjectivity was initially proposed in Henriques, Hollway, Urwin, Venn and Walkerdine's (1984) landmark critique of traditional psychology, *Changing the subject. Psychology, social regulation and subjectivity*. The aim of Henriques *et al.*'s work was to demonstrate how the individual–society dualism that functions at the heart of much of psychology reproduces and naturalises the idea of a rational self-contained self, freely choosing its life course. By rejecting the dualism, Henriques *et al.* wanted to point to the complexity of the relationship between the self and society in the production of identity and subjectivity.

Particularly influential on Henriques *et al.*'s work was Foucault's theoretical ideas about subjectivity being the product of discursive practices or epistemic regimes. According to this perspective a sense of self emerges not from an inner core but out of a complex of historical, cultural and political processes and practices. Identities are ascribed through positions in discourses. Individuals are seen to be located in and opting for a variety of different positions depending on the social, historical, political and economic aspects of their situations. Thus subjects are positioned within discursive practices. Hollway (1984) applied these ideas to an analysis of how discourses of gender and sexuality position women and men in different ways. For example, Hollway illustrated how what she called a 'male sexual drive' discourse positioned men as sexual aggressors and women as sex objects.

The notion of 'positioning' was also discussed by Davies and Harré (1990) as a replacement for the more conventional psychological concept of 'role' for understanding identity. Whereas the idea of role suggests a characteristic that is relatively fixed and unique to the individual, the idea of positioning captures the more dynamic and multiple locations that any one individual may inhabit during their lifetime. Positioning is the idea that:

> An individual emerges through the processes of social interaction, not as a relatively fixed end product but as one who is constituted and reconstituted through the various discursive practices in which they participate. Accordingly, who one is is always an open question with a shifting answer depending upon the positions made available within one's own and others' discursive practices and within those practices, the stories through which we make sense of our own and others' lives.
>
> (Davies and Harré, 1990, p. 46)

Elements of poststructuralism and positioning theory have been incorporated into a discursive approach to the study of identity (see Wetherell, 1998). Key aspects of the approach are: its focus on the constructed nature of social identity; the centrality of language (broadly defined) in the process of construction; and the idea that identity emerges at points where individuals engage with social/cultural meaning systems or discursive practices. Wetherell and Edley's (1998) discursive approach to gender identity as

142

social practices brings ideas about identity taken from poststructuralism and positioning theory together with those from ethnomethodology and conversation analysis. The approach they advocate was informed, in part, by an extensive study on men and masculinity (see Edley and Wetherell, 1995, 1997, 1999) which will be discussed next.

Discursive practices

The notion of practice was a key concept of the CofP framework in sociolinguistic work on gender and language, where communities of practice were understood as mediating the relationship between social identity and language variation. Wetherell and Edley (1998) also drew upon notions of practice in their theoretical approach to gender identities. One sense of practice they used was taken from poststructuralism and positioning theory. Thus individuals can be viewed as 'positioned' as masculine or feminine within gender discourses. For example, women who enjoy an active sex life tend to be positioned as slags within discourses of sexuality. Another sense of practice was drawn from Connell's (1987, 1995) theory of practice, a framework developed to understand the relationships between gender (particularly masculine identities), sexual politics and a patriarchal social structure. Connell viewed gender as emerging from people's everyday activities within a dynamic social environment. In this respect Connell's idea of practice has close links to the notion of practice used within the CofP framework.

A second view of practice that Wetherell and Edley (1998) embraced in their discursive approach to gender identity is that used in ethnomethodology and the more conversation analytic strands of discursive psychology. Within these approaches, practices are seen as the everyday activities or methods that people use to understand the world and make things happen. An excellent example of this sense of social practice was described in the last chapter – in Garfinkel's (1967) study of Agnes, whom he described as a practical methodologist of gender (see p. 100). So an ethnomethodological sense of practice consists of the routine, ongoing activities of everyday social interaction that accomplish gender. Wetherell and Edley argued that this second notion of practice is crucial to a social psychology of gender because it grounds and provides a context for the more theoretical ideas about discursive positions. Furthermore it begins to clarify, through the concepts of norms and accountability, how the constraints of the social environment operate.

An example of how the different senses of practice were combined in a single discursive study was Edley and Wetherell's (1997) research on how a subordinated group of school boys managed their masculine identity within the school social hierarchy, where rugby players dominated. At times during discussions the non-rugby boys invoked identities such as the 'new man' to subvert the dominance of the more conventional masculine identities of the sporty group of lads. However, in the constructions of the 'new man', traditional features of masculinity such as strength and fortitude (albeit in different forms from the rugby boys) were reproduced. Thus the marginalised boys, in their discussions, challenged the dominant position of the rugby boys, but at the same time they drew upon and reproduced conventional cultural notions of masculinity.

Billig *et al.*'s (1988) examination of the dilemmatic aspects of gender categories was an earlier example of research on discourse practices relevant to the study of gender. Billig *et al.* noted a fundamental dilemma associated with discussions about men and women. The dilemma arises from the contradictory discourses (or common-sense ideas) that all human beings are essentially 'the same' and also that all individuals are essentially 'different'. The availability of these contradictory notions means that making generalisations about people can always be countered by particular exceptions and vice versa. An important point is that generalisations and 'particularisations' have a moral status. There are tensions between beliefs and values of human equality and human variety. As a result, the extent of similarity or difference between people is always an ideological dilemma, and perhaps especially so for gender categories.

The contradictions between sameness and difference are not ones that can be resolved once and for all. Debates about gender difference in language are a good example of this! A realist approach might assume that issues of sameness or difference can be resolved. A discursive approach, however, influenced by a rhetorical perspective, examines how competing notions of gender and individual difference are used, in the same situation, or even by the same person, for argumentative purposes. Billig *et al.* (1988) illustrated the articulation of the dilemma of gender versus individual difference in a student discussion about the statement: 'there are some jobs men can do better than women'. Discussions of this question followed what Billig *et al.* referred to as a 'generalisation–particularisation chain', with each categorical statement about what women or men are generally like sparking a reference to individual differences or exceptions.

The 'fact' of being a man or a woman and what that means, at least in discussions about gender, is not fixed but a process of stabilising and destabilising notions of generalisations about gender and the specifics of individual women and men within the ongoing business of interaction. The contradictory purposes to which gender can be put were noted by Ehrlich (1998, 1999), when the tribunal member's status as a woman was used to justify claims that she was biased and not biased (see p. 137). Similarly, Marshall and Wetherell (1989) found variability and inconsistency in how gender identity was used in discussion of men's and women's suitability as lawyers. The similarity between women and men was used to support the argument that both make good lawyers. However, the differences between them were also used to argue that both women and men could make good lawyers. Notions of similarities and differences, like generalisations and particularisations, are examples of discourse practices that can be used in the formation and negotiation of gendered social identities.

Chapter summary

This chapter has focused on the relationships between language, discourse and identity assumed by different social psychological and sociolinguistic perspectives. Historically and conventionally, social psychological research on gender and language rests on essentialist and realist notions of identity. Language is treated as the site where identity is both expressed and reflected. The assumption of identity pre-existing language is shared by social identity theory and accommodation theories. Problems with this approach for the gender and language field are: the heterogeneity of women and of men; that few features of language directly and exclusively index (gender) identity; and the assumption of relevance and causality of gender identity to speech.

Sociolinguistic work on the relationship between gender identity and language has examined how broad social categories such as gender tend to correlate with linguistic variation. Feminists have been critical of the tendency for this work to treat gender as stable, coherent social groups with a monolithic and universal impact on language. The community of practice framework has been proposed as an alternative, where local social practices mediate the relationship between language and gender. However, the community of practice approach fails to consider the wider ideological forces influencing the practices that constitute doing gender within a local community. A style of discursive psychology advocated by Wetherell (1998) weaves together the sense of practice used in the conversation analytic approach, the sense used in the community of practice framework and the sense used in poststructural theories of discourse. A strength of this discursive approach is that it incorporates the influence of broader discourses and local practices on the constitution of gender identity.

7

FOLLOWING THE DISCURSIVE TURN

Twenty years after *Signs: Journal of Women, Culture and Society* published Kramer, Thorne and Henley's (1978) review essay on gender and language, Cameron (1998a) wrote another for the same journal. In it she suggested that, during the time spanning the two reviews, an interest in the topic had been undiminished. Indeed in the late 1990s there seemed to be a 'notable "burst" of publishing activity' (Cameron, 1998a, p. 945). Cameron attributed the renewed vigour of feminist language study to the discursive turn across the humanities and social sciences, where the socially constructed, discursive nature of life is stressed. In psychology the influence of the discursive turn is evident in the development of approaches that argue that language and not the mind is the best site for understanding human conduct (see Edwards, 1997; Potter, 1996; Potter and Wetherell, 1987). Feminist psychologists are playing key roles in the growth of discursive approaches, not least of all by developing analyses of the linguistic practices that produce and sustain social beliefs about gender (e.g. Edley and Wetherell, 1999; Gavey, 1992; Gill, 1993; Kitzinger, 2000a; Marshall and Wetherell, 1989; Weatherall and Walton, 1999).

The topic of gender and language is a multidisciplinary endeavour. However, in this book I have attempted to highlight psychology's contribution to the field. The 1978 review essay already mentioned, alongside psychologists Thorne and Henley's (1975) edited book *Language and sex: difference and dominance*, helped to establish a research agenda that still influences work in the field today. Furthermore the experimental, quantitative methods favoured by the majority of psychologists were, for a long time, the dominant approach used to test claims about the significance of sexist language and the nature of 'woman's language'. More recently, feminist psychologists have been developing comprehensive theoretical frameworks and innovative methodological approaches for examining gender as a product of discursive practices (see, for example, Wetherell and Edley, 1998). It is my hope that this book will encourage gender and language researchers from other disciplinary origins to engage with the ideas and methods being advanced by feminist discursive psychologists.

Looking back

The research agenda for gender and language was set early on and had two major components – sexism in language and gender differences in language use. Here I will give a brief overview of the kinds of questions that got asked in those two areas and briefly revisit the debates that arose about the answers. Then, in the next section, 'Taking stock', I will summarise the new insights that the discursive turn brought to those two areas. Finally, I will speculate about the future of research in the gender and language field.

Typically the topic of sexist language was considered distinct from that of gender differences in speech. Research on sexist language has been largely confined to two issues. One of those concerns was to detail the ways in which the English language could be considered sexist. A review of the different aspects of linguistic sex bias was given in Chapter 1. There is an impressive array of lexical, semantic and grammatical features of English that have been described as sexist. Two of the most written about and researched features are the use of masculine forms to refer to both women and men (i.e. masculine generics), and cultural naming practices. A more recent addition to the number of ways in which English is sexist is the suggestion that the implicit causality of verbs may contain a gender bias. LaFrance and Hahn (1994) found some evidence that more cause is attributed to the sentence subject when the sentence object is female than when the sentence object is male. Details about forms of sexist language aside, arguably one of the most important contributions of this thread of work has been to highlight that the relationships between words and the world are not neutral but deeply ideological. In the case of sexism, language is implicated in male dominance. An interest in the ideological nature of language has only become more widespread with the discursive turn (e.g. Billig *et al.*, 1988).

A second theoretical and empirical issue about linguistic bias was the relationships between sexist language, negative attitudes towards women and discrimination against them. Feminist psychologists' position on the relationship between sexist language and sexism marginalised them from many of their disciplinary colleagues. Predating social constructionist ideas in psychology, feminist psychologists researching language in the 1970s and 1980s endorsed the idea of linguistic relativity, where language shapes our understanding of the world. In contrast, the generally endorsed psychological view was that perception and cognitive processes were the primary influence on how people made sense of their world. The evidence used to support the idea that cognition and not language determined thought was cross-cultural studies which showed that colour perception was independent of the number of colour words available in a language (see Berlin and Kay, 1969).

Somewhat antithetical to the cognitive dominant view was feminist language research which has shown that the use of sexist language forms does influence people's comprehension of, recall of and response to linguistic messages. For example, research has consistently demonstrated that masculine generics are interpreted as being masculine-specific (Falk and Mills, 1996). Evidence of the significance of sexist language has been used to support policies for the use of non-sexist language forms in educational material and public documents. In New Zealand, school texts tend to be gender-inclusive and to avoid sex stereotypes. Government documents and university papers must comply with non-sexist language guidelines. However, sexist language forms are still common in everyday speech and written media (Holmes, 1993; Stirling, 1987).

The question of gender differences in language and what those differences reveal about women and men has been the second substantive thread in the gender and language field. Comparing the sexes has a long and rather inglorious history in psychology, which has led to a lively debate about whether sex differences should be examined in any type of behaviour. The major arguments in that debate, presented in Chapter 2, were illustrated by considering research on sex differences in verbal ability and voice. Compared with discussions of gender differences in speech styles, the areas of verbal ability and voice have received far less coverage in gender and language publications. Nevertheless they constitute two important elements in the broad topic of language use. Furthermore, they are two aspects of difference that have been typically considered as having biological rather than social origins.

Popular wisdom is that females' verbal ability is, on average, better than males'. Psychologists have tended to explain that difference in terms of sex differences in the brain's hemispheric specialisation. In fact much brain lateralisation research is predicated on the assumption of females' verbal and males' spatial superiority. Given popular wisdom and the dependence of brain lateralisation research on sex differences in verbal ability (and spatial ability), it is somewhat surprising to find that evidence for female verbal superiority is very weak (Hyde and Linn, 1988). The notion of sex differences in verbal ability has been subject to what Cameron (1997) referred to as a hall of mirrors effect: findings based on small-scale, badly designed studies are cited, discussed and popularised so that over time they become re-presented more and more as absolute facts. The 'fact' of female verbal superiority then becomes a self-fulfilling prophecy, where the strongest evidence of sex differences in verbal ability comes from young adults – where socialisation and not biology is the more plausible explanation for the difference.

The second candidate for biological causes of a sex difference is voice. The ability to recognise the sex of a speaker on the basis of verbal clues alone would seem to be clear evidence that men's voices differ from women's in essential ways. Indeed, there are numerous studies that have reported people's ability to accurately identify the sex of speakers on the basis of voice alone. However, explanations for that accuracy have been more difficult to establish. One possibility is that, on average, men have larger vocal cords, which result in a lower voice pitch, than women. However, vocal cord size alone does not explain correct voice identification because small men and large women are still accurately identified. Indeed, any simple physical differences have failed to account for sex differences in voice. Thus alternative explanations, such as social learning, must be considered. What Chapter 2 showed was that the two most likely features of sex differences in language to be biologically determined, are not. The limitations of biological explanations for gender differences are highlighted in feminist discussion of them, where they are shown to have more of an ideological than a material basis. For example, Gill (1993) found that the qualities of 'women's voice' were a justification for not employing them as DJs on prime-time radio shows.

Chapter 3 focused on what is one of the most popular and widely debated topics in the gender and language field – gender differences in speech style. The way in which the research findings are used repeats a pattern found in other areas that compare the sexes. Alleged differences are polarised as being typical of all women or all men; then those differences are used either overtly or more subtly to disadvantage women. Studies that aim to provide conclusive evidence of the features defining gender-specific speech styles have proliferated since Lakoff's (1973, 1975) claims about women's language successfully goaded more research on the topic. A phenomenal amount of published research has investigated virtually every possible source of linguistic variation for sex differences. Despite the research effort, overviews of the topic have concluded that there is a fundamental lack of agreement about the linguistic features that differentiate between women's and men's speech (Aries, 1996; Crawford, 1995; Simkins-Bullock and Wildman, 1991).

There are two explanations conventionally offered for the lack of definitive answers to questions of how speech style differentiates women from men. One is the form–function problem. The multiple functions associated with any single linguistic form mean that there is no simple relationship between the use of a linguistic feature and what that means about a person's speech. For example, a tag question (e.g. it's a lovely day *isn't it?*) may signal uncertainty or it may be a facilitative conversational device. Even when tag questions signal uncertainty it does not mean that the speaker has a powerless speech style. Edwards and Potter (1993) suggested that displaying a lack of confidence, through the use of features like tag questions, could be a powerful strategy to avoid being accountable for later statements that contradict earlier ones. So, a straightforward counting of linguistic forms in the utterances of men and women fails to be

149

informative about gendered speech styles because there is no one-to-one relationship between linguistic form and communicative function.

The second (conventional) explanation for the difficulty in pinning down gendered speech styles is the problem of context. Typically context is defined as the complement of factors that define the situation where an interaction takes place. Factors that have been investigated as influencing speaker's speech style are: whether a conversation is between members of the same gender or between women and men; whether the interactants are friends or strangers; and whether the setting is business or casual. So insufficient attention to how women's language use compares with men's in a variety of different situational contexts provides another explanation for the failure to establish definitive gender differences in speech. This second explanation is a boon for researchers committed to the idea of gender differences in speech. It provides the basis for an infinite number of studies, as there is a huge array of 'context' variables that would need to be investigated to establish how they influence the speech styles of women and men.

Despite a massive research effort there are no definitive descriptions of gender differences in speech. The lack of closure on the issue of what characterises women's speech compared to men's does not deter theorising about why gender differences in speech exist. Traditionally two explanations for alleged differences have been given; these can be glossed as the 'dominance' and 'difference' approaches. According to dominance perspectives, women's (alleged) hesitant, deferent and uncertain speech stems from their marginal and powerless social position. Hence gender and power are understood as interacting with each other, so that a woman with high status may use a speech style associated with men. The implication that men's style is associated with high status and is therefore a preferred communication style has been criticised (e.g. Kitzinger and Frith, 1999; West, 1995). In contrast, a difference explanation highlights women's conversational competence.

The difference or cultural explanation for gendered speech styles is based on the idea that boys and girls play in predominantly single-sex groups and as a result gender-specific cultures are thought to evolve with unique communication patterns (Maltz and Borker, 1982). A feminine subculture is based on values of closeness and equality, whereas a masculine one is based on dominance and competitiveness. Thus women develop a co-operative speech style and men a competitive one. The cultural explanation avoids the problem of viewing women's language style negatively. However, the idea that women's speech is co-operative and men's competitive is an extension of sex-role stereotypes to linguistic behaviour. These gender language stereotypes have fuelled a huge popular psychology industry that attributes heterosexual relationship problems to the difficulties associated with communicating across a 'cultural divide'. Miscommunication theory

150

provides the academic basis for best-selling self-help books such as Tannen's (1986) *That's not what I meant* and Gray's (1992) *Men are from Mars, women are from Venus.*

A focus on gender difference, taken to its extreme in miscommunication theory, hides the similarities in the way women and men communicate; it also hides the differences amongst women and amongst men (for example, of different ages, classes or ethnic origins). Thus a preoccupation with gender difference distracts attention away from the need to understand the variability and subtlety of the communicative practices of people across their life-span and in their different communities.

Despite intentions to the contrary, theories of gender difference in speech fail to engender social change for the better. The dominance explanation constructs a feminine speech style as deficient compared to a masculine style. The difference explanation merely extends sex stereotypes to language style. Despite these major problems there still appears to be a strong commitment to differentiating and describing women's and men's speech (e.g. Coates, 1996; Holmes, 1997). An important issue that needs further consideration is whether it is possible to conduct feminist research on gender without reproducing the very stereotypes and power dynamics that the work seeks to undermine.

Taking stock

For those already familiar with research in the gender and language field the above overview will have covered very well known territory. During the mid- to late 1980s it seemed that theory and research on gender and language were beginning to stagnate around the very issues that I have just described. However, from the late 1980s, ideas associated with the discursive turn were starting to be applied to gender and language research. Language was given a more strongly constitutive role than it had in the past. A significant realisation was that sexist language and gender differences in speech were not different issues but were both aspects of one process, the social construction of gender. The way gender is talked about and the way women and men speak can be understood as language practices that together produce and recreate what gender means.

The blurring of the boundaries imposed by the questions typically organising gender and language research has been one change brought about by the ideas associated with the discursive turn. I would like to consider here what other insights the discursive turn has brought to the founding questions. Remember, the original concerns were captured by Kramer, Thorne and Henley in their early review article when they asked 'Do women and men use language in different ways? In what ways does language – in structure, content and daily usage – reflect and help constitute sexual inequality? How can sexist language be changed?' (1978, p. 638).

The first part of Kramer *et al.*'s question asks about gender differences. The constructionist thrust of the discursive turn is a radical challenge to the question of whether women and men use language in different ways. An assumption underlying the questions of difference is that gender is an essence that gets reflected in speech. If there is an essential difference or set of differences and those differences are reflected in language then it would be theoretically possible to establish the stable and enduring features defining gender-specific speech styles. However, constructionist approaches view language and discourse as constituting gender, not reflecting it. Thus, being a man or a woman means, amongst other things, talking like one. From a constructionist perspective the failure of research to determine exactly what the gender differences in speech are is unsurprising. 'Women's speech' and men's speech' are not an empirical reality of how women and men speak. Rather, women's speech and men's speech are symbolic notions that are ideological. They function as standards or norms against which the ways women and men actually talk get judged. Thus a woman speaking with a low pitch may be accused of rejecting her femininity. They also represent a cultural ideal – how it is that women and men ought to sound.

The ideological dimension of notions about gendered speech styles underlies the reason why theories for gender differences in speech have turned to women's disadvantage. What counts as knowledge can be understood as an effect of the dominant cultural order – that is, power/ knowledge (Weedon, 1987). In a patriarchal social order, knowledge about women's and men's speech will support the status quo. Thus men's speech will be seen as the desirable standard or norm, and gendered speech will be consistent with stereotyped views about femininity and masculinity. Research on gender differences in general and on speech styles in particular has done little more than support and recreate women's disadvantage in society. The theoretical insight of the mutual constitution of power/ knowledge provides a compelling reason why the study of gender differ- ence should be abandoned, or at least treated with caution. The concept of gender difference can be understood as one of the mechanisms for creating and maintaining a social system where men and maleness are valued over women and femaleness.

A second aspect of Kramer *et al.*'s (1978) question was about how language reflects and constitutes sexual inequality. In hindsight this aspect of the question can seem quite naïve because from a constructionist perspective it is simply assumed that gender and sexual inequality are produced and sustained through the linguistic and discursive resources available to talk about them. However, in other ways the question can be read as anticipating a move away from the ideas about language that were current at that time. Consistent with the ideas that were dominant in psychology at the time, Kramer *et al.*'s question assumed that words would reflect a (sexist) social world that existed outside of language. However, in their question they also acknowledged that language is able to 'constitute' the social order.

The final part of Kramer *et al.*'s (1978) question asked how sexist language could be changed. This question can be interpreted in different ways. On the one hand it assumes that language is sexist – that particular lexical items and grammatical forms have fixed and stable meanings that are biased against women. Researchers holding this view designed studies to show that particular words for women had more negative associations than others (e.g. Kitto, 1989). However, a poststructuralist theory of meaning emphasises its indeterminacy and fluidity. Words or grammatical forms do not have enduring, fixed and stable meanings. Rather, the meanings of words depend on their relationship to, and associations with, other words. So, sexist language is not just a matter of the words used to refer to women; it is more about the meaning systems that function to restrict what women are and to perpetuate social beliefs that disadvantage them.

Kramer *et al.*'s (1978) suggestion that researchers investigate everyday language as an important site implies that they did not anticipate that an experimental approach could fully answer the questions they were asking about gender differences and sexist language. In the case of gender differences and speech, even the most carefully controlled studies have failed to establish any fixed and stable set of characteristics that differentiate the speech of women from the speech of men. However, research following the discursive turn takes up Kramer *et al.*'s suggestion by emphasising everyday talk as a central activity of social life and conversation as an important site for the production and recreation of gender.

A feminist thread that draws early and more recent work together is a recognition that language and discourse are ideological; they are implicated in the creation and maintenance of patriarchy. Highlighting and questioning linguistic practices that can be described as sexist remains now, as it did when Kamer *et al.* (1978) were writing, a strategy for challenging the status quo. The ideological nature of language and discourse requires feminists to 'make trouble' in order to threaten the social order.

Future directions

The theoretical approaches to gender that dominated the twentieth century viewed gender as residing in the minds of individuals, a result of biological sex differences and the internalisation of social norms associated with being female or male. Research sought to establish how gender influenced cognitive processes and patterns of behaviour. Many research studies have been conducted with the general aim of establishing stable and universal truths about the nature of women and men. One problem with seeking

153

generalisations about gender is the heterogeneity of people who are categorised as women or men. For example, no single physical characteristic or social experience is common to all women or all men. So any generalisations about gender downplay the variety within gender categories and emphasise differences between them. Thus one requirement of future work on language use is to attend to the diversity of speech styles amongst women and amongst men and to consider the similarities in the talk of the two groups.

Towards the end of the twentieth century there was an increasing (postmodern) scepticism that the scientific study of gender (amongst other things) could reveal truths about what women and men are really like and the kinds of speech styles they use. In psychology this scepticism has been fuelled by repeated documentation of the language of science being used to justify women's low status in society. Feminist psychologists have described how the 'fantasy life of the male psychologist' (Weisstein, 1968) and 'the mismeasure of woman' (Tavris, 1993) have resulted in a body of knowledge that distorts and exaggerates the characteristics of women and men (e.g. Grady, 1981; Unger, 1992). The development of feminist psychology has been one consequence of the dissatisfaction with 'male-stream' psychology. Feminist psychology is not a unified subdiscipline. Some forms support the use of scientific principles for understanding women, while others reject the possibility of neutral and value-free knowledge. Nevertheless all styles of feminist psychology share a recognition of women's social, political and economic disadvantage, and work towards challenging the cultural beliefs and social practices that limit the kinds of lives women can lead.

A relatively new insight that has emerged from feminist poststructuralist theory is that knowledge about how women and men are is part and parcel of cultural beliefs about how they should be (Butler, 1990a, 1993; Weedon, 1987). Thus the social categories of women and men can be understood as a product of beliefs about, and ways of referring to, gender. The idea of gender as a product rather than a cause of language challenges the assumptions upon which the vast majority of psychological work on gender and language rests. Furthermore it strikes at the very heart of everyday, common-sense notions of what it means to identify as a woman or a man. Feminist discursive research has begun to demonstrate the productivity of applying poststructural theoretical ideas to the study of gender. For example, Edley and Wetherell (1999) showed how competing ideas of men and masculinity (e.g. as breadwinner or as new man) were used in young men's conversations about fatherhood, in ways that reworked and recuperated beliefs about women's and men's traditional roles in domestic life. Discursive work on issues of concern to feminists (e.g. domestic violence, sexual abuse, reproductive rights and childcare) is still in its infancy and provides huge potential for future work.

Another comparatively recent idea for feminist psychology is that dominant beliefs about sex and gender are part and parcel of notions about sexuality. In a study of intersexuality, Kessler (1998) illustrated how beliefs in two and only two gender categories informed norms of sexuality. For example, decisions about designating an infant 'male' depended not only on the presence of a penis of a certain size, but also the requirement that the penis would be capable of becoming erect and penetrating a vagina. Research on gender and language has largely failed to draw links between gender and issues of sexuality. Livia and Hall's (1997) edited collection *Queerly phrased* is an exception. An examination of how ways of talking about gender produce and support heterosexual norms ought to be part of the agenda for feminist language research in the twenty-first century.

The general goal of feminist psychology – to understand and challenge the social practices that endorse and perpetuate the current patriarchal social order – straddles past, present and future work. The study of language and discourse is key to achieving that goal. However, one challenge for feminist language researchers is to critically engage with the increasing array of theoretical perspectives and analytic tools available to understand the social world. The innovative use of theory and method is a characteristic of feminist psychology, which means that it has the potential to make a valuable contribution to gender and language research (see, for example, Crawford and Kimmel, 2000; Wilkinson, 1986). Another challenge is to continue to develop cross-disciplinary dialogue within the gender and language field so that different perspectives are applied to the same issues. For example, discursive psychological approaches have not yet addressed the issue of phonological variation, which is at the heart of much feminist sociolinguistic research using a community of practice framework.

An aspect of discursive approaches in psychology is that language and discourse, not cognition, are considered the primary site for the study of psychological concepts such as gender identity. This discursive shift has profound implications for the study of gender and language. Instead of viewing gender as a relatively stable aspect of individuals which is reflected in language use, it is considered to be discursively constituted, worked up, contested and negotiated during interaction, depending on the business at hand. Therefore everyday talk becomes important in discursive approaches, because mundane interaction produces, and is a product of, patterns of social organisation.

An unfortunate consequence of research that has assumed the notion of 'women's language' as an empirical reality is that it has tended to endorse and perpetuate sex stereotypes. Thus the way women speak has been characterised as, at worst, powerless and, at best, relationship oriented. An ethnomethodological principle followed in the analytic mentality of conversation analysis may provide one way of escaping the historical tendency of gender and language research to endorse and perpetuate stereotyped

155

beliefs about the ways women and men speak. There has been some theoretical debate about the practical utility, political effectiveness and scholarly completeness of language research that limits its analysis to what a conversation demonstrably means to the participants (e.g. Kitzinger, 2000a; Schegloff, 1997; Speer, 1999; Stokoe, 1998; Wetherell, 1998). I have not been an impartial observer of this debate. Rather I have argued that the pervasive nature of gender as a social category means that it is always relevant in the interpretation of social behaviour (Weatherall, 2000a). Nevertheless, as a strategy to avoid reifying cultural beliefs about gender, the productiveness of using a conversation analytic mentality has yet to be systematically explored (but see Kitzinger, 2000a).

The idea that taken-for-granted notions of sex, gender and sexuality are not natural and inevitable consequences of biology or society but are constructed through language and discourse will, I think, be a general theme in future feminist research on gender and language. The pervasiveness and taken-for-grantedness of gender are a product of the linguistic and discursive resources available for its construction. However, the social practices that function to produce and maintain dominant notions of sex, gender and sexuality are yet to be fully understood. One task for feminist language researchers is to make the processes of doing gender visible – to demonstrate that sex/gender are not natural facts but products of the social practices that we engage in. Of course, many everyday rituals as well as social institutions are heavily vested in sex/gender as a fact. So uncovering the constructedness of sex/gender is very much a political as well as a scholarly exercise.

Concluding comments

The discursive turn has brought about a radical transformation in the ways gender and its relationship to language can be understood. Traditionally in gender and language research, like elsewhere in the social sciences, language was viewed as a mirror; it reflected the shared essences of individual women and men. Language was also thought to reflect society's beliefs and values about women and men. Now language about women and men and the way men and women speak can be understood as part of the same discursive process, the social construction of gender. Sex/gender no longer has to be viewed as something that we are. Rather it is something that we do, an interactional accomplishment that we achieve over and over again, in different ways, throughout the course of our lives. The idea that sex/gender is something done in social interaction is exciting for those committed to a feminist agenda because it means that there is a possibility of doing sex/gender differently. The ongoing challenge is to understand the social practices that create and maintain current norms of gender, so that we can work towards a post-patriarchal society.

REFERENCES

Alford, R. D. (1987). *Naming and identity: a cross-cultural study of personal naming practices.* New Haven, CT: HRAF.

Allen, R. C. (1985). *Speaking of soap operas.* Chapel Hill: University of North Carolina Press.

Allport, G. W. (1963). *Pattern and growth in personality.* New York: Holt, Rinehart, and Winston.

Antaki, C., and Widdicombe, S. (1998). Identity as an achievement and as a tool. In C. Antaki and S. Widdicombe (eds), *Identities in talk* (pp. 1–14). London: Sage.

Ardener, S. (ed.) (1975). *Perceiving women.* London: Malaby Press.

Aries, E. (1996). *Men and women in interaction: reconsidering the differences.* New York: Oxford University Press.

Aries, E. (1997). Women and men talking: are they worlds apart? In M. R. Walsh (ed.), *Women, men, and gender. Ongoing debates* (pp. 91–100). New Haven, CT and London: Yale University Press.

Augoustinos, M., and Walker, I. (1995). *Social cognition: an integrated introduction.* London: Sage.

Austin, J. L. (1962). *How to do things with words.* Oxford: Clarendon.

Bähr, G., and Weatherall, A. (1999). Women and their personal names. Making sense of cultural naming practices. *Women's Studies Journal, 15*(1), 43–63.

Baker, R. (1981). 'Pricks' and 'chicks': a plea for 'persons'. In M. Vetterling-Bragin (ed.), *Sexist language: a modern philosophical analysis* (pp. 161–182). Totowa, NJ: Rowman and Littlefield.

Baron, D. (1986). *Grammar and gender.* New Haven, CT: Yale University Press.

Barrett, R. (1997). The 'homo-genius' speech community. In A. Livia and K. Hall (eds), *Queerly phrased: language, gender, and sexuality* (pp. 181–201). New York: Oxford University Press.

Baumeister, R. F. (1988). Should we stop studying sex differences altogether? *American Psychologist, 43,* 1092–1095.

Bem, S. L. (1993). *Lenses of gender.* New Haven, CT: Yale University Press.

Bem, S. L., and Bem, D. J. (1973). Does sex-biased job advertising 'aid and abet' sex discrimination? *Journal of Applied Social Psychology, 3*(1), 6–18.

Bergvall, V. L. (1996). Divided minds: gender polarization in brain and language research. In N. Warner, J. Ahlers, L. Bilmes, M. Oliver, S. Wertheim, and M. Chen (eds), *Gender and belief systems: proceedings of the fourth Berkeley women and language conference* (pp. 11–23). Berkeley, CA: Berkeley Women and Language Group.

Bergvall, V. L., Bing, J. M., and Freed, A. F. (1996). *Rethinking language and gender research: theory and practice.* New York: Longman.

Berlin, B., and Kay, P. (1969). *Basic color terms: their universality and evolution.* Berkeley, CA: University of California Press.

Billig, M., Condor, S., Edwards, D., Gane, M., Middleton, D., and Radley, A. (1988). *Ideological dilemma. A social psychology of everyday thinking.* London: Sage.

Bing, J. M., and Bergvall, V. L. (1998). The question of questions: beyond binary thinking. In J. Coates (ed.), *Language and gender: a reader* (pp. 495–510). Oxford: Blackwell.

Block, J. H. (1976). Issues, problems and pitfalls in assessing sex differences: a critical review of the psychology of sex differences. *Merrill-Palmer Quarterly, 22,* 283–308.

Bodine, A. (1975). Androcentrism in prescriptive grammar: singular 'they', sex indefinite 'he', and 'he or she'. *Language in Society, 4,* 129–146.

Bohan, J. S. (ed.) (1992). *Seldom seen, rarely heard: women's place in psychology.* Boulder, CO: Westview Press.

Brabandt, S., and Mooney, L. (1989). Him, her, or either: sex of person addressed and interpersonal communication. *Sex Roles, 20*(1/2), 47–58.

Brannon, L. (1996). *Gender. Psychological perspectives.* Boston, MA: Allyn and Bacon.

Briere, J., and Lanktree, C. (1983). Sex-role related effects of sex bias in language. *Sex Roles, 9*(5), 625–633.

Brouwer, D. (1982). The influence of the addressee's sex on politeness in language use. *Linguistics, 20,* 697–711.

Broverman, I. K., Vogel, S. R., Broverman, D. M., Clarkson, F. E., and Rosenkrantz, P. S. (1972). Sex-role stereotypes: a current appraisal. *Journal of Social Issues, 28*(2), 59–78.

Brown, R., and Fish, D. (1983). The psychological causality implicit in language. *Cognition, 14,* 237–273.

Bucholtz, M. (1996). Geek the girl: language, femininity and female nerds. In N. Warner, J. Ahlers, L. Bilmes, M. Olicer, S. Wertheim, and M. Chen (eds), *Gender and belief systems* (pp. 119–131). Berkeley, CA: Berkeley Women and Language Group.

Bucholtz, M. (1999). 'Why be normal': language and identity practices in a community of nerd girls. *Language in Society, 28,* 203–223.

Bucholtz, M., and Hall, K. (1995). Introduction: twenty years after 'Language and woman's place'. In K. Hall and M. Bucholtz (eds), *Gender articulated: language and the socially constructed self* (pp. 1–22). London and New York: Routledge.

Bunzl, M. (2000). Inverted appellation and discursive insubordination: an Austrian case study in gay male conversation. *Discourse and Society, 2*(11), 207–236.

Burman, E., and Parker, I. (eds) (1993). *Discourse analytic research. Repertoires and readings of texts in action.* London and New York: Routledge.

Burnham, D. K., and Harris, M. B. (1992). Effects of real gender and labeled gender on adults' perception of infants. *Journal of Genetic Psychology, 153*(2), 165–183.

Buss, D. M. (1995). Psychological sex differences: origins through sexual selection. *American Psychologist, 50*(3), 164–168.

Buss, D. M. (1996). Paternity uncertainty and the complex repertoire of human mating strategies. *American Psychologist, 51*, 161–162.

Butler, J. (1990a). *Gender trouble: feminism and the subversion of identity.* New York: Routledge.

Butler, J. (1990b). Performative acts and gender constitution: an essay in phenomenology and feminist theory. In S. Case (ed.), *Performing feminisms: feminist critical theory and theatre* (pp. 270–282). Baltimore: Johns Hopkins University Press.

Butler, J. (1993). *Bodies that matter: on the discursive limits of sex.* New York: Routledge.

Butler, J. (1997). *Excitable speech: a politics of the performative.* London: Routledge.

Butruille, S. G., and Taylor, A. (1987). Women in American popular song. In L. P. Stewart and S. Ting-Toomey (eds), *Communication, gender, and sex roles in diverse interaction contexts* (pp. 179–188). Norwood, NJ: Ablex Publishing Co.

Caldas-Coulthard, C. R. (1995). Man in the news: the misrepresentation of women speaking in news-as-narrative discourse. In S. Mills (ed.), *Language and gender: interdisciplinary perspectives* (pp. 226–239). London: Longman.

Cameron, D. (1985). *Feminism and linguistic theory.* London: Macmillan.

Cameron, D. (1992). 'Not gender difference but the difference gender makes' – explanation in research on sex and language. *International Journal on Sociology of Language, 94*, 13–26.

Cameron, D. (1995). *Verbal hygiene.* London: Routledge.

Cameron, D. (1997). Theoretical debates in feminist linguistics: questions of sex and gender. In R. Wodak (ed.), *Gender and discourse* (pp. 21–36). London: Sage.

Cameron, D. (1998a). Gender, language, and discourse: a review essay. *Signs: Journal of Women in Culture and Society, 23*(4), 945–967.

Cameron, D. (1998b). 'Is there any ketchup, Vera?': Gender, power and pragmatics. *Discourse and Society, 9*(4), 437–455.

Cameron, D., McAlinden, F., and O'Leary, K. (1989). Lakoff in context: the social and linguistic functions of tag questions. In J. Coates and D. Cameron (eds), *Women in their speech communities* (pp. 74–93). London: Longman.

Caplan, P. J., MacPherson, G. M., and Tobin, P. (1985). Do sex-related differences in spatial abilities exist? *American Psychologist, 40*, 786–799.

Carli, L. (1990). Gender, language and influence. *Journal of Personality and Social Psychology, 59*, 941–951.

Chadhuri, A. (2000). Portrait of a lady. Is the L word OK? *Guardian (G2)*, 19 September, p. 6.

Coates, J. (1986). *Women, men and language.* London: Longman.

Coates, J. (1996). *Women talk.* Oxford: Blackwell.

Coates, J. (ed.) (1998). *Language and gender: a reader.* Oxford: Blackwell.

Cole, C. M., Hill, F. A., and Dayley, L. J. (1983). Do masculine pronouns used generically lead to thoughts of men? *Sex Roles, 9*(6), 737–749.

Condry, J. C., and Condry, S. M. (1976). Sex differences: a study in the eye of the beholder. *Child Development, 56*, 225–233.

Connell, R. W. (1987). *Gender and power*. Stanford, CA: Stanford University Press.

Connell, R. W. (1995). *Masculinities*. Oxford: Polity Press.

Connor, J., Byrne, F., Mindell, J., Cohen, D., and Nixon, E. (1986). Use of the titles Ms., Miss, or Mrs.: does it make a difference? *Sex Roles, 14*(9/10), 545–549.

Cooper, P. J. (1987). Sex role stereotypes in children's literature. In L. P. Stewart and S. Ting-Toomey (eds), *Communication, gender, and sex roles in diverse interaction contexts* (pp. 61–82). Norwood, NJ: Ablex Publishing Co.

Cooper, P. J. (1989). Children's literature: the extent of sexism. In C. M. Lont and S. A. Friedley (eds), *Beyond boundaries* (pp. 233–250). Fairfax, VA: G. Mason University Press.

Crawford, M. (1995). *Talking difference*. London: Sage.

Crawford, M., and English, L. (1984). Generic versus specific inclusion of women in language: effects on recall. *Journal of Psycholinguistic Research, 13*(5), 373–381.

Crawford, M., and Kimmel, E. (eds) (2000). *Innovations in feminist psychological research*. New York: Cambridge University Press.

Crowther, B., and Leith, D. (1995). Feminism, language, and the rhetoric of television wildlife programmes. In S. Mills (ed.), *Language and gender: interdisciplinary perspectives* (pp. 207–225). London: Longman.

Cutler, A., and Scott, D. R. (1990). Speaker sex and perceived apportionment of talk. *Applied Psycholinguistics, 11*(3), 253–272.

Daly, M. (1978). *Gyn/ecology: the metaethics of radical feminism*. Boston, MA: Beacon Press.

Daly, M., and Caputi, J. (1987). *Webster's first new intergalactic wickedry of the English language*. London: Women's Press.

Daly, N., and Warren, P. (2001). Pitching it differently in New Zealand English: speaker sex and intonation patterns. *Journal of Sociolinguistics, 5*, 85–96.

Davies, B., and Harré, R. (1990). Positioning: the discursive production of selves. *Journal for the Theory of Social Behaviours, 20*(1), 43–63.

de Beauvoir, S. (1952, reprint 1988). *The second sex*. London: Cape.

Derry, P. S. (1996). Buss and sexual selection: the issue of culture. *American Psychologist, 51*, 159–160.

Dion, K. L., and Schuller, R. A. (1990). Ms., and the manager: a tale of two stereotypes. *Sex Roles, 22*(9/10), 569–577.

Dubois, B. L., and Crouch, I. (1974). The question of tag questions in women's speech: they don't really use more of them, do they? *Language in Society, 4*, 289–294.

Duggan, D. A., Cota, A. A., and Dion, D. L. (1993). Taking thy husband's name: what might it mean? *Names, 41*, 87–102.

Duran, R. L., and Carveth, R. A. (1990). The effects of gender-role expectations upon perceptions of communicative competence. *Communication Research Reports, 7*(1), 25–33.

Eagly, A. H. (1994). On comparing women and men. *Feminism and Psychology, 4*(4), 513–522.

Eagly, A. H. (1995). The science and politics of comparing men and women. *American Psychologist, 50*(3), 145–158.

Eagly, A. H. (1997). Comparing women and men: methods, findings and politics.

In M. R. Walsh (ed.), *Women, men and gender. Ongoing debates* (pp. 24–32). New Haven, CT and London: Yale University Press.

Eakins, B. W., and Eakins, R. G. (1978). *Sex differences in human communication.* Boston, MA: Houghton Mifflin.

Eckert, P. (1988). Adolescent social structure and the spread of linguistic change. *Language in Society, 17*, 245–267.

Eckert, P. (2000). *Linguistic variation as social practice.* Malden, MA: Blackwell.

Eckert, P., and McConnell-Ginet, S. (1992). Think practically and look locally: language and gender as community-based practice. *Annual Review of Anthropology, 21*, 461–490.

Eckert, P., and McConnell-Ginet, S. (1995). Constructing meaning, constructing selves. Snapshots of language, gender and class from Belten High. In K. Hall and M. Bucholtz (eds), *Gender articulated: language and the socially constructed self* (pp. 469–507). New York: Routledge.

Edley, N., and Wetherell, M. (1995). *Men in perspective: practice, power and identity.* London and New York: Prentice Hall/Harvester Wheatsheaf.

Edley, N., and Wetherell, M. (1997). Jockeying for position: the construction of masculine identities. *Discourse and Society, 8*(2), 203–217.

Edley, N., and Wetherell, M. (1999). Imagined futures: young men's talk about fatherhood and domestic life. *British Journal of Social Psychology, 38*, 181–194.

Edwards, D. (1997). *Discourse and cognition.* London: Sage.

Edwards, D. (1998). The relevant thing about her: social identity categories in use. In C. Antaki and S. Widdicombe (eds), *Identities in talk* (pp. 15–34). London: Sage.

Edwards, D., and Potter, J. (1993). Language and causation: a discursive action model of description and attribution. *Psychological Review, 100*, 23–41.

Ehrlich, S. (1998). The discursive reconstruction of sexual consent. *Discourse and Society, 9*(2), 149–171.

Ehrlich, S. (1999). Communities of practice, gender and representation of sexual assault. *Language in Society, 28*, 239–256.

Ellis, L. (1991). A synthesised (biosocial) theory of rape. *Journal of Consulting and Clinical Psychology, 59*, 631–642.

Ellis, L. (1993). Rape as a biosocial phenomenon. In G. N. Hall, R. Hirschman, J. R. Graham, and M. S. Zaragosa (eds), *Sexual aggression: issues in aetiology, assessment, and treatment* (pp. 17–41). Washington, DC: Hemisphere.

Epstein, C. F. (1988). *Deceptive distinctions: sex, gender, and the social order.* New Haven, CT: Oxford University Press.

Epstein, C. F. (1997). The multiple realities of sameness and difference: ideology and practice. *Journal of Social Issues, 53*(2), 259–278.

Falk, E., and Mills, J. (1996). Why sexist language affects persuasion: the role of homophily, intended audience, and offense. *Women and Language, 19*(2), 36–43.

Fausto-Sterling, A. (1986). *Myths of gender: biological theories about women and men.* New York: Basic Books.

Fausto-Sterling, A. (1993). The five sexes. Why female and male aren't enough. *Science* (March/April), 20–25.

Fausto-Sterling, A. (1997). Beyond difference: a biologist's perspective. *Journal of Social Issues, 53*(2), 233–258.

Fishman, P. M. (1977). Interactional shitwork. *Heresies, 2*, 99–101.

Fitzpatrick, M. A., Mulac, A., and Dindia, K. (1995). Gender-preferential language use in spouse and stranger interaction. *Journal of Language and Social Psychology, 14*(1–2), 18–39.

Freed, A. F., and Greenwood, A. (1996). Women, men, and type of talk: what makes the difference? *Language in Society, 25*, 1–26.

French, M. (1992). *The war against women*. London: Penguin Books.

Frith, H., and Kitzinger, C. (1997). Talk about sexual miscommunication. *Women's Studies International Forum, 20*(4), 517–528.

Gal, S. (1991). Between speech and silence: the problematics of research on language and gender. In M. di Leonardo (ed.), *Gender at the crossroads of knowledge: feminist anthropology in the postmodern era* (pp. 175–203). Berkeley, CA: University of California Press.

Gal, S. (1995). Language, gender, and power: an anthropological review. In K. Hall and M. Bucholtz (eds), *Gender articulated: language and the socially constructed self* (pp. 169–182). New York: Routledge.

Gardner, C. B. (1980). Passing by: street remarks, address rights, and the urban female. *Sociological Inquiry, 50*(3–4), 328–356.

Garfinkel, H. (1967). *Studies in ethnomethodology*. Cambridge, MA: Polity Press.

Gavey, N. (1989). Feminist poststructuralism and discourse analysis: contributions to feminist psychology. *Psychology of Women Quarterly, 13*, 459–475.

Gavey, N. (1992). Technologies of heterosexual coercion. *Feminism and Psychology, 2*, 325–352.

Geraghty, C. (1991). *Women and soap opera: a study of prime time soaps*. Cambridge: Polity Press.

Giles, H., and Coupland, N. (1991). Language in context. In H. Giles and N. Coupland (eds), *Language: contexts and consequences* (pp. 1–31). Milton Keynes: Open University Press.

Giles, H., and Smith, P. M. (1979). Accommodation theory: optimal levels of convergence. In H. Giles and R. St Clair (eds), *Language and social psychology* (pp. 45–65). Oxford: Blackwell.

Gill, R. (1993). Justifying injustice: broadcasters' accounts of inequality in radio. In E. Burman and I. Parker (eds), *Discourse analytic research: repertoires and readings of texts in action* (pp. 75–93). London: Routledge.

Gill, R. (1995). Relativism, reflexivity and politics: interrogating discourse analysis from a feminist perspective. In S. Wilkinson and C. Kitzinger (eds), *Feminism and discourse. Psychological perspectives* (pp. 165–186). London: Sage.

Gilligan, C. (1982). *In a different voice: psychological theory and women's development*. Cambridge, MA: Harvard University Press.

Goffman, E. (1976). *Gender advertisements. Studies in the anthropology of visual communication*. New York: HarperCollins.

Gough, B. (1998). Men and the discursive reproduction of sexism. Repertoires of difference and equality. *Feminism and Psychology, 8*(1), 25–49.

Graddol, D., and Swann, J. (1989). *Gender voices*. Oxford: Blackwell.

Grady, K. (1981). Sex bias in research design. *Psychology of Women Quarterly, 5*(4), 628–636.

Gray, J. (1992). *Men are from Mars, women are from Venus*. London: Thorsons.

Gray, J. (1995). *Mars and Venus in the bedroom: a guide to lasting romance and passion*. New York: HarperCollins.

Greene, K., and Rubin, D. L. (1991). Effects of gender inclusive/exclusive language in religious discourse. *Journal of Language and Social Psychology, 10*(2), 81–98.

Greer, G. (1970). *The female eunuch*. London: Landsborough.

Gross, R. M. (1996). *Feminism and religion: an introduction*. Boston, MA: Beacon Press.

Gumperz, J. J. (1982). *Discourse strategies*. Cambridge: Cambridge University Press.

Haan, J., and van Heuven, V. J. (1999). *Male vs female pitch range in Dutch questions*. Paper presented at the thirteenth international congress of phonetic sciences, San Francisco.

Hall, K. (1995). Lip service on the fantasy lines. In K. Hall and M. Bucholtz (eds), *Gender articulated: language and the socially constructed self* (pp. 183–216). London and New York: Routledge.

Halperin, D. M. (1995). *Saint=Foucault. Towards a gay hagiography*. New York and Oxford: Oxford University Press.

Halpern, D. F. (1986). *Sex differences in cognitive abilities*. Hillsdale, NJ: Lawrence Erlbaum Associates.

Halpern, D. F. (1992). *Sex differences in cognitive abilities* (2nd edn). Hillsdale, NJ: Lawrence Erlbaum Associates.

Halpern, D. F. (1994). Stereotypes, science, censorship and the study of sex differences. *Feminism and Psychology, 4*(4), 523–530.

Hamilton, M. C. (1988). Masculine generic terms and misperception of AIDS risk. *Journal of Applied Social Psychology, 18*(14), 1222–1240.

Hamilton, M. C. (1991). Masculine bias in the attribution of personhood. *Psychology of Women Quarterly, 15*, 393–402.

Hamilton, M. C., Hunter, B., and Stuart-Smith, S. (1992). Jury instructions worded in the masculine generic: can a woman claim self-defense when 'he' is threatened? In J. C. Chrisler and D. Howard (eds), *New directions in feminist psychology: practice, theory, and research* (Vol. 13, pp. 169–178). New York: Springer.

Hannah, A., and Murachver, T. (1999). Gender and conversational style as predictors of conversational behaviour. *Journal of Language and Social Psychology, 18*(2), 153–195.

Haraway, D. J. (1991). *Simians, cyborgs and women: the reinvention of nature*. London: Free Association Press.

Harding, S. (1986). *The science question in feminism*. Milton Keynes: Open University Press.

Harding, S. (ed.) (1992). *Feminism and methodology: social science issues*. Bloomington, IN: Indiana University Press.

Hare-Mustin, R. T., and Marecek, J. (eds) (1990). *Making a difference: psychology and the construction of gender*. New Haven, CT: Yale University Press.

Hare-Mustin, R. T., and Marecek, J. (1994). Asking the right questions: feminist psychology and sex differences. *Feminism and Psychology, 4*, 531–537.

Harré, R. (1980). What's in a nickname? *Psychology Today* (January), 79–84.

Hawes, T., and Thomas, S. (1995). Language bias against women in British and Malaysian newspapers. *Australian Review of Applied Linguistics, 18*(2), 1–18.

163

Hayashi, R. (1997). Hierarchical interdependence expressed through conversational styles in Japanese women's magazines. *Discourse and Society, 8*(3), 359–389.

Healey, J. M., Waldstein, S., and Goodglass, H. (1985). Sex differences in the lateralization of language discrimination vs language production. *Neuropsychologia, 23*(6), 777–789.

Heilman, M. E. (1975). Miss, Mrs., Ms., or none of the above. *American Psychologist* (April), 516–518.

Henley, N. (1977). *Body politics. Power, sex and nonverbal communication.* Englewood Cliffs, NJ: Prentice Hall.

Henley, N. (1987). This new species that seeks a new language: on sexism in language and language change. In J. Penfield (ed.), *Women and language in transition* (pp. 3–25). New York: State University of New York Press.

Henley, N. (1989). Molehill or mountain? What we know and don't know about sex bias in language. In M. Crawford and M. Gentry (eds), *Gender and thought* (pp. 59–77). New York: Springer Verlag.

Henley, N., and Kramarae, C. (1991). Gender, power, and miscommunication. In N. Coupland, H. Giles, and J. M. Wiemann (eds), *'Miscommunication' and problematic talk* (pp. 18–43). Newbury Park: Sage.

Henley, N., Gruber, B., and Lerner, L. (1988). *Studies on the detrimental effects of 'generic' masculine usage.* Paper presented at the proceedings of the Eastern psychological association conference, Boston.

Henley, N., Miller, M., and Beazley, J. (1995). Syntax, semantics, and sexual violence: agency and the passive voice. *Journal of Language and Social Psychology, 14*(1–2), 60–84.

Henriques, J., Hollway, W., Urwin, C., Venn, C., and Walkerdine, V. (1984). *Changing the subject. Psychology, social regulation and subjectivity* (2nd edn). London: Routledge.

Henton, C. G. (1989). Fact and fiction in the description of female and male speech. *Language and Communication, 9*(4), 299–311.

Hepburn, A. (1999). Postmodernity and the politics of feminist psychology. *Radical Psychology, 1*(2), 1–18.

Heritage, J. (1984). *Garfinkel and ethnomethodology.* Oxford: Polity Press.

Hier, D. B., Yoon, W. B., Mohr, J. P., Price, T. R., and Wolf, P. A. (1994). Gender and aphasia in the stroke data bank. *Brain and Language, 47*, 155–167.

Hill, A. O. (1986). *Mother tongue, father time: a decade of linguistic revolt.* Bloomington, IN: Indiana University Press.

Hollway, W. (1984). Gender difference and the production of subjectivity. In J. Henriques, W. Hollway, C. Urwin, C. Venn, and V. Walkerdine (eds), *Changing the subject. Psychology, social regulation and subjectivity* (2nd edn, pp. 26–59). London: Routledge.

Hollway, W. (1994). Beyond sex differences: a project for feminist psychology. *Feminism and Psychology, 4*(4), 538–546.

Holmes, J. (1984). Hedging your bets and sitting on the fence: some evidence for hedges as support structures. *Te Reo, 27*, 47–62.

Holmes, J. (1992). *An introduction to sociolinguistics.* London: Longman.

Holmes, J. (1993). Chairpersons and goddesses: non sexist usages in New Zealand English. *Te Reo, 36*, 99–113.

Holmes, J. (1997). Story-telling in New Zealand women's and men's talk. In R. Wodak (ed.), *Gender and discourse* (pp. 263–293). London: Sage.

Holmes, J. (1999). Preface. *Language in Society, 28,* 171–172.

Holmes, J. (ed.) (2000). *Gendered speech in social context: perspectives from town and gown.* Wellington, NZ: Victoria University Press.

Holmes, J., and Meyerhoff, M. (1999). The community of practice: theories and methodologies in language and gender research. *Language in Society, 28,* 173–183.

Holmes, J., and Meyerhoff, M. (eds) (in press). *Blackwell handbook for language and gender.* Oxford: Blackwell.

Hopper, R., and LeBaron, C. (1998). How gender creeps into talk. *Research on Language and Social Interaction, 31*(1), 59–74.

Hughes, D. L., and Casey, P. L. (1986). Pronoun choice for gender-unspecified agent words: developmental differences. *Language and Speech, 29*(1), 59–67.

Hyde, J. S. (1990). Meta-analysis and the psychology of sex differences. *Signs: Journal of Women and Culture in Society, 16*(1), 55–73.

Hyde, J. S. (1994). Should psychologists study sex difference? Yes, with some guidelines. *Feminism and Psychology, 4*(4), 507–512.

Hyde, J. S., and Linn, M. C. (1988). Gender differences in verbal ability: a meta-analysis. *Psychological Bulletin, 104*(1), 53–69.

Hyde, J. S., and Plant, E. A. (1995). Magnitude of psychological gender differences: another side to the story. *American Psychologist, 50*(3), 159–161.

Jacobson, M. B., and Insko, W. R. (1985). Use of nonsexist pronoun as a function of one's feminist orientation. *Sex Roles, 13*(1/2), 1–7.

James, D. (1996). Derogatory terms for women and men: a new look. In N. Warner, J. Ahlers, L. Bilmes, M. Oliver, S. Wertheim, and M. Chen (eds), *Gender and belief systems. Proceedings of the fourth Berkeley women and language conference* (pp. 343–354). Berkeley, CA: Berkeley Women and Language Group.

James, D., and Clarke, S. (1993). Women, men and interruptions: a critical review. In D. Tannen (ed.), *Gender and conversational interaction* (pp. 231–280). New York: Oxford University Press.

James, D., and Drakich, J. (1993). Understanding gender differences in amount of talk: a critical review of research. In D. Tannen (ed.), *Gender and conversational interaction* (pp. 281–312). New York: Oxford University Press.

James, J. B. (1997). What are the issues involved in focussing on difference in the study of gender? *Journal of Social Issues, 53*(2), 213–232.

Jansen, S. C., and Sabo, D. (1994). The sport/war metaphor: hegemonic masculinity, the Persian Gulf War, and the New World Order. *Sociology of Sport Journal, 11,* 1–17.

Jespersen, O. (1911). *A modern English grammar* (Vols 1 and 2).

Jespersen, O. (1922). *Language: its nature, development, and origin.* London: Allen and Unwin.

Johnson, L. (1994). Try a little togethern (English terms for women). *The Economist, 331*(7860), 86.

Johnson, M. E., and DowlingGuyer, S. (1996). Effects of inclusive vs exclusive language on evaluations of the counselor. *Sex Roles, 34*(5–6), 407–418.

Keenan, E. (1974). Norm-makers and norm-breakers: uses of speech by men and women in a Malagasy community. In R. Bauman and J. Sherzer (eds), *Explorations in the ethnography of speaking* (pp. 125–143). New York: Cambridge University Press.

Kertesz, A., and Benke, T. (1989). Sex equality in intrahemispheric language organization. *Brain and Language, 37,* 401–408.

Kessler, S. J. (1998). *Lessons from the intersexed.* New Brunswick, NJ: Rutgers University Press.

Kessler, S. J., and McKenna, S. (1978). *Gender: an ethnomethodological approach.* New York: Wiley.

Key, M. R. (1975). *Male/female language.* Metuchen, NJ: Scarecrow Press.

Kimura, D. (1983). Sex differences in cerebral organisation for speech and praxic functions. *Canadian Journal of Psychology, 37,* 19–35.

Kimura, D. (1992). Sex differences in the brain. *Scientific American, 267,* 81–87.

Kissling, E. A. (1991). Street harassment: the language of sexual terrorism. *Discourse and Society, 2*(4), 451–460.

Kitto, J. (1989). Gender reference terms: separating the women from the girls. *British Journal of Social Psychology, 28,* 185–187.

Kitzinger, C. (1994). Sex difference: feminist perspectives. *Feminism and Psychology, 4*(4), 501–596.

Kitzinger, C. (2000a). Doing feminist conversation analysis. *Feminism and Psychology, 10*(2), 163–193.

Kitzinger, C. (2000b). How to resist idiom. *Research on Language and Social Interaction, 33*(2), 121–154.

Kitzinger, C., and Frith, H. (1999). Just say no? The use of conversation analysis in developing a feminist perspective on sexual refusal. *Discourse and Society, 10*(3), 293–316.

Kitzinger, C., and Thomas, A. (1995). Sexual harassment: a discursive approach. In S. Wilkinson and C. Kitzinger (eds), *Feminism and discourse: psychological perspectives* (pp. 32–48). London: Sage.

Kline, S. L., Stafford, L., and Reiss, J. C. (1996). Women's surnames: decisions, interpretations, and associations with relational qualities. *Journal of Social and Personal Relationships, 13,* 593–618.

Knight, H. M. (1992). Gender interference in transexuals' speech. In K. Hall, M. Bucholtz, and B. Moonwomon (eds), *Locating power* (pp. 312–317). Berkeley, CA: University of California Press.

Kramarae, C. (1982). Gender: how she speaks. In E. Ryan and H. Giles (eds), *The social psychology of language: attitudes towards language variation in social and applied contexts* (pp. 84–97). London: Chaucer Press.

Kramarae, C. (1990). Changing the complexion of gender in language research. In H. Giles and W. P. Robinson (eds), *Handbook of language and social psychology* (pp. 345–361). Chichester and New York: Wiley.

Kramer, C. (1978). Male and female perceptions of male and female speech. *Language and Speech, 20*(2), 151–161.

Kramer, C., Thorne, B., and Henley, N. (1978). Perspectives on language and communication. *Signs: Journal of Women in Culture and Society, 3*(3), 638–651.

Kyratzis, A., and Guo, J. (1996). 'Separate worlds for girls and boys?': Views from US and Chinese mixed-sex friendship groups. In D. I. Slobin, J. Gerhardt, A.

Kyratzis, and J. Guo (eds), *Social interaction, social context, and language* (pp. 555–577). Mahwah, NJ: Lawrence Erlbaum Associates.

LaFrance, M., and Hahn, E. (1994). The disappearing agent: gender stereotypes, interpersonal verbs, and implicit causality. In C. Roman, S. Juhasz, and C. Miller (eds), *The women and language debate: a sourcebook* (pp. 348–363). New Brunswick, NJ: Rutgers University Press.

Lakoff, R. (1973). Language and woman's place. *Language in Society, 2,* 45–80.

Lakoff, R. (1975). *Language and woman's place.* New York: Harper and Row.

Lakoff, R. (1990). *Talking power: the politics of language.* New York: Basic Books.

Laqueur, T. (1990). *Making sex: body and gender from Greeks to Freud.* Cambridge, MA: Harvard University Press.

Lawrence, S. G., Stucky, N. P., and Hopper, R. (1990). The effects of sex dialects and sex stereotypes on speech evaluations. *Journal of Language and Social Psychology, 9*(3), 209–224.

Lees, S. (1983). How boys slag off girls. *New Society, 13,* 51–53.

Lees, S. (1997). *Ruling passions: sexual violence, reputation, and the law.* Buckingham and Philadelphia: Open University Press.

Leet-Pellegrini, H. M. (1979). Conversational dominance as a function of gender and expertise. In H. Giles, W. P. Robinson, and P. M. Smith (eds), *Language: social psychological perspectives* (pp. 97–104). Oxford: Pergamon.

Lemert, C., and Branam, A. (1997). *The Goffman reader.* Malden, MA: Blackwell.

Levi, J. (1995). Last one across is a big girl's blouse: an examination of language use and gender in outdoor activities. *Journal of Adventure and Outdoor Leadership, 12*(1), 25–26.

Livia, A. (1995). 'I ought to throw a buick at you': fictional representations of butch/femme speech. In K. Hall and M. Bucholtz (eds), *Gender articulated* (pp. 245–278). New York: Routledge.

Livia, A., and Hall, K. (1997). *Queerly phrased. Language, gender and sexuality.* New York and Oxford: Oxford University Press.

Lott, B. (1997). The personal and social correlates of a gender difference ideology. *Journal of Social Issues, 53*(2), 279–298.

Maccoby, E. E., and Jacklin, C. N. (1974). *The psychology of sex differences.* Stanford, CA: Stanford University Press.

MacKay, D. G. (1979). Language, thought and social attitudes. In H. Giles, W. P. Robinson, and P. M. Smith (eds), *Language. Social psychological perspectives* (pp. 89–96). Oxford: Pergamon.

MacKay, D. G., and Fulkerson, D. C. (1979). On the comprehension and production of pronouns. *Journal of Verbal Learning and Behaviour, 18,* 661–673.

Maltz, D. N., and Borker, R. A. (1982). A cultural approach to male–female miscommunication. In J. Gumperz (ed.), *Language and social identity* (pp. 196–216). Cambridge: Cambridge University Press.

Marecek, J. (1995a). Psychology and feminism: can this relationship be saved? In D. C. Stanton and A. J. Stewart (eds), *Feminisms in the academy* (pp. 101–132). Ann Arbor, MI: University of Michigan Press.

Marecek, J. (1995b). Gender, politics, and psychology's ways of knowing. *American Psychologist, 50*(3), 162–163.

Marshall, H., and Wetherell, M. (1989). Talking about career identities: a discourse analysis perspective. In S. Skevington and D. Baker (eds), *The social identity of women* (pp. 106–130). London: Sage.

Martin, E. (1991). The egg and the sperm: how science has constructed a romance based on stereotypical male–female roles. *Signs: Journal of Women in Culture and Society, 16*, 485–501.

Martyna, W. (1980a). Beyond the he/man approach: the case for non-sexist language. *Signs, 5*(3), 482–493.

Martyna, W. (1980b). The psychology of the generic masculine. In S. McConnell-Ginet, R. Borker, and N. Furman (eds), *Women and language in literature and society* (pp. 69–78). New York: Praegar.

McArthur, L. A., and Eisen, S. V. (1976). Achievements of male and female storybook characters as determinants of achievement behaviour by boys and girls. *Journal of Personality and Social Psychology, 33*, 463–473.

McConnell, A. R., and Fazio, R. H. (1996). Women as men and people: effects of gender-marked language. *Personality and Social Psychology Bulletin, 22*(10), 1004–1013.

McConnell-Ginet, S. (1983). Intonation in a man's world. In B. Thorne, C. Kramarae, and N. Henley (eds), *Language, gender and society* (pp. 69–88). Rowley, MA: Newbury House.

McConnell-Ginet, S., Borker, R., and Furman, N. (eds). (1980). *Women and language in literature and society*. New York: Praegar.

McGuire, W. J., and McGuire, C. V. (1992). Psychological significance of seemingly arbitrary word-order regularities: the case of kin pairs. In G. R. Semin and K. Fiedler (eds), *Language, interaction and social cognition* (pp. 214–236). London: Sage.

McMillan, J. R., Clifton, A. K., McGrath, D., and Gale, L. (1977). Women's language: uncertainty or interpersonal sensitivity and emotionality. *Sex Roles, 3*(6), 545–559.

McMinn, M. R., Lindsay, S. F., Hannum, L. E., and Troyer, P. K. (1990). Does sexist language reflect personal characteristics? *Sex Roles, 23*(7/8), 389–396.

McNabb, S. L. (1986). Stereotypes and interaction conventions of Eskimos and non-Eskimos. In Y. Y. Kim (ed.), *Interethnic communication: recent research* (pp. 21–41). Newbury Park, CA: Sage.

Messner, M. M., Duncan, M. C., and Jansen, K. (1993). Separating the men from the girls: the gendered language of televised sports. *Gender and Society, 7*(1), 121–137.

Michard, C., and Viollet, C. (1991). Sex and gender in linguistics: fifteen years of feminist research in the United States and Germany. *Feminist Issues, 11*(1), 53–88.

Miller, C., and Swift, K. (1976). *Words and women*. New York: Anchor Press.

Mills, S. (1995). *Language and gender: interdisciplinary perspectives*. New York: Longman.

Moonwomon, B. (1985). Toward the study of lesbian speech. In S. Bremner, N. Caskey, and B. Moonwomon (eds), *Proceedings of the first Berkeley women and language conference* (pp. 96–107). Berkeley, CA: Berkeley Women and Language Group.

Moonwomon-Baird, B. (1997). Toward the study of lesbian speech. In A. Livia and

K. Hall (eds), *Queerly phrased: language, gender, and sexuality* (pp. 202–213). New York: Oxford University Press.

Morawski, J. G. (1990). Toward the unimagined: feminism and epistemology in psychology. In R. T. Hare-Mustin and J. Marecek (eds), *Making a difference: psychology and the construction of gender* (pp. 150–183). New Haven, CT: Yale University Press.

Morgan, E. (1972). *The descent of woman.* London: Corgi.

Mott, H., and Petrie, H. (1995). Women's workplace interactions: women's linguistic behaviour. *Journal of Language and Social Psychology, 14*(3), 324–336.

Moulton, J., Robinson, G. M., and Elias, C. (1978). Sex bias in language use: 'neutral' pronouns that aren't. *American Psychologist* (November), 1032–1036.

Mulac, A., and Bradac, J. J. (1995). Women's style in problem solving interaction: powerless, or simply feminine? In P. J. Kalbfleisch and M. J. Cody (eds), *Gender, power, and communication in human relationships* (pp. 83–104). Hillsdale, NJ: Lawrence Erlbaum Associates.

Mulac, A., and Lundell, T. L. (1986). Linguistic contributors to the gender-linked language effect. *Journal of Language and Social Psychology, 5*, 81–101.

Mulac, A., Lundell, T. L., and Bradac, J. J. (1986). Male/female language differences and attributional consequences in a public speaking situation: toward an explanation of the gender-linked language effect. *Communication Monographs, 53*, 115–129.

Murdock, N. L., and Forsyth, D. R. (1985). Is gender-biased language sexist? A perceptual approach. *Psychology of Women Quarterly* (1), 39–41.

Ng, S. H. (1990). Androcentric coding of *Man* and *His* in memory by language users. *Journal of Experimental Social Psychology, 26*, 455–464.

Ng, S. H. (1991). Evaluation by females and males of speeches worded in the masculine, feminine, or gender-inclusive reference form. *International Journal of Applied Linguistics, 1*(2), 186–197.

Ng, S. H., and Bradac, J. J. (1993). *Power in language.* London: Sage.

Ng, S. H., Chan, K. K., Weatherall, A., and Moody, J. (1993). Polarized semantic change of words associated with females and males. *Journal of Language and Social Psychology, 12*(1/2), 66–80.

Nikander, P. (1995). The critical potential of discursive social psychology. *Nordiske Udkast, 2*, 3–15.

Nilsen, A. P. (1977a). Linguistic sexism as a social issue. In A. P. Nilsen, H. Bosmajian, H. C. Gershuny, and J. P. Stanley (eds), *Sexism in language* (pp. 1–25). Urbana, IL: National Council of Teachers.

Nilsen, A. P. (1977b). Sexism in children's books and elementary classroom materials. In A. P. Nilsen, H. Bosmajian, H. C. Gershuny, and J. P. Stanley (eds), *Sexism in language* (pp. 161–179). Urbana, IL: National Council of Teachers.

O'Barr, W. M., and Atkins, B. K. (1980). 'Women's language' or 'powerless language'? In S. McConnell-Ginet, R. Borker, and N. Furman (eds), *Women and language in literature and society* (pp. 93–110). New York: Praegar.

Ochs, E. (1992). Indexing gender. In A. D. Duranti and C. Goodwin (eds), *Rethinking context: language as an interactive phenomenon* (pp. 335–358). Cambridge: Cambridge University Press.

Ohara, Y. (1992). Gender dependent pitch levels: a comparative study in Japanese and English. In K. Hall, M. Bucholtz, and B. Moonwomon (eds), *Locating power. Proceedings of the second Berkeley women and language conference* (Vol. 2, pp. 469–477). Berkeley, CA: University of Berkeley.

Okamoto, S. (1994). 'Gendered' speech styles and social identity among young Japanese women. In M. Bucholtz, A. C. Liang, L. Sutton, and C. Hines (eds), *Cultural performances. Proceedings of the third Berkeley women and language conference* (pp. 569–581). Berkeley, CA: University of Berkeley.

Okamoto, S. (1995). 'Tasteless' Japanese: Less 'feminine' speech among young Japanese women. In K. Hall and M. Bucholtz (eds), *Gender articulated. Language and the socially constructed self* (pp. 297–325). London and New York: Routledge.

Otta, E. (1997). Assigning a name to a child: gender differences in two overlapping generations. *Journal of Psychology, 131*(2), 133–142.

Pauwels, A. (1998). *Women changing language.* New York: Addison Wesley Longman.

Penelope, J. (1990). *Speaking freely: unlearning the lies of the father tongue.* New York: Pergamon.

Penfield, J. (1987). *Women and language in transition.* Albany, NY: State University of New York Press.

Peplau, L. A., and Conrad, E. (1989). Beyond nonsexist research: the perils of feminist methods in psychology. *Psychology of Women Quarterly, 13,* 379–400.

Petrie, H., and Johnson, C. L. (1991). *On the psychology of personal names: a boy named Sue?* Paper presented at the British Psychological Society London Conference, City University, London.

Phillips, B. S. (1990). Nicknames and sex role stereotypes. *Sex Roles, 23*(5/6), 281–289.

Pomerantz, A., and Fehr, B. J. (1997). Conversation analysis. In T. VanDijk (ed.), *Discourse studies: a multidisciplinary introduction* (pp. 64–91). London: Sage.

Potter, J. (1996). *Representing reality. Discourse, rhetoric and social construction.* London: Sage.

Potter, J., and Wetherell, M. (1987). *Discourse and social psychology: beyond attitudes and behaviour.* London: Sage.

Potts, A. (1998). The science/fiction of sex: John Gray's 'Mars and Venus in the Bedroom'. *Sexualities, 1*(2), 153–173.

Poynton, C. (1989). *Language and gender: making the difference.* Oxford: Oxford University Press.

Rakow, L. F., and Kramarae, C. (eds) (1990). *The revolution in words: righting women, 1868–1871.* New York: Routledge.

Rancer, A. S., and Dierks-Stewart, K. J. (1987). Biological and psychological gender differences in trait argumentativeness. In L. P. Stewart and S. Ting-Toomey (eds), *Communication, gender, and sex roles in diverse interaction contexts* (pp. 18–30). Norwood, NJ: Ablex Publishing.

Riger, S. (1997). From snapshots to videotape: new directions in research on gender differences. *Journal of Social Issues, 53*(2), 395–408.

Ryan, E. (1979). Why do low-prestige language varieties persist? In H. Giles and R. St Clair (eds), *Language and social psychology* (pp. 145–157). Oxford: Blackwell.

Sachs, J. (1975). Cues to the identification of sex in children's speech. In B. Thorne

170

and N. Henley (eds), *Language and sex: difference and dominance* (pp. 152–171). Rowley, MA: Newbury House.

Sattel, J. (1983). Men, inexpressiveness, and power. In B. Thorne, C. Kramarae, and N. Henley (eds), *Language, gender and society* (pp. 118–124). Rowley, MA: Newbury House.

Schegloff, E. A. (1997). Whose text? Whose context? *Discourse and Society, 8*(2), 165–187.

Scheuble, L., and Johnson, D. R. (1993). Marital name change: plans and attitudes of college students. *Journal of Marriage and the Family, 55*, 747–754.

Schneider, J. W., and Hacker, S. L. (1973). Sex role imagery and use of the generic 'Man' in introductory texts: a case in the sociology of sociology. *The American Psychologist, 8*, 12–18.

Schulz, M. R. (1975). The semantic derogation of woman. In B. Thorne and N. Henley (eds), *Language and sex: difference and dominance* (pp. 64–75). Rowley, MA: Newbury House.

Semin, G. R., and Fiedler, K. (1988). The cognitive functions of linguistic categories in describing persons: social cognition and language. *Journal of Personality and Social Psychology, 54*(4), 558–568.

Seth-Smith, M., Ashton, R., and McFarland, K. (1989). A dual-task study of sex differences in language reception and production. *Cortex, 25*, 425–431.

Shaywitz, B. A., Shaywitz, S. E., Pugh, K. R., Constable, R. T., Skudlarski, P., Fulbright, R. K., Bronen, R. A., Fletcher, J. M., Shankweller, D. P., Katz, L., and Gore, J. C. (1995). Sex differences in functional organization of the brain for language. *Nature, 373*(6515), 605–609.

Sherif, C. (1979). Bias in psychology. In J. Sherman and E. T. Beck (eds), *The prism of sex: essays in the sociology of knowledge* (pp. 93–133). Madison, WI: University of Wisconsin Press.

Shields, S. (1975). Functionalism, Darwinism, and the psychology of women: a study of social myth. *American Psychologist, 30*, 739–754.

Siaan, G. (1994). *Gender, sex and sexuality: contemporary psychology and perspectives*. London: Taylor & Francis.

Silverstein, L. B. (1996). Evolutionary psychology and the search for sex differences. *American Psychologist, 51*, 160–161.

Simkins-Bullock, J. A., and Wildman, B. G. (1991). An investigation into the relationships between gender and language. *Sex Roles, 24*(3/4), 149–160.

Skevington, S., and Baker, D. (eds) (1989). *The social identity of women*. London: Sage.

Smith, P. M. (1979). Sex markers in speech. In H. Giles (ed.), *Social markers in speech* (pp. 109–146). Cambridge: Cambridge University Press.

Smith, P. M. (1985). *Language, the sexes and society*. New York and Oxford: Blackwell.

Speer, S. A. (1999). Feminism and conversation analysis: an oxymoron? *Feminism and Psychology, 9*(4), 471–478.

Speer, S. A., and Potter, J. (2000). The management of heterosexist talk: conversational resources and prejudiced claims. *Discourse and Society, 11*(4), 543–572.

Spender, D. (1980). *Man-made language*. Boston and London: Routledge and Kegan Paul.

Spender, D. (1995). *Nattering on the net: women, power and cyberspace.* Melbourne: Spinifex.

Stanley, J. P. (1977). Gender-marking in American english: usage and reference. In A. P. Nilsen, H. Bosmajian, H. C. Gershuny, and I. P. Stanley (eds), *Sexism in language* (pp. 43–74). Urbana, IL: National Council of Teachers.

Stannard, U. (1977). *Mrs Man.* San Francisco, CA: Germainbooks.

Stirling, L. (1987). Language and gender in Australian newspapers. In A. Pauwels (ed.), *Women and language in Australian and New Zealand society* (pp. 108–128). Sydney: Australian Professional Publications.

Stokoe, E. H. (1998). Talking about gender: the conversational construction of gender categories in academic discourse. *Discourse and Society, 8*(2), 217–240.

Stokoe, E. H. (2000). Toward a conversation analytic approach to gender and discourse. *Feminism and Psychology, 10*(4), 590–601.

Stokoe, E. H., and Smithson, J. (2001). Making gender relevant: conversation analysis and gender categories in interaction. *Discourse and Society, 12*, 217–244.

Strathern, M. (1992). *After nature: English kinship in the late twentieth century.* Cambridge: Cambridge University Press.

Stringer, J. L., and Hopper, R. (1998). Generic 'he' in conversation. *Quarterly Journal of Speech, 84*, 209–211.

Stubbe, M., Lane, C., Hilder, J., Vine, B., Vine, E., Holmes, J., Marra, M., and Weatherall, A. (1999). *Multiple discourse analyses of a workplace interaction* (Wellington Working Paper in Linguistics 11): Victoria University of Wellington.

Stubbe, M., Lane, L., Hilder, J., Vine, E., Vine, B., Holmes, J., Marra, M., and Weatherall, A. (in press). Multiple discourse analyses of a workplace interaction. *Discourse Processes.*

Sutton, L. A. (1995). Bitches and skankly hobags. In K. Hall and M. Bucholtz (eds), *Gender articulated* (pp. 279–296). London and New York: Routledge.

Swann, J. (1992). *Girls, boys and language.* Oxford and Cambridge, MA: Blackwell.

Tannen, D. (1986). *That's not what I meant: how conversational style makes or breaks relationships.* New York: Ballantine Books.

Tannen, D. (1990). *You just don't understand: women and men in conversation.* New York: Ballantine Books.

Tannen, D. (1997). Women and men talking: an interactional sociolinguistic approach. In M. R. Walsh (ed.), *Women, men, and gender* (pp. 82–90). New Haven, CT and London: Yale University Press.

Tavris, C. (1992). *The mismeasure of woman.* New York: Simon and Schuster.

Tavris, C. (1993). The mismeasure of woman. *Feminism and Psychology, 3*, 149–168.

Thaler, B. (1987). Gender stereotyping in the comic strips. In L. P. Stewart and S. Ting-Toomey (eds), *Communication, gender, and sex roles in diverse interaction contexts* (pp. 189–199). Norwood, NJ: Ablex Publishing Co.

Thomson, R., and Murachver, T. (2001). Predicting gender from electronic discourse. *British Journal of Social Psychology, 40*, 193–208.

Thorne, B. (1990). Children and gender: construction of difference. In D. Rhode (ed.), *Theoretical perspectives in sexual difference* (pp. 100–113). New Haven, CT: Yale University Press.

Thorne, B., and Henley, N. (1975). An overview of language, gender and society. In B. Thorne and N. Henley (eds), *Language and sex: difference and dominance* (pp. 5–42). Rowley, MA: Newbury House.

Thorne, B., Kramarae, C., and Henley, N. (eds) (1983). *Language, gender, and society.* Rowley, MA: Newbury House.

Titscher, S., Meyer, M., Wodak, R., and Vetter, E. (2000). *Methods of text and discourse analysis.* London: Sage.

Trudgill, P. (1972). Sex, covert prestige and linguistic change in the urban, British English of Norwich. *Language in Society, 1,* 179–195.

Uchida, A. (1992). When 'difference' is 'dominance': a critique of the 'anti-power-based' cultural approach to sex differences. *Language in Society, 21*(4), 547–568.

Unger, R. (1992). Will the real sex differences please stand up? *Feminism and Psychology, 2*(2), 231–238.

Ussher, J. (1992). Sex differences in performance: fact, fiction or fantasy? *Handbook of Human Performance, 3,* 63–94.

Vetterling-Braggin, M. (ed.) (1981). *Sexist language: a modern philosophical approach.* Totawa, NJ: Rowman and Littlefield.

Walby, S. (1990). *Theorizing patriarchy.* Oxford: Blackwell.

Wallston, B. S., and Grady, K. E. (1985). Integrating the feminist critique and the crisis in social psychology: another look at research methods. In V. O'Leary, R. H. Unger, and B. S. Wallston (eds), *Women, gender, and social psychology* (pp. 7–33). Hillsdale, NJ: Lawrence Erlbaum Associates.

Walsh, M. R. (ed.) (1997). *Women, men and gender: ongoing debates.* New Haven and London: Yale University Press.

Weatherall, A. (1996). Language about women and men: an example from popular culture. *Journal of Language and Social Psychology, 15*(1), 59–75.

Weatherall, A. (1998). Re-visioning gender and language research. *Women and Language, 21,* 1–9.

Weatherall, A. (2000a). Gender relevance in talk-in-interaction and discourse. *Discourse and Society, 11*(2), 290–292.

Weatherall, A. (2000b). *Shifting from gender and language to gender and discourse.* Paper presented at the 7th International Conference of Language and Social Psychology, Cardiff, Wales.

Weatherall, A., and Walton, M. (1999). The metaphorical construction of sexual experience in a speech community of New Zealand university students. *British Journal of Social Psychology, 39,* 479–498.

Weatherall, A., Gavey, N., and Potts, A. (in press). Whose words are they anyway? *Feminism and Psychology.*

Weedon, C. (1987). *Feminist practice and poststructuralist theory.* Oxford: Blackwell.

Weisstein, N. (1993). Psychology constructs the female; or the fantasy life of the male psychologist (with some attention to the fantasies of his friends, the male biologist and the male anthropologist). *Feminism and Psychology, 3,* 195–210.

West, C. (1995). Women's competence in conversation. *Discourse and Society, 6*(1), 107–131.

West, C., and Zimmerman, D. H. (1987). Doing gender. *Gender and Society, 1,* 125–151.

Wetherell, M. (1998). Positioning and interpretative repertoires: conversation analysis and post-structuralism in dialogue. *Discourse and Society, 9*(3), 387–412.

Wetherell, M., and Edley, N. (1998). Gender practices: Steps in the analysis of men and masculinities. In K. Henwood, C. Griffin, and A. Phoenix (eds), *Standpoints and differences: essays in the practice of feminist psychology* (pp. 156–174). London: Sage.

Wetherell, M., Stiven, H., and Potter, J. (1987). Unequal egalitarianism: a preliminary study of discourse and employment opportunities. *British Journal of Social Psychology, 26*, 59–71.

Whorf, B. (1956). *Language, thought and reality: selected writings of Benjamin Lee Whorf,* ed. J.B. Carroll. Cambridge, MA: MIT Press.

Widdicombe, S. (1995). Identity, politics and talk: a case for the mundane and the everyday. In S. Wilkinson and C. Kitzinger (eds), *Feminism and discourse: psychological perspectives* (pp. 106–127). London: Sage.

Widdicombe, S. (1998). Identity as an analyst's and a participant's resource. In C. Antaki and S. Widdicombe (eds), *Identities in talk* (pp. 191–207). London: Sage.

Widdicombe, S., and Wooffitt, R. (1995). *The language of youth subcultures: social identity in action.* Hemel Hempstead: Harvester Wheatsheaf.

Wilkinson, S. (1986). Sighting possibilities: diversity and commonality in feminist research. In S. Wilkinson (ed.), *Feminist social psychology: developing theory and practice* (pp. 7–24). Milton Keynes: Open University Press.

Wilkinson, S., and Kitzinger, C. (1995). *Feminism and discourse.* London: Sage.

Williams, J., and Giles, H. (1978). The changing status of women in society: an intergroup perspective. In H. Tajfel (ed.), *Differentiation between social groups* (pp. 431–446). London: Academic Press.

Wilson, E., and Ng, S. H. (1988). Sex bias in visual images evoked by generics: a New Zealand study. *Sex Roles, 18*(3/4), 159–168.

Wodak, R. (ed.) (1997). *Gender and discourse.* London: Sage.

Wolfson, N., and Manes, J. (1981). 'Don't "Dear" me!'. In S. McConnell-Ginet, R. Borker, and N. Furman (eds), *Women and language in literature and society* (pp. 79–91). New York: Praegar.

Wood, J. (1997). *Gendered lives: communication, gender, and culture* (2nd edn). Belmont, CA: Wadsworth.

Zhan, C. J. (1989). The bases for differing evaluations of male and female speech: evidence from ratings of transcribed conversation. *Communication Monographs, 56*(1), 59–74.

Zimmerman, D. H. (1992). The interactional organization of calls for emergency assistance. In P. Drew and J. Heritage (eds), *Talk at work: interaction in institutionalised settings* (pp. 418–469). Cambridge: Cambridge University Press.

Zimmerman, D. H., and West, C. (1975). Sex roles, interruptions, and silences in conversation. In B. Thorne and N. Henley (eds), *Language and sex: difference and dominance* (pp. 105–129). Rowley, MA: Newbury House.

Zweigenhaft, R., Hayes, K., and Hagan, M. (1980). The psychological impact of names. *Journal of Social Psychology, 110*, 203–210.

INDEX

175